NEW PARENTS HANDBOOK

DR MIRIAM STOPPARD

NEW PARENTS' HANDBOOK

Miriam Stoppard Brand Manager	Lynne Brown
Editor	Angela Baynham
Designer	WHSmith Brand Design/Edward Kinsey
Senior Editor	Julia North
Production	Wendy Penn

WITH THANKS TO THE ORIGINAL TEAM:

Senior Managing Editor	Corinne Roberts
Senior Managing Art Editor	Lynne Brown
Senior Editor	Nicola Adamson
Senior Art Editor	Karen Ward
Project Editor	Claire Cross
DTP Designer	Rajen Shah
Production	Martin Crowshaw

Published in Great Britain in 2002
For WHSmith by Dorling Kindersley, a Penguin Company,
80 Strand, London, WC2R 0RL

A CIP catalogue record for this book is available from the British Library.

ISBN 0 751347906
Reproduced by Colourscan, Singapore
Printed and bound in Italy by Graphicom

See Dorling Kindersley's complete catalogue at www.dk.com

LONDON, NEW YORK, MUNICH, MELBOURNE and DELHI

CONTENTS

INTRODUCTION

Having a baby these days is quite different from the past. For one thing parenting is often shared – it may even be equal – and sometimes it's reversed, when a father becomes a househusband. Nowadays fathers figure much more in baby and childcare to the benefit of all – mum, baby and dad himself. So this book pays more attention to Dad's role and Dad's needs than most other baby books.

CELEBRATING DADS

I make no apology for giving dads prominence throughout the book. Fathers figure on every page because mothers and babies need involved, active dads. Men are as good at fathering as women are at mothering; there's no qualitative difference between the two. Fathering instincts are strong and only need a little encouragement to flower. Babies love being nurtured by fathers as well as mothers; it follows that parenting should be equal and shared. You may think sharing the care of your baby is difficult, but it needn't be! Parents can share all the aspects of baby care with a little planning and a generous heart. After all, baby care means loving your baby, encouraging your baby, teaching your baby, watching your baby grow and develop, and establishing bonds with your baby that in all probability will be the strongest you ever make with anyone. Who in their right mind would miss out on it? More and more dads aren't prepared to be deprived of this unique relationship. And when they're fully involved with their baby, a little miracle happens along the way – their relationship with their baby's mother flourishes too.

BRINGING UP BABY IS A PARTNERSHIP

To help both parents become fully involved, I've included special panels that give the mother's point of view on one side of the page and the father's point of view on the other. Arranging information in this way has a special purpose: it can help you gain insight into what your partner may be feeling on a particular question, or might want to say but is reluctant to make demands. Looking at the pages together may help you to get a discussion going. Communication is the key to a successful relationship, so hopefully these panels will enable you to talk things through and be generous about the other's way of looking at things. Above all, couples whose relationship is on a sound footing and who embrace parenthood as a true partnership are doing the best for their baby, who will grow up secure in the love of both parents. Shared care means there'll be time for your baby, time for yourselves and time when, as well as being a family, you're just a couple – but with the knowledge that together you have produced and nurtured a wonderful baby.

There's much evidence to show that the unborn baby benefits from having a relaxed, calm mother who can take obstacles in her stride. Other research demonstrates that the most important factor in determining whether a pregnant woman is tranquil or not, is a caring, interested, supportive partner. And here we have come to the reason for my writing this book. It is not just for first-time mothers, but for couples — mothers and fathers.

YOUR BABY AND YOUR RELATIONSHIP

It's important to emphasize how a baby will affect your relationship. Few couples think about the impact their new baby will have on their lives, their work, their emotions and their feelings for one another. With the care of their baby as top priority, parents can easily give too little consideration to looking after themselves. Both new mothers and new fathers will find their world turned upside down by the advent of a baby. This may create tensions and strains, which, if unspoken and unresolved could drive a wedge between them. It's a huge leap from being a couple to becoming a family. A child-free man is very different from a father, and different things are expected of him. If they're honest, most men admit to experiencing difficulties in making the transition to fatherhood. By the same token, a mother is a very different person from a child-free woman, who was probably pretty confident and independent before she became pregnant. Now she may be apprehensive and come to feel isolated. She has to cope with a baby who is completely dependent upon her, which can bring with it a perceived loss of identity. This in turn may lead to confusion, resentment and irritation towards her partner. The good news is it's possible for both of you to pick your way through this potential minefield of new feelings and responsibilities. But it isn't always easy and it requires a lot of give and take to smooth the path. Perhaps now, more than at any other time, each of you has to be aware of and sensitive to the needs of the other and actively look for ways of showing you care.

A REASSURING WORD

While my main aim is to give new parents the confidence to follow their own instincts in fashioning their particular brand of family life, and to be open and loving with one another so that their relationship is enriched by their new baby, there's no doubt that first-time parents can find some bits of advice quite useful. So I've tried to be helpful in matters with which most young families have problems. Issues like where to have your baby, how to stay healthy during pregnancy, what to expect during labour, how to establish breastfeeding and cope with broken nights or an inconsolably fretful baby are all covered. While love for your baby can begin from the moment of birth, her care is a skill that you'll be learning throughout this first year of life, and understanding how she develops is a crucial part of it. All new parents feel anxious and inept to begin with, but if you share the worries as well as the joys, you're less likely to strain your relationship and more likely to grow closer — as a family.

CHAPTER ONE

DECIDING TO BE A
PARENT

When a couple decides to have a baby they're making a commitment to becoming parents with all the responsibilities that entails. Not only are you creating a completely new person you are taking on an entirely new and different role, and a role that lasts a lifetime. The implications of your new family and your place in it are many, so it's worth asking yourself some searching questions about how you see yourself as a parent and how it will affect you as a person and what you want from life.

THE CHANGING FAMILY

HOW ROLES ARE CHANGING

At their most basic, the terms "mother" and "father" describe a range of biological facts. A mother produces ova (eggs) and gives birth to children. A father's sperm fertilize the ova and contribute half his child's genes. But these are obviously not the only differences. Human beings belong to a species where there is fairly clear "sexual dimorphism", in which the physical differences between men and women evolved to enable men (being bigger and stronger) to protect women.

NO NEED FOR BRUTE STRENGTH
For thousands of years, men used their biological role to claim privilege and authority, but today the traditional roles of mother and father are about as relevant to modern parents as flint tools and mammoth traps. Those roles evolved to adapt to circumstances that simply don't exist any more. Modern technology has done away with the need for brute strength and nowadays women and children generally don't need their menfolk to protect them from incoming marauders.

INVOLVING MEN IN PARENTING
Since the 1970s it has been increasingly recognized that men should be more involved in the upbringing of their children. This is sometimes seen as a spin-off from the women's movement, but this misses the point. The equal investment of men in the rearing of their children shouldn't just be the result of women refusing to be captive to outmoded social convention, but the outcome of men's determination to claim their right to one of the most humanizing of human activities: the nurture, guidance and bringing to independent maturity of a child.

WHEN YOU DECIDE TO HAVE A BABY, you are creating a new social unit; instead of being two people who may have made a commitment to each other, but who essentially keep their individuality, you become a family. The helplessness and long infancy of human babies means they need constant protection: the family has evolved to make sure that happens. Although the family shows huge variations in structure, there is nowhere in the world where it doesn't exist. But a child knows nothing about structure – all she knows is the quality of care, interest and love she receives from within her family.

HOW IT USED TO BE

Until two or three generations ago, the family was usually based on the extended model. People were part of a large grouping of three or four generations, extending outwards to include cousins. When people's lives were less mobile, and they lived and worked in one small area, face-to-face contact was possible on a daily basis. This larger family unit could act as a support group for its members, particularly in the case of child rearing.

THE EXTENDED FAMILY
Four generations were gathered together for this photograph – an example of the traditional extended family that was already becoming a rarity by the 1920s, when this photograph was taken.

THE FAMILY TODAY

In the past fifty years, this extended family grouping has largely broken down. Increasingly rapid technological change produced a labour market that demanded mobility; people wanted to go where the jobs were, or were forced to do so through economic necessity. Leaving home meant leaving the extended family network and possibly settling where there were no relations at all to lean on for financial and emotional support. At the same time, increased prosperity allowed people to set up their own homes, whereas in the past they may have remained in the family home, even when married. This broad social movement saw the rapid spread of the isolated nuclear family: just mother, father and children. Even when embedded within an extended family, this unit can be a hothouse of troubled emotions; on its own, its long-term survival is more likely to be precarious.

NEW FAMILY GROUPINGS

Since the 1960s, women have increasingly developed a degree of financial independence that made them less likely to hang on to the last remnant of a marriage just because they didn't think they could provide for themselves and their children on their own. Liberal attitudes to welfare have also played their part in the transformation of the traditional family; as the nuclear family – detached from its older members or more tenuous branches – became the norm rather than the exception, so the divorce rate increased, giving rise to a variety of less orthodox family structures.

DIVORCE AND REMARRIAGE

Many divorced or separated people have not turned their backs on marriage or partnership as such, but only on the one they found intolerable. A good proportion of them is prepared to have another try, thus often creating a step-family (see p. 123). As with the nuclear family, the step-family has been around for a long time (and hasn't always had a very good press), but its recent growth has been quite dramatic.

SINGLE PARENTS

The one-parent family is a much maligned institution. It is true that it has often grown out of unhappy situations and the pressures, not least financial, on the lone parent are great. But many single-parent families are thriving and vigorous units that are bound by particularly close ties, and that offer the children involved continuity, stability and happiness (see p. 120).

A NEW KIND OF PARENTING

Not only has the composition of the traditional family changed in recent times, but also how it functions. Whereas fathers used to be protectors, having little direct involvement in day-to-day child care, their importance as equal partners is now being recognized – side by side with women's increasing role as equal or even primary financial provider. In recent years an alternative family arrangement has developed where the father cares for home and family by choice, while his partner earns the daily bread (see p. 154). One reason why such families are often strong and successful units is that they take account of both partners' talents and generally come out of careful discussion and planning. But whatever the practicalities of any individual family unit, providing a stable, loving and open environment in which to bring up children is probably the only important constant.

THE NUCLEAR FAMILY
The majority of modern families plan the number of children they have, and both parents want to become involved, to a greater or lesser degree, in child care.

11

WHAT IS A FATHER?

No-one has a problem in defining a mother's role. Mothers care for children: they feed, comfort, dress and bathe; they encourage, teach, carry, undress, put to bed, and maybe sing to sleep. We know this because it's what we experienced as children. Defining the role of a father is more problematic.

FINDING A ROLE MODEL

Much as we may love our fathers, the way we experienced them as children is not necessarily how we hope our own children will experience their fathers. Men are constantly being exhorted to become fully involved in nurturing their children, but few have any role model to demonstrate what this actually means. To put it bluntly, what we want is for fathers to be more like mothers.

BABIES DON'T DIFFERENTIATE

Babies and young children don't see any difference in male and female nurturing. They experience comfort, warmth, and security from two adults and, though they soon learn to tell them apart, they don't make value judgments based on a notion of what mothers' and fathers' roles ought to be. Apart from breastfeeding, there is nothing a woman can do for a baby that can't be done by a man.

THE NEED FOR PARENTING

Babies don't need mothering and fathering, they need parenting. They need the most important adults in their lives to be models of what parents do for their children; when this is achieved, the next generation of fathers will not be at a loss as to what a father's role should be. Care for a child is indivisible; she will only compartmentalize her needs if this is what she learns from her experiences.

WHY BE A PARENT?

MOTHER

While it's recognized that a mother's role has changed, unfortunately it's taking longer to break down stereotypes of fathering. It's a good idea to be clear about your own attitude to make sure it doesn't reinforce these traditional ideas.

ATTITUDES TO FATHERING

■ In the past it was assumed that fathers came home from work expecting the home to be clean, the children ready for bed and a meal on the table. It's a myth that's died hard, but it's hard to believe that many modern mothers would entertain it.

■ Many women still expect their partners to handle all the family finances, sometimes to their disadvantage. However, couples should find an equitable way to share their financial burdens.

■ It's often assumed that men do all the heavy work associated with parenthood. However, while a man must do this when his partner is pregnant and the baby is young, women are fitter and stronger than they used to be and these tasks can be shared.

■ Women still tend to take on the chores while their partners play with the baby, even when both parents work. But both of you should try to find time to play with your baby, and share the housework equally.

■ Some women hide behind their partners when disciplining their children, but, "I'll tell your father when he gets home" is both out-dated and a cop-out. Attitudes to discipline should be agreed and consistently applied by both parents (see p. 157).

YOU MAY NEVER do anything more important than bring up a child. However satisfying your career, however important your job, whatever prowess you have achieved in sport or leisure activities or in voluntary work, your achievement in bringing up a happy child is matchless; what's more, no-one else can claim the credit. As your child's first – and lifelong – carer, teacher, coach, supporter, counsellor, trainer, promoter and fan, you have an enormous responsibility. If you approach parenthood realistically, you'll find it's a role that is rewarding in a way that is unlike anything else.

FOLLOWING YOUR INSTINCTS

The instinct to bear children is a strong one, and luckily the joy and fulfilment felt by the majority of parents far outweigh some of the inconveniences and compromises they may have to accept. Although this isn't always so, making the decision to have a child usually comes from within a close, loving relationship between two people who decide that they would like to express their mutual affection in having a baby. This is just as well – you're unlikely to have made the decision because you're attracted by the notion of reduced free time, never being able to put yourself first, sleeplessness, going everywhere with a baby survival kit or forking out for designer infant trainers! If you think carefully about the changes brought about by parenthood, you'll realize that it's your genes that are pushing you relentlessly towards recreating yourselves in the form of children. Nowadays, people don't like to admit that they might be at the beck and call of basic urges and tend to dress them up as something more refined. That's fine, so long as we remember that we can also push back and say no to parenthood. For some, that can be the best decision, because having a baby is a commitment like no other.

MORE THAN JUST NATURE

Aside from for biological reasons, people also want to have a baby for fulfilment and personal achievement. Human beings are social animals, and the way they think and act always has a social element. This is shown most clearly in human parenthood in the case of adoption where (usually) two people voluntarily make a commitment to assume all the rights and duties of natural parents, while being genetically unrelated to the child (see p. 122). Adoption also illustrates the depth of the emotional need that people feel to nurture, educate and, above all, love a child. What you give to your babies and children in time, love, understanding and example will constantly be repaid as you watch them grow and develop over the months and years. Every child is genetically the sum of his parents, but he is also a unique personality in his own right, and knowing that you have been the primary influences and educators in allowing that personality to take shape and mature is deeply enriching as well as being a major achievement.

SOCIAL AND ECONOMIC PRESSURES

In a society where everyone goes to school, everyone expects to go to school. Similarly, when everyone except a small minority has children, people expect to have children. It's as though a person has to have a reason for remaining childless, rather than the opposite. In the past, when families tended to live close together, in the same street or village if not actually in the same house (see p. 10), there were quite important economic reasons for having children. As soon as they were old enough to work, children made a vital contribution to the family's economic welfare, and parenthood was also a guarantee of being cared for in old age.

CHANGING DEMANDS

In the much more fragmented society in which we live today, children aren't expected to contribute to the family income (at least until they have finished their education), and the state has taken over some of the basic responsibilities for the elderly, or people make their own provision for old age. As a result, the economic demands of the family are now directed downwards, from parents to children, instead of the other way round. Bringing up children today can be a costly business, and not just financially. For the first time in history, large numbers of women can achieve a whole range of satisfactions outside parenthood and the home; and with safe methods of contraception, they can also choose when and whether they want to have children. This doesn't mean that large numbers of women are opting out of motherhood, though some are; but what they are doing is fitting having and bringing up children into lives where work and a career are also seen as theirs by right.

A QUESTION OF UPBRINGING

Having begun to consider parenthood seriously, the first thing to realize before you go further is that having a baby is just the overture to bringing up a child. It isn't too difficult to imagine having a baby – the excitement, the celebrations, the delighted grandparents, the supportive friends and family. It is almost impossible to visualize bringing up a child if you haven't done it. The demands in time, energy and emotion are almost limitless, unless of course the first thing you're going to teach your toddler is how to use the remote control for the TV and video. This isn't an option for most people because, even before you become parents, you'll have some idea of the kind of people you hope your children will grow up to be, and of the upbringing that will make this idea a reality.

A FIRM FOUNDATION

Upbringing begins from the moment of birth. For a baby or young child, everything is a learning experience, so how you care for your baby is influential from day one. It's worth looking at the background of someone you know who is independent but has a large capacity to love and interrelate with others, who is effective and confident, who recognizes that there is such a thing as the general good and wants to contribute to it. You'll probably find that person found the world an accepting, loving, encouraging, reasonable and respectful place from birth. His parents made him feel that way, and the foundation for everything he has become was provided by them in his first year of life.

FATHER

When you're considering whether you're ready to be a parent, it is worth questioning your own ideas of parenthood, and whether what you think of as a mother's role isn't just as applicable to fathers.

ATTITUDES TO MOTHERING

■ While it's true that most of the people who stay at home with children are still women, many are now returning to work within months of the birth. In addition, a significant minority of fathers are becoming primary carers of their children (see p. 154).

■ Recent surveys continue to show that women, even full-time working mothers, do most of the chores in the home. Ask yourself if this is fair; cooking is increasingly seen as gender-free, and in any partnership day-to-day cleaning should always be shared.

■ As the children grow up, tasks like dealing with carers and teachers, taking and fetching from school, used to be seen exclusively as a mother's responsibility. But most fathers realize that being involved in their children's life and education is important, and they're fitting activities like the school run, helping in the classroom or taking their child to the doctor into their working day.

■ It used to be thought that mothers put children to bed, but most fathers know that the bath and story routine is enjoyable, especially if they've been away from their children all day.

■ The idea – prevalent not so long ago – that it was somehow demeaning for a man to push a pram is now laughable. Not only are men happy to be seen doing this, but they are also more than happy to take their children to the supermarket to do the weekly shopping without their partners.

13

YOUR ATTITUDE TO PARENTING

However right it may seem at the time, the decision to have a child needs the same reasoned, clear-eyed evaluation you would give to buying a house or a new car. It may be quite illuminating to ask yourselves the following questions, even if, in the event, your pregnancy is unplanned. If the answer to more than five is "yes", you may need to think about your whole attitude to parenting:

■ Do you already have ambitions for your children's future?

■ Are you uncertain about how parental actions affect children?

■ Have you still got to work out some of your views on parenting?

■ Do you think that after the birth, instinct will take over and you'll know exactly how to behave towards your child?

■ Are you worried that your partner sees parenting roles differently to you?

■ Do you believe in a strict routine for newborn babies?

■ Do you think a baby would benefit from such a routine?

■ Can you spoil a young baby?

■ Do you believe that babies cry for no reason?

■ If you're both intending to work after the birth, will you leave investigating child care until then?

■ Are your views on baby care at odds with those of your partner?

■ Will you find it difficult to tolerate the measure of disorder a new baby may bring to your home?

■ Do you foresee any conflict with grandparents or other relatives about the way you intend to care for your baby?

All of these topics are discussed elsewhere in this book. Parenting is not an exact science, but the advice given here should help you to clarify your own thinking.

TIMING IT RIGHT

IF YOU ARE WAITING for everything to be just right before you have your baby, you may as well give up now and take up a hobby instead. It's rare for a couple to feel that the perfect moment has arrived to have a child, but now that men and women have control over their fertility, it gives time for all the options to be considered.

MAKING THE DECISION

For many people, finance and accommodation may be the most pressing issues when making the decision whether or not to become parents. Others may look at their personal freedom, and how having a child may affect it. In today's society, where more and more women are finding satisfaction in the progress of their careers, making the decision to break off and have a child can be extraordinarily difficult. Although many companies – and countries – are providing increasingly generous maternity leave and benefits, this may not compensate for the fact that having a baby could delay your career prospects, especially if you want to spend more than a few months at home with your baby. This is one reason why many women, particularly those with satisfying or high-powered jobs, are waiting to start a family at least until their thirties, when they feel that they've reached a level of achievement that enables them to stand back from their careers with confidence.

MAKING SPACE FOR PARENTHOOD

Men also need to think about how their work commitments may impact upon their relationship with their children. Many older men who become parents for a second time in a new relationship have acknowledged that they regretted having missed out on their first family's childhood because pressures of work effectively separated them from their children. Childhood passes quickly and you only have one chance with any child, so think about how much time you will be able to give to her.

PRACTICAL CONSIDERATIONS

It's quite feasible to bring up a child in anything upwards from a two-room apartment – if there's a separate space for the baby, that's ideal. If you're thinking of moving into a larger home to accommodate future children, try to move before you become pregnant; otherwise it's best to wait until after your baby is born. You don't want the double pressure of a new baby and moving house. No-one pretends there isn't a financial implication to parenthood, but the cost of having a baby is largely dependent on what a couple see as essential. Be assured that no baby in a carrycot with one or two loving parents ever lay awake wondering why she didn't have a smart crib with Brahms' lullaby wafting from the attached electronic musical box. Nevertheless, it makes good sense to make the best of what's on offer. Look at your likely overall income and expenditure once the baby is born, taking account of benefits available (see p. 160), and plan accordingly. Whenever your purse allows you to shop, invest in the basic minimum (see p. 68); leave luxuries until you can really afford them.

PARTNERSHIP OR MARRIAGE

If you're in a long-term stable relationship but unmarried, you probably had good reason for choosing this kind of partnership. Now that you are considering parenthood, is there a case for reconsidering your position? Have either or both of you anything to gain from marrying and, more importantly, has your prospective child? One of the reasons most commonly given by prospective parents for marrying before the baby is born is that it ensures the father is the legal parent of his child. The legal situation may vary from country to country, so formal marriage may not necessarily be the only option for you, but clearly neither of you would want to encounter problems in gaining access to your child in the event of your relationship breaking down and leading to a split. However unlikely this may seem at present, no one can foretell the future and most couples would want to guarantee that their baby always has the equal benefit of both parents, even if at some time they may not live together any more.

CHANGING RELATIONSHIPS

Sometimes new parents have not bargained for the fact that their relationship with family and friends will change. More importantly perhaps, the dynamics of their own relationship will also change. No time is better spent before you even start trying for a baby than in exploring together what these differences might be (see p. 108). Policy made in advance needn't be written in stone, but not having a policy means that you haven't even got a starting point for tackling problems.

Grandparents You both know the personalities of the prospective grandparents and you may already see difficulties ahead because their views and attitudes may not be the same as yours. You'll find later on that agreement with grandparents about how you're going to set limits for your child is invaluable. It's also a good idea to agree that you'll both gently but firmly resist any attempt by them to dictate methods of parenting to you. You can, however, ask them to help you to implement yours. But it's also wise to listen to their views or you may be passing up good advice based on real experience. It's also true that many grandparents find it easier to have a relaxed and freer relationship with their grandchildren than they had with their own children, to the benefit of all concerned.

Your friends If you want to hang on to your child-free friends or those who have older children, look at their relationship with others who have recently become new parents. Keep a weather eye out for the vacant, glazed look that lets you know they find a baby's wicked way with rusks less than fascinating. Once you have children you may not be available to your friends as much as you were before, so they'll appreciate it if you retain your identity as a friend rather than a parent while you're with them. Bear in mind also that you'll meet other people with babies with whom you'll forge new friendships, based on the shared experience of new parenthood.

The impact at work Try also to rehearse in advance what difference the advent of the baby may have at work. You may never have clock-watched in your life before now, but it's difficult not to when you're aching to get back to your baby – and this is just as true for fathers as it is for mothers. However, your colleagues, no matter how sympathetic, have the right to assume that you'll be as good value as you were before. If you can see possible pitfalls, be up front and negotiate; you won't always be a new parent and lost trust is difficult to re-establish.

QUESTIONING YOUR REASONS

When making any decision, it can be useful to put into words some of the half-formulated thoughts and questions that rest in the corners of the mind. Even if you think you both really want a baby because you love each other and it's the natural thing to do, it's still sensible to think about all the issues. The following questions don't have right or wrong answers, but provide what I hope will be a useful starting point for you:

- Does the idea of having a baby seem to be the instinctive next step for you both, arising from your positive commitment to each other as a couple?

- Have you always taken it for granted that one day you would have children?

- Do you just want a child, or do you want a child specifically with your partner?

- Does one of you want this baby more than the other? If so, what effect has this had on your relationship?

- Do you want to have a baby because you think it will help to cement your relationship with your partner?

- What images do you conjure up when thinking about life with your baby? Do they include sleepless nights and dirty nappies?

- What will you miss most about being a couple rather than a trio?

- Have you any firm personal ambitions that could be compromised by having a baby?

- Do you want a baby to make up for areas in you life that you find unsatisfactory?

- Is any part of your motivation to please family members, such as grandparents?

- Are you and your partner quite clear about the commitment each of you will make to the baby?

15

CHAPTER TWO

PREPARING TO BE A
PARENT

Most parents have mixed feelings at the
news that a baby's on the way. Naturally
there's great excitement and elation at first
but then you may feel apprehensive and
anxious about the prospect ahead of you.
Fortunately there's nine months for you to
get used to the idea of having a baby in the
house while you follow the month-by-month
changes taking place in Mum's body and how
the baby is developing inside her. Partnership
is the key in the run-up to labour and the
birth itself, with Dad's role as chief coach
and birth assistant being pivotal.

PLAN FOR PREGNANCY

W HEN YOU MAKE THE DECISION to become parents, it makes sense to prepare yourselves in advance. To have a healthy baby, research shows that by far the most important factors are your own fitness and nutrition. This means fathers too: every baby is 50 per cent her father and so that half has to be the healthiest and best that it can be.

MOTHER

It's sensible to think ahead about the best time to conceive (see right). Your due date will be calculated as 40 weeks from the first day of your last period, so you need to take that into account when planning pre-pregnancy fitness.

WHY FITNESS IS IMPORTANT
There is a phenomenal build up over the 40 weeks of pregnancy; the statistics are staggering. Here are a few: the womb increases in volume (muscle) 1000 times; the womb increases in weight (protein) 30 times; individual muscle fibres of the womb increase 40 times in length; the work done by a mother's heart increases 50 per cent; the volume of a mother's blood increases by one third; a mother's kidneys filter 50 per cent more blood than before.

PREVENTING ANAEMIA
If you're anaemic, your heart is overworked, which can affect your baby. A blood test would reveal anaemia and it may be necessary to take iron supplements.

AVOIDING BIRTH DEFECTS
Folic acid has been found to reduce the risk of some birth defects like spina bifida. It's advisable to start increasing folic acid intake three months before you stop contraception, and for three months after you conceive. Good food sources are green leafy vegetables, cereals and bread; or, alternatively, take supplements.

IF YOU HAVE A MEDICAL PROBLEM
If you take regular drugs for a medical condition, let your doctor know before you try for a baby, as the dose may have to be changed once you're pregnant (see p. 33).

TIMING THE BIRTH

If you're serious about starting a family, ideally you should begin to think about it at least a year before the time you'd like your baby to be born. It's a good idea to allow at least three months to get your bodies to peak pre-conception fitness (see opposite). There are other issues you may want to take into account as well, such as the timing of the birth. If you're planning to move house, or know that work commitments are going to take you away from home at a specific time of year, you'll want to avoid allowing these to clash with the possible arrival of your baby. Some parents may even want to take account of whether their baby is born in winter or summer: most education systems involve an autumn start to the academic year and there is evidence to suggest that some children born in the summer, the youngest in their school year group, may not achieve as well academically as the older and more mature children who are born in the winter. This doesn't just affect the early years; it can sometimes last well into the teens.

DELAYING PARENTHOOD
More and more women are now delaying childbearing into their thirties or even early forties. A pregnant woman over 35 will be monitored more closely, but women's general health and fitness has improved enormously in recent years and the older pregnant mother is no longer likely to have the same risks of earlier generations. In addition, couples starting a family in their thirties are more likely to have planned the baby, be in a stable relationship and be financially secure. However, leaving conception until your mid-thirties or later does increase the time you might have to wait to conceive – an average of six months when you're 35, as opposed to four months when you're 25 (see p. 20).

WHEN TO STOP CONTRACEPTION

If you've been using straightforward barrier methods such as the condom or diaphragm, you can safely conceive as soon as you stop using them. However, most doctors recommend at least one normal period after ceasing other forms of contraception, before you try to conceive.

The pill The best plan is for you to stop taking the pill three months beforehand, but a month would do, so long as you have one normal period before you start a baby.

Intra-uterine device (IUD) The same timescale would apply to an IUD, so have it removed three months before you intend to get pregnant. Have at least one normal period before stopping all contraception – use a barrier method in the meantime.

18

HOW FITNESS HELPS YOU BOTH

As a prospective mother, the fitter you are, the more easily your body will be able to cope with the stresses and strains of pregnancy (see box opposite). But fitness and lifestyle may also change a man's ability to father a child, by affecting sperm production (see box below). Try to think about your general health and lifestyle at least three months before you're planning to stop contraception. As well as helping to improve your fitness, it will increase your chances of conceiving without delay and of having a healthy baby.

A HEALTHY DIET

Adjusting your diet shouldn't require uncomfortable changes. Your staple diet should include good quality carbohydrates such as wholewheat bread, rice and potatoes. Keep your animal fat intake down by changing to skimmed milk and low fat cheeses, and use olive or sunflower oil for cooking. Eat lots of fresh fruit and vegetables every day (see p. 34). Don't skip meals, avoid processed foods, outlaw the liquid lunch and eat a hearty breakfast, though not a fried one.

TAKING EXERCISE

Exercise makes a contribution to becoming a healthy potential parent, so if you don't already do so, start a gentle exercise programme together, such as jogging, swimming or gym sessions. Try for 20 minutes' exercise that increases your heartrate at least three times a week. However, bear in mind that very strenuous training or dieting may reduce fertility.

ROUTINE HEALTH PRECAUTIONS

WHAT TO LOOK AT	HOW TO IMPROVE
SMOKING	Smoking reduces fertility, especially in men as it lowers their sperm count. Give up before you try for a baby; smoking during pregnancy – direct or passive – harms your unborn child.
ALCOHOL	Alcohol can damage both sperm and the ovum, so prospective parents should consume no more than five units a week for women, 10 for men. (One unit=one small glass of wine or a half pint of beer.)
DRUGS AND MEDICATION	Many medicinal and street drugs affect fertility. In particular, cannabis reduces sperm production; the effects can take months to wear off. Consult your doctor if you're taking regular medication.
PRE-PREGNANCY SCREENING	Well before trying for a baby, check for rubella (German measles) immunity and get immunized if necessary; have a cervical smear test and any treatment; check for sexually transmitted diseases.
ENVIRONMENTAL FACTORS	Before conceiving, and once you stop contraception, make sure you avoid X-rays, hot saunas, and pollutants such as dioxins and PCBs (found in many garden and household products).

FATHER

It may seem obvious to you that your partner's fitness and lifestyle will have a bearing on her ability to conceive, but you need to be aware that your own fitness is also a crucial factor. If you aren't fit, you may not donate the best genetic material to your child in your sperm, so it's a responsibility you can't shirk.

WHY YOUR LIFESTYLE MATTERS
Whatever you think about your sexual prowess, it may bear no relation at all to your ability to father a child. Male fertility not only depends on the number of sperm produced, but also on the health of that sperm. This is affected by all sorts of lifestyle factors, such as smoking, alcohol and drugs (see left), and also stress. Try to re-order your life if it's stressful, and look at your diet and physical fitness.

19

GENETIC COUNSELLING

Seek advice and have tests in advance if a genetic disorder runs in your family. Examples of heritable conditions include cystic fibrosis, thalassaemia, muscular dystrophy and haemophilia.

WHAT HAPPENS IN COUNSELLING
The counsellor explains the condition and your family background and shows you the pattern of inheritance through past generations. Not all carriers of a defective gene get the condition: if it's recessive it can be masked by a healthy version, whereas a dominant gene will always show up. With a dominant gene the chances of your baby being affected are one in two, with a recessive gene they are one in four.

INCREASING CHANCES OF CONCEPTION

Once you've stopped using contraceptives and your periods are normal (see p. 18), the following tips might help you conceive more quickly:

■ Try to have intercourse during your most fertile period (see right).

■ Your fertile period is signalled by the texture of your cervical mucus, which becomes clear, thin and slippery, making it easier for the sperm to swim up through your cervix. Ovulation usually occurs 24 hours after this type of mucus is at its most profuse.

■ Avoid love-making for a couple of days before your fertile period to help build up to an optimum number of sperm.

■ The "missionary position" (man on top) is thought by some to be most effective for conception, particularly if you lie down for half an hour or so after you've had intercourse.

■ Cut down on your intake of caffeine – there's some evidence to suggest that it can interfere with the ability of the embryo to implant in the wall of the uterus.

CONCEPTION

Conceiving a baby is the ultimate expression of a loving sexual relationship between partners, who have made the decision together, without pressure from each other. You could conceive within a few months of making the decision to stop using contraception, especially if you have intercourse at your most fertile time of the month.

WHEN YOU'RE FERTILE

A woman is fertile only when she is ovulating – when an egg has been released from her ovum. This is nearly always 14 days after the first day of the last menstrual period. You can therefore predict ovulation by tracking your periods in a diary, or you can do an ovulation test on your urine, which may be helpful if you don't have a regular 28-day cycle. Three-quarters of all couples who have unprotected intercourse will conceive within nine months, and 90 per cent in 18 months, but from the age of about 25, the fertility of both men and women does start to wane.

WHAT HAPPENS WHEN YOU CONCEIVE

As the ovum can survive for 36 hours and sperm for 48 hours, your fertile period can last for about three days. When ovulation and intercourse overlap, sperm swim up through the cervix and uterus to meet the ovum, and fertilization with one sperm usually happens in the upper end of the Fallopian tube. It then takes 3–4 days for the fertilized cell (called a zygote) to reach the uterus and implant in the endometrium – the specially prepared uterine lining. The process of implantation is called nidation; the fertilized egg, now called a blastocyst, burrows into the lining and quickly forms a primitive placenta; seven days after ovulation, the blastocyst is embedded and growing.

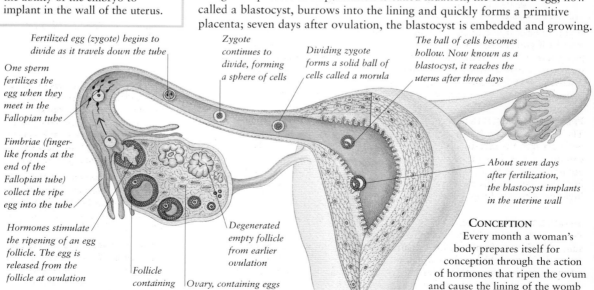

Fertilized egg (zygote) begins to divide as it travels down the tube

One sperm fertilizes the egg when they meet in the Fallopian tube

Fimbriae (finger-like fronds at the end of the Fallopian tube) collect the ripe egg into the tube

Hormones stimulate the ripening of an egg follicle. The egg is released from the follicle at ovulation

Follicle containing developing egg

Degenerated empty follicle from earlier ovulation

Ovary, containing eggs (ova) which are released at every menstrual cycle

Zygote continues to divide, forming a sphere of cells

Dividing zygote forms a solid ball of cells called a morula

The ball of cells becomes hollow. Now known as a blastocyst, it reaches the uterus after three days

About seven days after fertilization, the blastocyst implants in the uterine wall

CONCEPTION

Every month a woman's body prepares itself for conception through the action of hormones that ripen the ovum and cause the lining of the womb to thicken in order to nourish the tiny embryo.

FINDING OUT IF YOU'RE PREGNANT

Many women suspect that they are pregnant within days of conception, but the single most obvious indicator is a missed period, and anyone who has a regular menstrual cycle will realize something has happened once they are three or four days late. Other women may not realize for two or three weeks, especially if they continue to have so-called "withdrawal" bleeding, where pre-pregnancy hormones still present in the body cause a weak menstrual bleed. They may, however, suspect that they are pregnant from other physical signs (see below). Either way, you'll probably want to confirm it as soon as possible with a pregnancy test.

PREGNANCY TESTS
Commercially produced pregnancy tests are now widely available – though often expensive – and can confirm whether or not you are pregnant from the day your period is due. However, if you can wait a day or two longer, you'll get a more reliable result; a false positive is unlikely, but you may wrongly test negative if you try too early. You can also ask your doctor to do the test.

OTHER SIGNS OF PREGNANCY
You may experience other signs within days of missing your period that will alert you to the possibility of successful conception:
- Tender, heavy breasts that may tingle a little. Your bra may seem a touch too tight, the veins on your breasts more prominent than usual and your nipples and areolae may seem redder than usual.
- A feeling of nausea. Although often called "morning sickness", it may happen at any time of the day.
- A super-sensitive sense of smell, and a metallic taste in your mouth.
- The need to pass urine more frequently than usual.
- Feeling incredibly tired, especially in the evening.

WAITING A LONG TIME TO CONCEIVE

If you've been trying to conceive for 12 months without success (or eight months if you're over 35), you could approach your doctor to talk about being referred for investigations into your fertility. Finding out that you are unable to conceive without help can be very stressful, but many couples discover that taking this first step is in itself an antidote to stress and they may go on to conceive before their appointment with the specialist.

PREPARING YOURSELVES FOR FERTILITY INVESTIGATIONS
The test process can be long and difficult, so both partners must enter willingly into the investigation. Before you embark on it, you should think carefully about the strain (including perhaps financial) of what you are about to do. Many relationships have crumbled under the stress of infertility investigations, and living with the uncertainty, and the unpleasant and invasive tests, can be extremely hard.

SHARING THE RESPONSIBILITY
Be aware that your ability as a couple to conceive – your fertility – is the sum of both your fertilities. Investigations may indicate a problem that will probably be treatable, and it's worth remembering that in as many as half of infertile couples, the problem lies with the man. Infertility is nobody's fault, you share it. Don't apportion blame, feel resentment or guilt, or you'll drive a wedge between you that may make conception even more elusive.

BOY OR GIRL?

I'm not in favour of trying to select a boy or girl baby. Nature does very well in maintaining a balance of about 103 boys to 100 girls and we shouldn't interfere with that. With advances in ultrasound and foetal cell investigations, you may be able to find out the sex of your baby during pregnancy, although this deprives you of the lovely surprise of finding out your baby's sex at the birth.

WHAT DETERMINES A BABY'S SEX?
Men produce sperm with 22 chromosomes plus either one X (female) or one Y (male) sex chromosome. Women's ova also have 22 corresponding chromosomes, but they only produce an X sex chromosome. A zygote fertilized by an X sperm grows up to be a girl, a Y sperm results in a boy.

IS IT POSSIBLE TO INFLUENCE A BABY'S SEX?
Although no method with any scientific validity has been developed, by noting the different characteristics of X and Y sperm, it's possible to suggest a way of increasing your chances of conceiving the gender you want:

- X sperm are larger and slower than Y sperm.

- X sperm live longer than Y sperm.

- To increase the chances of an X sperm fertilizing the ovum and conceiving a girl, intercourse should be two to three days prior to ovulation, as only female sperm survive long enough to meet the ovum when it's finally released.

- There's a higher chance that a Y sperm will fertilize an ovum on the day of ovulation because it will reach the ovum more quickly, and the baby will be a boy.

- Frequent ejaculation lowers the proportion of Y sperm, so a girl is likely. Infrequent sex increases the proportion of Y sperm and the chances of a boy.

21

PREGNANCY AFTER MISCARRIAGE

The trauma of a miscarriage, stillbirth (see p. 33) or even a termination in the past, can affect how you both feel about your current pregnancy.

REKINDLING GRIEF

Even if your earlier pregnancy or pregnancies were some time ago, you may find being pregnant again rekindles your need to grieve. Talk through your feelings to your partner or a close friend: if you work through this old grief now, you'll find it easier to welcome your new baby when she's born.

RELIVING THE PAST

If you had a miscarriage, you'll both find it very difficult to be relaxed about the new pregnancy. In particular, you may find the weeks around the time you lost your last baby very difficult to get through. Take heart from the fact that the vast majority of women who miscarry go on to have a healthy child next time around.

AFTER A TERMINATION

If you had a termination due to abnormality, you're likely to be offered diagnostic tests in this pregnancy as soon as practically possible. Again, take heart from the fact that many such problems are extremely unlikely to recur. If your termination was for other reasons, you may suffer feelings of guilt that you're going ahead with this current pregnancy. It's important to talk about this rather than bottling up feelings that may affect your relationship with your new baby.

AFTER A STILLBIRTH

If you had a stillbirth, you'll probably be wondering whether or not this baby is alive and find the end of your new pregnancy almost unbearable. Although you'll be monitored carefully, talk your fears through with your consultant – you may very well be able to have the baby some days or even weeks before the due date.

ADJUSTING TO PREGNANCY

THE CHANGE FROM BEING AN INDIVIDUAL to becoming a parent is one of the most profound you'll ever experience; a woman is different from a mother; a father is not the same as a man. It's an essentially positive and deeply satisfying experience – but you're going to find it shattering, exhausting and incredibly hard work too.

THINKING AHEAD

Your pregnancy is a time to ponder on the great changes ahead – for each of you as individuals and for you both as a couple. In many ways it's impossible to describe exactly what's ahead in pregnancy until you're there, but it's certainly true that you can be as prepared as it's possible to be by asking questions, reading, and talking to friends who've already gone through it.

YOUR DIFFERING REACTIONS

Men and women respond differently to the news of pregnancy; elation may fade into fear, anxiety or depression at the thought of the responsibilities looming, and the changes that are unavoidable. Changes in relationships can be threatening at the best of times. Those that take place in early pregnancy are particularly taxing because they have to be played out when the mother is feeling tired and possibly anxious, and the father may be feeling ambivalent about the new situation (see p. 24). Use the months ahead to prepare, as much as possible, for what's in store, but try to enjoy your pregnancy, too. Life will, after all, never be the same again. If you can, go away for a weekend or have a holiday when you're between four and seven months pregnant – it will give you plenty of time and space to share your feelings together, and in the years ahead you'll probably look back on it as the end of your old way of life, in the run up to the exciting new times ahead.

FEELINGS ABOUT PREGNANCY

You've got approximately nine months to examine your feelings as dispassionately as possible, and following the progress of the pregnancy is helpful here (see p. 30). At first, the physical changes common to most pregnant women may colour your view of the pregnancy. Many women find the physical discomforts of the first three months – tiredness, nausea, tender breasts – occur almost as soon as the pregnancy has been confirmed, sometimes within a few days of missing a period (see p. 20). This can take couples by surprise, turning initial delight into apprehension and uncertainty. However, this reaction is usually temporary, lasting about 12 weeks; after this you'll suddenly realize that you're not waking up with nausea and a fuzzy head, that you're full of energy and that instead of just looking thicker around the waist, you're developing a recognizable "bump" that announces your pregnancy to the rest of the world, and of which you can be proud!

PLANNED OR UNPLANNED

Whether the pregnancy was planned or not has a bearing on your attitude to it. An unplanned pregnancy may be welcomed by one partner more than the other (and this is often the father rather than the mother), or both of you could be ambivalent about it, especially if you have financial worries. Whether your pregnancy is planned or unplanned, there may well be implications for your career, especially if you work for a company that doesn't have a sympathetic attitude to parenthood. This is more important for working women than men, but experience shows that it is possible to resume a career even when you've had a long break for birth and child care (see p. 148). Once you know you're pregnant, talk to your employer about the options as soon as possible to find out what maternity leave is on offer (see p. 160). This will help to allay any fears you have about your career prospects that might tarnish how you feel about your pregnancy as a whole.

IF YOUR PREGNANCY WAS ASSISTED

Your attitude to your pregnancy is bound to be affected if you've had to wait a long time to conceive, and perhaps had treatment to assist conception. You'll feel an enormous sense of relief that your longed-for baby is at last on the way, but may worry about doing anything that may lead to miscarriage, so that there's a tendency to treat the pregnancy like an illness. Try to avoid this; most specialists in assisted conception will hand their patients over to the normal maternity services once the pregnancy is established – if anything is going to go wrong, it is most likely to happen in the first eight to ten weeks, and you'll have been warned about this. Even if you've had to endure quite lengthy and invasive treatments to achieve the pregnancy, try not to dwell on them and look forward instead to the birth of your healthy baby.

GIVING THE NEWS

You might both want to tell everyone straight away that you're having a baby; on the other hand you might want to hug your secret to yourself for a while. You may surprise yourself at how it comes out, depending on who you're telling, because many people find admitting they are about to become parents to a third party seems to make it real for the first time. The unqualified support of friends and family can help to overcome any feelings of doubt; alternatively you may find yourself confessing to your closest friend your ambivalence to the whole thing, even though on the surface you appear to be delighted. Once the news is out, bear in mind that in the event of a miscarriage, the more people you have told, the more distressing it may be for you if you have to explain that you've lost the baby (see p. 33).

PRE-BIRTH BONDING

Although it's wonderful to be able to see your baby moving when you have your first scan (see p. 29), most women feel that the bonding process really begins once they feel it. Though this may not happen until about 16 weeks in a first pregnancy, it's an advantage you have which your partner lacks – so share your feelings as much as possible and encourage him to feel your tummy. First sensations of movement often coincide with a change in energy levels, so you'll probably be feeling better about yourself and the baby than you ever thought possible to start with.

FATHER

The physical changes of pregnancy can affect your partner's attitude to it. Being prepared for what may happen should help you deal with the low moments she may have as they crop up.

YOUR PARTNER'S FEELINGS

■ Exhaustion is a common feature of early pregnancy – it's probably caused by all the hormones your partner's body is suddenly having to deal with. Encourage her to take things easy, and look forward to the middle months when she'll probably feel incredibly energetic and wide awake; the "bloom" of pregnancy at this time will make your partner look wonderful – so make sure you tell her!

■ The effect of pregnancy hormones combined with the whole idea of becoming a parent could make her much more emotional than usual; she'll cry easily at a "weepie" film or a tragic story in the news. Don't mock her – be sympathetic.

■ She may worry about the fact that she'll inevitably be gaining weight. Don't draw attention to this; be positive about how she looks and compliment her. It's a very bad idea to diet in pregnancy, but she doesn't need to eat for two either. Most of the fat laid down in pregnancy is stored to nourish breastfeeding, and is burnt off remarkably quickly once she starts feeding after the birth; encourage her with this information (see p. 70).

■ Your partner may feel that she's lost control of her life by getting pregnant because there's always someone else with ideas on what's best for her. Don't add to this – she knows her body best and when it comes to decision time, she's got the last word.

23

THE EXPECTANT FATHER

MOTHER

You may not think your relationship with your partner will change before the baby is born, but it will, so you should be prepared for this.

UNDERSTANDING YOUR PARTNER
■ It is very easy for men to feel left out so make sure you involve your partner as much as possible.

■ Don't expect him to feel the same way as you. Expecting a baby is an external experience for him and it may be very difficult for him to empathize with the invisible changes taking place within you. Remember, his day-to-day life will be much the same and there won't be such an obvious change for him until after your baby is born.

■ Talk to your partner about how you are feeling. You may have big mood swings and go through periods of feeling insecure and unattractive. Don't take it out on him – it's not his fault. Rather than bottling it up and allowing it to come out in an argument, sit down with your partner and explain how you are feeling.

AFFECTION AND SEX
■ Your partner may be anxious about your wellbeing and treat you as if you are ill. This kind of attention can be suffocating so tell your partner if you don't like it. Also, remind him that you are as keen as he is not to do anything to endanger the baby. Equally, if your partner is not giving you enough attention, tell him when you need a cuddle.

■ Your desire to have sex may change at different stages of your pregnancy. If you do not want intercourse, tell your partner.

ONE OF THE MOST EXCITING MOMENTS of your life will probably be when you find out that you are going to be a father. The emotional impact for you will be just as real as it is for your partner, but it's often underestimated and you are likely to find that once the initial excitement has worn off, people stop asking you how *you* are feeling. It is, however, important to talk about your emotions, even if it is only to your partner, and to get involved in the pregnancy and birth plans. Make it as big a part of your life as you can – it is, after all, something that is happening to both of you, not just your partner.

UNDERSTANDING YOUR CONFLICTING EMOTIONS

The pregnancy may not seem real for the first couple of months – not least because your partner will physically look the same. Don't worry if you feel differently from her about the pregnancy; it is an internal experience for her and an external one for you, and you don't suddenly become one person with one set of feelings just because you are having a baby together. However, once you see that your partner's body has begun to change and, later, when you have felt the baby move, the idea of having a baby will become more real. It is at this time that your feelings of joy and excitement may be replaced by fears and worries; whatever your family set-up, it is normal for a man to begin to worry about being able to provide for his family. Having a child can be an extra financial burden, especially if your partner is going to give up her job, but try not to make life-changing decisions, such as getting a new job or seeking promotion. It's difficult to know whether you'll want extra responsibility a year down the line, once you are a parent. Remember, as a father, you have more than just material possessions to offer your child.

HOW YOU CAN PARTICIPATE

Being an expectant father is the one time in your life when you are quite likely to feel out of control. This feeling of being an outsider will not be helped by the way other people treat you: well-meaning female friends and relatives may unconsciously push you out of what they see as their territory. You may also find that the professionals, such as obstetricians and midwives, direct their conversations at your partner more than you.

TAKE THE INITIATIVE
Don't step back and allow your female relatives and friends to be more involved than you. Tell your own friends and colleagues: you may be subject to a certain amount of teasing but, equally, people may view you as more responsible and mature. Try to find out as much as you can about the pregnancy so that you can understand the changes taking place in your partner's body. If possible, go with her to the scans so that you can see your baby developing, talk about the fact you are going to be a father and ask as many questions as you want – most of all, enjoy it!

24

TAKING AN ACTIVE ROLE

WHAT TO DO	HOW IT CAN HELP YOU
TALK TO YOUR PARTNER	The best way to understand how your partner is feeling, and what is going on in her body, is to talk to her. Ask her what it feels like to feel the baby move; discuss your plans for the birth together; find out if she's got particular discomforts. She'll appreciate your interest.
GO TO ANTENATAL CLASSES	If you go to antenatal classes (especially father-only sessions), you will have an opportunity to learn about the birth and talk through your own concerns. This will help you to work out the best way to support your partner and enable you to be more involved in birth choices.
TALK TO OTHER FATHERS	Get to know the other expectant fathers at antenatal classes – they will probably be feeling the same as you and be glad to have someone to talk to. Talk to friends and colleagues who have babies; find out what their experience was like and ask their advice.
READ ABOUT PREGNANCY AND PARENTING	Read pregnancy and parenting books and any leaflets you are given. The more you understand about what's going on during the pregnancy, the more familiar it will become and it can help you to understand how your partner is feeling. It will also enable you to ask the right questions.
ASK QUESTIONS	Go to antenatal appointments with your partner so that you can meet the professionals and be present at the examinations. As a first-time parent, there will be things you don't understand and need to know about. If you ask questions of professionals, they are more likely to involve you.

PLAN FOR THE BIRTH TOGETHER

You will need to discuss with your partner the type of birth that she wants (see p. 26) and decide what your involvement will be. You will also need to talk to your employer about taking time off to go to the antenatal appointments as well as the birth, and to enable you to spend some time at home after the baby is born.

THE BIRTH PLAN

Discuss the issues raised by the birth plan (see p. 27) with your partner, but don't impose your views. If your partner feels strongly about certain issues, for example, she wants to try for a drug-free labour (see p. 41), try to respect her feelings, but insist on discussing the advantages and disadvantages. Look forward to being present at the birth. Remember, witnessing the birth of your child is probably one of the most precious things you will ever experience and holding your baby in the first few seconds of life is proven to help with future bonding between father and child.

PRENATAL BONDING

You can never start bonding with your baby too early. Babies can hear sounds outside the womb by five or six months; if you talk to your baby, he will bond to your voice while he is still in the womb and, in fact, he can hear your low-pitched voice more clearly than his mother's. Don't feel awkward – think about the life you've created and love it. To help you to bond with your baby:

■ Gently massage your partner's tummy and feel your baby move.

■ Talk and coo softly to your baby, and kiss and nuzzle him through your partner's skin.

■ Use inner tubes of toilet rolls to listen to the heartbeat.

■ Go to scans with your partner to see your baby develop (see p. 29).

25

BEING INVOLVED

It's your baby too. You have every right to be involved in all aspects of the pregnancy and to:

■ Be open about your feelings.

■ Express your concerns without fear of misinterpretation.

■ Talk candidly to your partner about sex so that it does not become an issue.

■ Be party to all arrangements and plans for the birth.

■ Go to antenatal classes.

■ Go to antenatal appointments so that you can hear your baby's heartbeat and see him move on the ultrasound monitor.

■ Visit the hospital and delivery room with your partner.

■ Contribute to the birth plan.

■ Meet any professionals involved.

■ Be present at the birth.

ANTENATAL CLASSES

It's immensely helpful and supportive for you both to attend a series of antenatal classes.

WHAT CLASSES DO
They will help explain a lot of the choices available both before, during and after the birth of your baby. As well as telling you about labour, birth and baby care, you'll meet other expectant parents with due dates near yours, with whom you can share experiences.

WHERE TO FIND CLASSES
If you're planning a hospital delivery, hospital-based classes can be useful as they'll help familiarize you with procedures and will include a tour of the labour ward. Community classes may be run by community midwives, providing "shared" care (see right) in your local health or community centre or at your doctor's surgery. Parent education networks or active birth groups (see p. 163) are usually run in teachers' own homes and are much more likely to focus on natural childbirth and alternative birth options than classes that are run by hospitals or midwives.

PREPARATION FOR BIRTH
Antenatal classes give you a chance to learn techniques to prepare you for labour and birth well in advance.

Your partner can practise different techniques for relieving pain

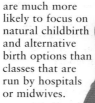

OPTIONS FOR ANTENATAL CARE

NOWADAYS, CHOICE IS THE WATCHWORD of maternity care, although how wide the choice is will depend on what's available in your area. Looking at your antenatal options also means looking ahead to your birth options. Although the majority of births do take place in hospital, this needn't automatically mean a high-tech managed labour.

WHO CAN DELIVER CARE?

Once you know you're pregnant, your first call will probably be to your family doctor. He or she may confirm the pregnancy with another test, take your blood pressure and ask you about when your last period was, to work out the due date. Your doctor will tell you the different options for antenatal care available in your area and you can also talk through where the baby will be born as these are often linked. Don't feel you have to make your mind up on any of these issues immediately: go away and think about the possibilities before finalizing details.

Shared care Antenatal care may be offered by your family doctor, in association with community midwives and the hospital. Routine checks will be done by your doctor and the community midwife, and you'll go to the hospital for specialist checks such as ultrasound. This type of care is helpful if you live some distance from the hospital. However, you may not have met the midwife who delivers your baby in the hospital before the event.

Midwives care In some places, antenatal care is given almost entirely by community or hospital midwives working in teams, or under the Domino system (see opposite). They are based either at a local health centre or hospital and can also arrange home births. You'll be able to build up a relationship with the midwives who will also deliver your baby.

Independent midwives If you want to be cared for solely by midwives, you might want to consider hiring an independent one. This is expensive, but it does enable you to arrange your care, labour and birth exactly as you want it.

Hospital care In some areas this may still be the only option. You'll receive your care from hospital-based doctors and midwives. It will be competent, but may lack the informality of other options. However, if you have any complications, have an existing medical condition, or are having twins, it's probably the wisest option.

Lean on a pillow over a chair-back

Experiment at classes with different labour positions

WHERE TO HAVE YOUR BABY?

Thinking about antenatal care also means deciding where you want your baby to be delivered. Whatever type of antenatal care you're having, you'll be booked in to the hospital at the first appointment (see overleaf). If you want to have a home birth, it may need a certain amount of negotiation with your doctor or midwives. Either way you need to look at the options side by side with those for antenatal care.

HOSPITAL BIRTH

Having a first baby in hospital feels right to many couples, and is usually the recommendation of the medical profession. There's plenty of back-up on hand if things aren't straightforward, and in most hospitals there's access to the full range of pain relief.

Advantages Having your baby in hospital doesn't necessarily mean opting for high-tech: many hospitals have special low-tech birthing rooms where you'll be free to walk around in labour and where intervention will be kept to a minimum. Many hospitals have pools for pain relief (see p. 41), though it's difficult to ensure you'll get to use one as you can't usually pre-book them. In some areas, under a scheme known as "Domino", a midwife comes to your home once you're in labour, accompanies you to hospital, delivers your baby and returns with you to your home as little as four hours later. If you like the idea of being back with your family at home as soon as possible, but want the medical back-up for the delivery itself, this option could be ideal for you.

Disadvantages It's important to realize that having a baby in hospital does mean agreeing to childbirth policies that may cramp your style. You will, for example, be required to have your baby's heartbeat electronically monitored, at least for a time, which may make it difficult for you to remain active and upright throughout, if that's what you'd hoped for.

HOME BIRTH

Although numbers are rising, only a tiny percentage of births happen in the home, and much depends on the attitude of your own doctor and community midwives. Despite evidence showing that a planned home birth is as safe as a hospital birth, some doctors are reluctant to co-operate and you may have to seek out an independent midwife to help you achieve it (see opposite).

Advantages Home is a more relaxed place to have a baby than hospital. You're far less likely to need emergency treatment if you remain active as far into labour as you can. Your chances for a straightforward, problem-free delivery at home are good, even if this is your first child.

Disadvantages You don't have immediate access to emergency treatment, so if anything untoward happens or your labour fails to progress, you might need to be transferred to hospital. You also won't have access to pain relief such as an epidural and, in some countries, pethidine (see p. 41).

DELIVERY IN A BIRTH CENTRE

Birth centres are usually sited near hospitals, but are completely self-contained and designed to have a less medical feel. They may be staffed by family doctors and community midwives or run solely by midwives. Staff often don't wear uniforms, and you'll probably be given your own room in which to spend your labour, give birth and then remain after the delivery. These centres can provide an excellent halfway house, giving you the informality of a home birth with the safety net of high-tech care nearby.

YOUR BIRTH PLAN

Once you've considered all your antenatal care and birth options, and have some clear ideas of what you would like to happen during your labour and birth, it's worth preparing a simple birth plan in consultation with your doctor and midwife. This should be kept with your hospital notes. It's probably best to wait until you're about 32–36 weeks pregnant before discussing the details; by that time you'll probably have discovered whether there are any special factors associated with your pregnancy that might make some of your requests difficult to achieve. You also need to be prepared to be flexible because things may not go according to plan on the day. Your birth plan might include the following:

■ Who you want to be present at the birth with you.

■ Your views on interventions such as induction, the artificial speeding up of labour (see p. 48), and foetal monitoring (see p. 42).

■ Your views on active labour, and whether you would like the possibility of using a birthing pool to help cope with labour (see p. 41).

■ Your preferences for pain relief (see p. 41), and the use of breathing and relaxation techniques you've been practising during your pregnancy.

■ Whether you mind student doctors or midwives being present during your labour and birth, if it is a teaching hospital.

■ What position you might adopt to deliver your baby (see p. 44).

■ Whether you would prefer not to have an episiotomy (see p. 45) if the delivery is normal.

■ Whether you mind if the delivery of your placenta is speeded up with syntometrine or whether you'd prefer it to be delivered naturally (see p. 46).

27

YOUR ANTENATAL CARE

THE PHYSICAL EXAMINATION

At every antenatal appointment, various checks will always be done to rule out potentially dangerous medical conditions.

BLOOD PRESSURE
A rise in blood pressure could mean you're at risk of pre-eclampsia, a potentially serious circulatory disorder (see p. 32).

URINE TEST
A urine sample will be tested for the presence of protein, which could mean an infection or, later, pre-eclampsia; glucose or sugar, which could signal diabetes; and ketones, chemicals which indicate you're not eating enough.

ABDOMINAL CHECK
The midwife will feel your abdomen to check the size of your uterus. She'll also listen to your baby's heartbeat, using either a Pinard stethoscope (which looks like an ear trumpet) or a sonicaid, an electronic stethoscope that amplifies the baby's heartbeat so you can hear it (see below).

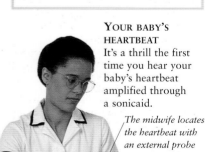

YOUR BABY'S HEARTBEAT
It's a thrill the first time you hear your baby's heartbeat amplified through a sonicaid.

The midwife locates the heartbeat with an external probe

W HICHEVER KIND OF ANTENATAL CARE you choose, there will be certain procedures that any midwife or doctor will follow throughout your pregnancy when caring for you. In general, antenatal checks are to ensure that all is going well with your pregnancy – that you are healthy, and that your baby is growing properly.

YOUR FIRST APPOINTMENT

Often known as the booking-in appointment, your first antenatal session may be quite long, lasting as much as an hour. It may be at your home, at the local health centre or doctor's surgery, or at a hospital clinic. A midwife will take a detailed medical history, and will ask a long list of questions about your general health, your family's health, and your gynaecological and obstetric history. She will also ask whether or not this baby was planned, how long ago you stopped using contraceptives or what contraceptive you were using when you got pregnant, and the date of the first day of your last menstrual period. The midwife will also talk to you generally about how your pregnancy is going and ask you how you are feeling. She'll offer you advice – often backed up by booklets you can take away to digest at home – on issues like diet, exercise and maternity benefits. You will also be able to discuss your thoughts on what kind of delivery you'd like, though it's still early days and nothing will have to be decided at this time unless you're absolutely sure (see previous page). You will probably be asked to bring a urine sample to each appointment.

THE BLOOD TEST

You'll probably have some blood taken, which will be sent to the laboratory for analysis. Ask the midwife exactly what your blood will be checked for and why; it's routinely checked for iron content, blood group and rhesus status, rubella immunity, blood sugar levels and sexually transmitted diseases. Other tests, such as one to check whether you've been exposed to toxoplasmosis (a parasitic disease that may affect your unborn baby) may also be available. Blood isn't usually tested at every appointment, but in certain situations you will be asked to give blood again at later appointments (see opposite), and many hospitals test routinely at 28 and 36 weeks.

FUTURE APPOINTMENTS

Your routine antenatal check-ups will generally be shorter than your booking-in appointment, but if you're attending them at a hospital clinic you may need to set aside a couple of hours each time as queues can easily build up if another appointment overruns. Between appointments, it's a good idea to write down any questions you may have as you think of them, and keep them with your record card; otherwise you're likely to forget them. You'll be given a schedule of appointments, but you can always ask for an additional appointment if you have any worries.

ULTRASOUND SCANS

Ultrasound is now offered routinely to almost all pregnant women, as it enables the baby's gestational age to be measured very accurately and can also detect visible abnormalities. Many hospitals offer two scans, one at about 12 weeks and the other at 16 to 20 weeks. The scans are carried out at the hospital, and your partner should be allowed into the examination room with you; this is a wonderful opportunity for a father to relate to his growing baby as you'll be able to see it moving about. The operator slowly scans across your abdomen with a hand-held instrument called a transducer that detects sound waves bounced off your uterus and baby's body. These are transmitted to a computerized monitor for visual interpretation. After the scan you may be offered a picture – your first photo of your baby!

HAVING AN ULTRASOUND SCAN

As you lie comfortably on a bed, gel is spread over your abdomen. The transducer is passed gently to and fro across your abdomen and the image transmitted to a nearby visual monitor.

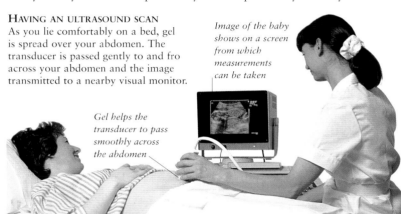

Image of the baby shows on a screen from which measurements can be taken

Gel helps the transducer to pass smoothly across the abdomen

29

SPECIALIST SCREENING AND DIAGNOSTIC TESTS

TEST	HOW IT IS DONE	WHAT IT CAN TELL YOU
NUCHAL SCAN	A fairly new non-invasive screening scan done at 11–13 weeks, measuring the thickness of the "nuchal pad" in the baby's neck.	A thick nuchal pad may mean a higher risk of chromosomal defects, so you'll be offered a test such as amniocentesis later.
TRIPLE (OR BART'S) TEST	This blood test (non-invasive to the baby) screens you for the risk of Down's syndrome. It is done at 15–16 weeks along with a scan.	Hormone levels indicate the risk of your baby being affected; if it is greater than 1 in 250, you'll be offered a diagnostic test.
AFP TEST	A screening blood test that checks the level of alpha-fetoprotein (AFP) at about 15–18 weeks.	A higher or lower level than usual may indicate Down's syndrome or spina bifida.
CHORIONIC VILLUS SAMPLING	A diagnostic test, in which a cannula (tube) is passed through the cervix at about 10–12 weeks to take cells from the developing placenta.	The cells are examined to check the baby's chromosomes for any abnormalities. This technique carries a small risk of miscarriage.
AMNIOCENTESIS	A diagnostic test done at about 15 weeks. Guided by ultrasound, a needle takes a sample of amniotic fluid through the abdominal wall.	Chromosomes in foetal cells can be checked for abnormalities such as Down's syndrome. There's a small risk (1 in 200) of miscarriage.
FETAL BLOOD TEST (CORDOCENTESIS)	This rare diagnostic test is carried out after about 18–20 weeks. It takes blood from the umbilical cord.	Blood is tested for abnormal chromosomes or infections. There's a miscarriage risk of about 1–2 per cent.

MOTHER

The knowledge that your baby is growing inside you is really exciting, so don't let minor complaints get you down.

COPING WITH COMMON COMPLAINTS

■ Feeling sick is most common in the first three months. It may happen in the morning, but by no means always, and you may also vomit. Eating little and often rather than big meals helps. Avoid foods that make you feel nauseous. If you're vomiting incessantly, consult your doctor.

■ You're more likely to get cramp in your legs or feet. It's not known exactly why, but you can relieve it by pulling your toes up hard towards your ankle.

■ Constipation is a common problem, caused by the presence of hormones that slow down the workings of the large intestine. Make sure you eat plenty of fibre, exercise regularly, and drink plenty of water. Iron pills may make it worse.

■ Later in pregnancy, you may suffer from indigestion or heartburn, because your enlarging womb is pressing on your stomach. You can prevent this by eating smaller meals more often, sitting up straight when eating, and avoiding spiced foods. Sipping milk, especially at night, can help if you have heartburn.

■ Haemorrhoids – swollen varicose veins that protrude from the back passage – occur in pregnancy due to pressure from the baby, especially if you're constipated and strain to open your bowels. Eat plenty of fibre and avoid standing for long periods. Apply an ice pack or cold wet flannel to ease discomfort. Consult your doctor if they become very painful or prolapse.

30

THE PROGRESS OF PREGNANCY

HAVING A BABY GROWING INSIDE YOU is like being part of a real-life miracle. Sometimes you'll pat your bump and feel you can hardly believe your child is in there – it seems so amazing and extraordinary. Take time to ponder on the wonder of what's happening; you'll both be laying the foundations for a baby who feels secure and wanted.

FOLLOWING YOUR PREGNANCY

No part of a woman's body escapes when she's carrying a baby, and you both need to keep that in mind. For instance, tender breasts that are getting ready for breastfeeding need to be treated gently by a father when he caresses them; the growing uterus pressing on your internal organs means that you must never be too far from a toilet during the last three months of pregnancy. The guide that follows is only a brief outline of the complex changes going on inside your body.

WHAT'S HAPPENED BY THREE MONTHS

The first three months of pregnancy (the first trimester) are tremendously important in laying the foundations of your baby's healthy development, although there are few visible signs of your baby's phenomenal growth.

YOU
- You'll really start to gain weight; any morning sickness will soon disappear.
- The uterus is rising out of the pelvis and can be felt.
- The risk of miscarriage is almost zero now.
- Your heart is working flat out and will continue to do so right up to labour.

YOUR BABY
- She has a fully formed body, complete with fingers, toes and ears.
- Her eyes move, though her eyelids are closed.
- Her body is covered with fine hair.
- She wriggles if poked – her muscles are growing.

WHAT'S HAPPENED BY SIX MONTHS

The period from about the third to the sixth month (the second trimester) is when pregnancy sickness ends, your baby really grows and you begin to feel her move. You're brimming with energy, vitality and well-being.

YOU
- You're putting on about 0.5kg (12oz) weight per week.
- Your uterus is a good 5cm (2 in) above the pelvis.
- You may have bouts of indigestion.
- From about 16 weeks, you'll feel the baby move.

YOUR BABY
- Her hearing is acute, she can recognize your voice.
- She's becoming better proportioned – her body is catching up on her head.
- She's well muscled but thin.
- Her lungs are maturing fast.

WHAT'S HAPPENED BY NINE MONTHS (FULL TERM)

The final 12 weeks or so of pregnancy, known as the third trimester, are when the baby puts on fat in preparation for birth and the brain and lungs mature in preparation for independent life.

YOU
- You may feel a "lightening" as your baby's head drops into the pelvis.
- It's more difficult to find a comfortable position for sleep.
- You visit the antenatal clinic every week.
- Your breasts secrete clear-coloured nutritious colostrum.

YOUR BABY
- She weighs about 2.7–3.5kg (6–8lb) and she measures 35–38cm (14–15in) from crown to rump.
- Her head is "engaged", lying just on top of your cervix.
- The placenta is 20–25cm (8–10in) across and there is 1.1 litres (2 pints) of amniotic fluid.
- Her breasts may be swollen due to the action of your hormones.

PREGNANCY AT A GLANCE
It's useful to be able to visualize what is happening by the end of each of the three phases, or trimesters, of pregnancy, so that you understand why certain complaints may occur (see opposite).

FATHER

Although you're experiencing the pregnancy secondhand, following its progress helps you to become emotionally attached to your unborn baby.

THE PROGRESS OF PREGNANCY
■ Accompanying your partner to antenatal appointments (see p. 28) enables you to find out together how your baby is growing.

■ Remember that the baby is part of you as well as your partner. It's amazing to think that a single cell created from your sperm and your partner's ovum (see p. 20) can develop so rapidly.

■ Understanding and learning about the impact of the growing baby and uterus on your partner's body helps you to be sympathetic when she suffers the inevitable discomforts caused by the pregnancy (see box opposite).

31

AT THREE MONTHS
Your uterus is about the size of a grapefruit and can just be felt above the pubic bone. All your baby's organs are formed and virtually impervious to the potential dangers, such as an infection and medication.

The foetus is recognizably human, and all her internal systems are in place

AT SIX MONTHS
Your baby's organs are fully formed, her face is that of a newborn, and she sucks her thumb. Your uterus is poised for labour. You may notice Braxton Hicks contractions (see p. 40).

Hearing is developed; she may respond to noise. Skin is red and thin, with little fat beneath it

Below: Size of the baby's hand in relation to your hand at six months.

AT NINE MONTHS (FULL TERM)
You'll find you get breathless because your baby is now so big. Her eyes are open and she's fat and healthy. If your baby is a boy, his testes have descended.

By full term, the baby is usually positioned head downwards

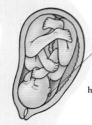

Below: Size of the baby's hand in relation to your hand at full term.

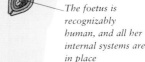

"SMALL FOR DATES"

After reviewing the date of your last period and your expected date of delivery, both your heights, and scans of the baby, your pregnancy may be pronounced "small for dates". This is no cause for alarm, but for reassurance doctors will keep an eye on you by:

■ Giving you weekly ultrasound scans for a while to ensure all's well and to check the placenta.

■ Checking on the baby's heartrate for any sign of strain.

■ Discussing with you the possibility of delivering your baby by Caesarean section (see p. 50), to prevent the baby having to go through a vaginal delivery.

PRE-ECLAMPSIA

Pre-eclampsia is a potentially serious condition that can affect as many as one in ten women, especially first-time mothers and women carrying more than one baby. It's unique to pregnancy, starting at any time in the second half. It's not known precisely what causes it, but it does tend to run in families.

HOW IT AFFECTS YOU

Pre-eclampsia is symptomless, but raised blood pressure and protein in the urine detected at an antenatal visit, may alert staff to its presence. It arises in the placenta and so the baby may grow more slowly than normal. The pregnancy can't be restored to normal, but delivery of the baby and placenta ends the disease. Admission to hospital allows close monitoring of mother and baby so that delivery can be arranged before serious complications arise. For almost every mother, delivery of her baby reverses all the effects.

DIFFICULT PREGNANCIES

ALTHOUGH THE MAJORITY OF PREGNANCIES proceed without incident, occasionally things don't go according to plan. When something unexpected happens or there's cause for concern at your antenatal check-up, you're both going to feel extremely concerned about it, especially if all has gone well up to this point. Until now you may have been confident, perhaps had even taken for granted, that all would be straightforward. Now, suddenly, the pregnancy seems to be in question, and you may feel apprehensive and confused. It helps enormously to face what's ahead together and to get as much information as you can.

CAUSES FOR CONCERN

Some worrying development, like vaginal bleeding, may strike out of the blue; a "small for dates" baby (see above left) or high blood pressure (pre-eclampsia – see below left) may be diagnosed at a routine antenatal check. Whatever the cause for concern, get a full explanation from your doctor or consultant, and it may need both of you to insist on this.

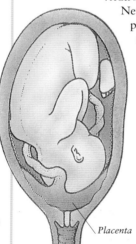

VAGINAL BLEEDING

Never ignore vaginal bleeding at any stage of your pregnancy. Although it's always worrying, close medical supervision can help avoid serious problems.

Bleeding in the first three months Bleeding in early pregnancy doesn't mean you'll lose your baby. You may not yet have high enough hormone levels to subdue your periods. You may have a condition like cervical erosion or polyps, neither of which are likely to interfere with your pregnancy. Contact your doctor or hospital as soon as possible so you can be referred for a scan; if the heart is beating well, bleeding will probably stop and pregnancy continue normally. You'll need to rest and forego sex for a while.

Bleeding in later pregnancy It's rare to bleed late in pregnancy, but it's serious since it may indicate problems with the placenta such as placenta praevia or approaching placental abruption. Placenta praevia means the placenta is positioned in the lower part of the womb, possibly across the cervix (see left). Placental abruption means that the placenta is beginning to separate from the uterine wall. Both conditions can be confirmed by ultrasound scanning, and hospital admission for observation and subsequent Caesarean delivery (see p. 50) will be necessary.

Placenta

PLACENTA PRAEVIA
The placenta embeds close to or across the cervix, where pressure from the baby may cause vaginal bleeding.

PREGNANCY AND PRE-EXISTING MEDICAL CONDITIONS

Any existing medical condition means that your pregnancy will be carefully monitored to safeguard you and your baby. Medical conditions like asthma, epilepsy, heart disease or kidney disease don't in themselves make pregnancy and labour difficult. If you take care of yourself, have meticulous antenatal supervision and prepare yourself for in-patient hospital care in the last ten weeks of pregnancy, the chances are you'll have a normal birth.

DIABETES

Sugar – a sign, but not proof, of diabetes – may appear in your urine at any time in pregnancy. The most common reason for this is a change in the way the kidney handles sugar in pregnancy: no treatment is needed. "Latent" diabetes can do the same thing and can be controlled with diet alone, though you'll be checked more frequently at the antenatal clinic. Pre-existing diabetes needs strict supervision because your insulin needs may change and your dose will be adjusted. Babies of diabetic mothers tend to be large so you may be induced early or your baby may be delivered by Caesarean section (see p. 50).

MULTIPLE PREGNANCY

Carrying more than one baby will undoubtedly mean you have more professional attention and more antenatal appointments during your pregnancy. The diagnosis of twins, triplets or more will be confirmed with an ultrasound scan, and the news may take a lot of getting used to, but there's a lot of help and support for you both.

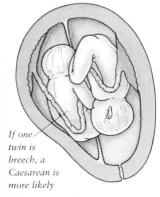

If both twins are head down, it's more likely that both will be delivered vaginally

If one twin is breech, a Caesarean is more likely

HOW TWINS LIE
Twins normally lie both head down, or one head down and one breech. How they lie may affect the way your delivery is managed (see p. 49).

HOW YOU MAY FEEL

Nausea Multiple pregnancies often cause severe nausea, even vomiting, in the first three months. Eat little and often, and drink plenty of fluids – drinks containing glucose or glucose tablets may boost energy levels if you feel too sick to get calories from food.

Increasing size You get bigger faster than a mother with one baby because, as well as carrying two babies, you produce more amniotic fluid.

Backache Be careful about posture and avoid carrying or lifting heavy weights, because the additional levels of pregnancy hormones mean your pelvic ligaments can soften and stretch, and become painful.

Fatigue You'll tire very easily, and this may be made worse by anaemia. Rest, eat meat and take folic acid and iron supplements.

Indigestion This may be worse than in a single pregnancy (see p. 30) because your stomach is squashed against your diaphragm. Have nourishing drinks and soups and eat frequent small meals.

LOSING YOUR BABY

No-one can imagine the grief of a couple losing a longed-for baby. For your own sakes, seek counselling so that you can grieve fully and finally come to terms with your loss.

EARLY MISCARRIAGE
A miscarriage in the first few weeks is more common than you might think – in fact one in three of first pregnancies. It usually happens because there was something amiss with the foetus or perhaps it had not implanted correctly. Early miscarriage may not be accompanied by much pain, although you may suffer severe period-like cramps. However, you're both going to feel really let down, and a woman has to deal with sudden hormonal changes that can make her very emotional.

LATE MISCARRIAGE
This occurs between 13 and 24 weeks, usually because of placental problems or a weakened cervix that opens due to the weight of the growing foetus. You have a mini-labour to expel the foetus with whatever pain relief you choose.

STILLBIRTH
Losing your baby at or close to full term is very hard to bear, but nowadays you'll be given a chance to hold your baby if you want to, to name him and to give him a proper funeral.

DEALING WITH YOUR LOSS
Whatever the reason for your loss, your distress needs careful handling: it's a bereavement that may be complicated by feelings of guilt and blame that could trigger depression or drive a wedge between you as a couple. Talk about your feelings to each other and to your doctor; ask her to explain the reasons for your loss, but accept that no-one may know exactly why your baby died. Above all, look forward to the future; most couples who have lost a baby go on to become proud parents of healthy babies.

33

BALANCING YOUR DIET

To provide for your baby's needs as well as your own, note the following tips about your diet:

■ Complex carbohydrates such as pasta, potatoes or pulses (beans and lentils) are needed for energy.

■ Protein is needed for your baby's growth. Eat fish and poultry, dairy produce, wholegrain cereals, seeds and pulses.

■ Don't cut out fats altogether, but don't eat too much either. You'll get enough from dairy products and normal cooking methods.

■ Get vitamin C daily from raw fresh fruit and vegetables, and the B complex from wholegrains, nuts and pulses, green vegetables, dairy products, eggs, oily fish and meat.

■ Iron maintains red blood cells; it's found in red meat, fish, egg yolks, apricots and cereals.

FOOD SAFETY

Scrupulous kitchen hygiene (see p. 97) is essential as some infections transmitted in food are hazardous during pregnancy:

■ Listeria is a rare bacterium found in products made with unpasteurized milk, liver, undercooked meat and pre-cooked meals. Avoid these products as infection during pregnancy may result in miscarriage or stillbirth.

■ Salmonella is a bacterium infection found in eggs and chicken that causes fever, abdominal pain and severe diarrhoea. It's destroyed by thorough cooking.

■ Toxoplasmosis is caused by a parasite in cat and dog faeces, and also in raw meat. It can cause birth defects. Cook meat thoroughly, wash your hands after handling pets and wear gloves when gardening.

TAKING CARE OF YOURSELF

PREGNANCY IS NOT AN ILLNESS, it's a natural part of life and women's bodies are designed to accommodate it. But your body does have to work hard to provide for your growing baby, so it's important to pay attention to nutrition and exercise that help you build stamina, maintain your energy levels and minimize discomfort.

WEIGHT AND DIET

Your body uses up a lot of energy during pregnancy and you need to eat well to fuel your requirements and those of your growing baby. You could reasonably increase your intake of food by 200–300 calories a day and expect to put on 9–15kg (20–30lbs) in weight, much of which is accounted for by the baby, uterus and amniotic fluid. Pregnancy is not a time to go on a diet, but you should also forget the myth about "eating for two"; the rule is to eat to satisfy your hunger, and no more. Later in pregnancy you may find you simply can't take in much food at any one time so eat little and often. Keep healthy snacks such as dried fruit, rice cakes, crispbreads and hard fruits in your bag, car or office, and low-fat cheese and yogurt, raw vegetables, fresh fruit and unsweetened fruit juice in the refrigerator at home.

BODY MAINTENANCE

The pregnancy hormones have profound effects on teeth, hair, nails and skin, so don't be surprised by some temporary changes.

Teeth Progesterone makes the gums soft so they may bleed more easily. Take care of your teeth and gums, and visit your dentist at the beginning of your pregnancy. Make sure you tell him you are pregnant in case he wants to take X-rays, as these are dangerous to the developing embryo.

Hair and nails Straight hair can become curly, and vice versa. Hair grows and falls in phases – pregnancy often prolongs the growth phase, making thin hair thick and glossy, whereas thick hair may become dry and unmanageable. The downside is that you'll experience hair loss after the birth, although it'll grow back eventually. Although they grow faster, nails also become brittle. Keep them short and use rehydrating creams to keep them moist.

Skin Oestrogen gives your skin the legendary bloom of pregnancy, but dry skin becomes drier and greasy skin more oily. Patches of brown pigment (chloasma) may appear on your face and neck but will eventually fade. All skins deepen in colour with browning of the nipples and a line down the abdomen. Tiny dilated capillaries (spider naevi) on the face are common but disappear later. Stretch marks on the breasts, thighs and abdomen are very common; they're related to the breakdown of protein in the skin by the high levels of pregnancy hormones. Because of this, rubbing in oils and creams doesn't help, but most marks will fade after the birth.

DEALING WITH FATIGUE

Fatigue is a periodic problem during pregnancy, especially during the first three months and the last six to eight weeks. Its extent may take you by surprise, especially during the first few weeks – it's the kind of tiredness where you feel you don't even have the energy to blink, but just stare straight ahead. You're sleepy in the early stages of pregnancy because you're sedated by the high levels of progesterone. Your metabolism speeds up to deal with the demands of your baby and the extra work all your organs are called on to do. Later on in pregnancy you're tired because your whole body is working flat out 24 hours a day, and you're having to carry extra weight around that puts a strain on your heart, lungs and muscles.

WAYS OF COPING
- Never stand when you can sit, never sit when you can lie.
- If possible, put your feet up whenever you sit – if you're in the office invert a wastebin or box under the desk.
- Sleep anywhere; put your head down on your desk during the lunchbreak; close your eyes on the bus or train home after work.
- When you're at home, plan specific rest times and let nothing interfere with them; some people like to lie down after lunch, others find they need to rest in the late afternoon or early evening.
- Lie in every weekend.
- Go to bed early at least three times a week.
- Find ways to help you drop off, such as watching TV or reading.
- Lie down and listen to music – not too loud as your baby can hear it.
- Find different comfortable resting positions for instant relief of tiredness. Try lying on the floor on cushions with your feet on a bed, sofa or chair and your knees at right angles, or take up the first-aid recovery position with cushions under your knees and upper body (see below).

Relaxation Use whatever technique you can to relax – you're going to need at least 30 minutes a day from now on and it will be so refreshing if you teach yourself to let go in seconds. You'll probably be taught relaxation techniques at your antenatal classes (see p. 26), and there are plenty of books and tapes to guide you. Practise with your partner, if possible; it will be good for both of you and learning to relax is an essential part of most of the techniques used for the natural control of pain during labour (see p. 43).

POSITION FOR RELAXATION
This position takes the weight off your back and allows free blood circulation, increasing the supply of oxygen to your baby.

Support your head with pillows

Pillows between the legs support the upper knee

ON YOUR OWN

If you decided at the outset that you wanted to have a baby but not a continuing relationship with the baby's father, fair enough. However, most women facing pregnancy and parenthood on their own did not make that choice and if you find that this is your reality, allow yourself to work through your feelings of disappointment and even outrage.

COPING WITH YOUR FEELINGS
At a time when women naturally expect support, comfort and the shared pleasure of contemplating parenthood, you are experiencing the very opposite. Ideally, explore your feelings with a friend or, even better, a professional counsellor who will help you to isolate each issue and deal with it.

BEING POSITIVE
Once you have embarked upon your pregnancy, you must be ruthless about avoiding those people who may not take a positive view of either you or your condition. Since you do not have the most obvious form of support, a partner, the last thing you need is negativity, no matter where it is coming from.

LOOKING AFTER YOURSELF
Try not to neglect your health; when you're on your own, it's only too easy to skip meals or opt for easy snacks because you can't be bothered to cook. Make sure you go to all your antenatal check-ups. The health professionals are there to help you and if you need extra support, they will help you find it.

FEELINGS TOWARDS YOUR BABY
If you are feeling hostile towards the baby's father, try not to associate this feeling with your unborn baby; it's not her fault. You've taken on a challenge, but you can give her the best start in life: by deciding to have her without the support of a partner, you have already demonstrated how committed you are to her.

PELVIC FLOOR EXERCISES

The pelvic floor consists of muscles and fibrous tissue suspended like a funnel from the pelvic bones. The layers of muscle are thickest at the perineum, where there are openings for the urethra, vagina and anus, which the pelvic floor muscles also support. If you don't know where your pelvic floor muscles are, you can locate them by stopping your flow of urine in midstream: the muscles you are using are those of your pelvic floor.

EXERCISING YOUR PELVIC FLOOR
The pelvic floor is put under strain by pregnancy, when the presence of hormones causes it to soften and relax. You can keep it toned by doing the following simple exercise routine daily:

■ Pull in your pelvic floor muscles, then let them go quickly; do this five times.

■ Pull the muscles in and hold for a count of five, then let them go slowly; repeat this five times.

■ Finally, do the first, quick exercise five more times.

Restart these exercises after your baby is born to minimize the risk of prolapse.

PRECAUTIONS

Before any exercise session, do some stretches to warm up: keep your back straight, breathe evenly and flex your feet. Your ligaments are softened through the action of the pregnancy hormones so take it easy and don't twist suddenly, to protect your back. Stop at once if you become breathless, dizzy or overheated, or feel pain. Avoid dehydration by drinking plenty of water, and cool down afterwards with further gentle stretches.

EXERCISE IN PREGNANCY

Both you and your baby benefit from exercise: your blood starts circulating freely, there's a blast of oxygen to your baby's brain, exercise hormones such as endorphins give you both a wonderful high and your baby loves the swaying motion. Exercise increases your strength, suppleness and stamina, which will make pregnancy easier and equip you for the rigours of labour. But exercise in pregnancy is not just about fitness. It helps you to understand your body, to believe in its power, and it gives you the key to relaxation so that you can cope with fatigue and prepare yourself for the actual birth.

WHOLE-BODY EXERCISE
Try to incorporate some exercise into your day, beginning gradually, at a pace that is comfortable. Always stop if you get out of breath or feel pain. Whole-body exercise is best as it tones up your heart and lungs, so walking and swimming are excellent. Dancing is good too as long as it's not too energetic. Yoga is ideal because it stretches tight muscles and joints and also relieves tension. Yoga methods can help with labour and pain relief too.

EXERCISE TO AVOID
Pregnancy is not a time to start learning an energetic contact sport; however you can continue sporting activities for a while if you're already fit and play often. Don't engage in sports like skiing, cycling or horse riding after 20 weeks because balance may become a problem from that time. Take it easy on very energetic sports like tennis or squash and don't do heavy work-outs at the gym, especially tough abdominal exercises.

PREPARING FOR LABOUR

Help yourself to prepare for labour and birth by introducing your body to some exercises and postures that will help when the baby is coming. You'll be taught different techniques at your antenatal classes (see p. 26), but it's a great help if both of you can learn the exercises so that your partner can help and encourage you to practise at home.

POSTURES TO PREPARE FOR BIRTH
If you're hoping to have an active birth, it's a good idea to begin learning the postures as early as possible. There are different techniques you can follow, that may be taught in locally-run active birth classes. An active birth means keeping mobile rather than being confined to the bed, and using breathing and relaxation techniques to help control the pain of labour.

Tailor sitting Sit up with your back straight (lean against a wall if necessary), with the soles of your feet together. This opens up the hip joints.

Squatting Squat down on your haunches as low as possible, supporting your back against a wall or sofa – or lean against your partner when he is sitting in a chair. Squatting stretches and relaxes the birth canal, and when it comes to the delivery you may well find that this is the position that you adopt naturally, since it will help you bear down (see p. 44).

All fours Getting down onto all fours is very helpful during pregnancy when you have a bad back, especially if you combine it with a few gentle pelvic tilts (see above left). Put a pile of cushions in front of you so can rest on them with your head on your arms, and ask your partner to massage your back. Many women also find this a comfortable position for backache during labour, and for the actual delivery of the baby (see p. 44).

LOOKING AFTER YOUR BACK

The hormones of pregnancy soften your ligaments in preparation for the birth; the problem is that this also makes them more susceptible to strain during pregnancy, and your back is the most vulnerable.

Shoulders straight and relaxed

Buttocks tucked in keeps back straight

STANDING POSTURE

As pregnancy progresses, good posture becomes increasingly important, otherwise you'll have a tendency to bend your spine to balance the bump in front, leading to an arched back and slumped shoulders. Try to avoid this by keeping a straight back, tucking your buttocks under and tilting your pelvis forward. Remember to drop your shoulders to avoid tensions in your neck.

CARRYING AND LIFTING

Avoid carrying a heavy bag for long periods; this can put a strain on your shoulders and neck. If you need to lift something from floor level, always bend your knees and keep a straight back, lifting the object high against your chest. Never bend down or twist from the waist; you could damage your lower back. After lying down, always get up by pushing yourself up onto your hands first and then move into a kneeling position if you're on the floor, or swing your legs over the edge of the bed.

SITTING POSTURE

Sitting badly for long periods can be as bad for your back as poor posture when standing. If you have to sit for a long time, such as at the office, make sure you use a firm, straight backed chair and sit well back with your feet flat on the floor or raised slightly on a footstool. Sitting badly, slumped in your chair, forces your baby up against your diaphragm and stomach, constricts your lungs and causes breathlessness and indigestion.

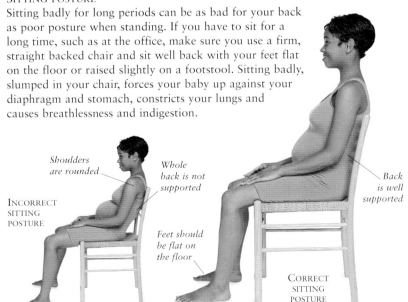

Shoulders are rounded

Whole back is not supported

INCORRECT SITTING POSTURE

Back is well supported

Feet should be flat on the floor

CORRECT SITTING POSTURE

FATHER ♂

Making sure you look after your partner's wellbeing during pregnancy is good for your unborn baby, good for your relationship and essential to your partner's long-term physical and emotional health. Try the suggestions below, but don't treat her like an invalid!

HOW YOU CAN HELP

■ Your partner's hair and skin will look marvellous, especially during the middle trimester, from four to seven months. Tell her how good she looks to boost her self-esteem. Towards the end of the pregnancy she may begin to get very bored and feel uncomfortable and unattractive; encourage her to go out and treat herself at this time.

■ Encourage your partner to eat and drink well. Get involved in the shopping and cooking, if you haven't done so before. The basic advice on diet (see p. 34) doesn't just apply to pregnant women – it will also do you good to adjust your diet in line with it.

■ Give your partner opportunities to rest: bring her breakfast in bed at weekends; make sure visitors aren't invited when she normally likes to rest, whether it's after lunch or early evening. Put the television in the bedroom, if there isn't one there already, so she can watch in bed.

■ Do the heavy lifting so that your partner doesn't strain her back or other muscles softened by pregnancy hormones (see left). If she does lift something, make sure she bends her legs, rather than bending from the waist. Carry the shopping and climb the ladder to paint the ceiling (yes, it's true that pregnant mothers have been known to do this during the burst of energy that often presages birth – see p. 40).

37

CHAPTER THREE

GETTING TO KNOW
YOUR NEW BABY

You will relive the moment of your baby's
birth over and over again for the rest of
your life. It's a moment like no other – moving,
emotional, thrilling and fulfilling. Bringing a
new life into the world is a very special
occasion drawing you close as a couple,
sharing your love for your baby and feeling for
the first time the intimacy of your new family.
The moments immediately after the birth are
very precious so it's worth orchestrating them
so that you each hold the baby very close next
to your skin (Dads – take your shirt off)
and start bonding with your new baby.

COUNTDOWN TO BIRTH

MOTHER

Your due date is only a guide so be prepared for labour to start any time from 36 weeks. Keep the telephone numbers of your partner, your midwife and the hospital delivery ward by the telephone at all times. Have your bag packed (see below) or get everything ready for a home delivery (see p. 44).

WHAT YOU NEED FOR HOSPITAL
◼ Your hospital notes.

◼ A large T-shirt or short, loose nightdress for labour.

◼ Socks in case you're chilly immediately after delivery.

◼ For labour you may also need a hot-water bottle to relieve backache, bottled mineral water and a natural sponge to suck, a water spray bottle to cool your skin, and a hand mirror to see your baby's head as it appears.

◼ Two front-opening nightdresses or pyjamas, a dressing gown and a pair of slippers.

◼ Two packets of super-strength sanitary pads and several pairs of cotton pants to hold them in place.

◼ Properly-fitted nursing bras and disposable breast pads.

◼ Washbag with toiletries, face flannel or sponge and a couple of bath towels.

◼ For your baby you'll need to pack stretch suits or nightdresses and vests (see p. 82), a packet of first size nappies and nappy changing equipment (see p. 76).

◼ You may also need a blanket or shawl in which to wrap your baby, as most hospitals only supply basic cot bedding.

Y OU'VE REACHED THE 38TH WEEK of pregnancy and your due date is fast approaching; if you're the expectant mother, the days may seem to drag by, and you probably feel uncomfortably large and cumbersome. If you're the expectant father, you'll be on edge every time the telephone rings because it could be the call you've been waiting for.

GETTING READY

Although pregnancy is said to last 40 weeks, this is only a convenient method of calculation – it's quite normal for a baby to be born anything between 38 and 42 weeks. If your baby hasn't been born by the official due date, don't worry. Most doctors aren't in a hurry to induce a baby if the mother is healthy and there are no obvious problems such as raised blood pressure. This is the time for a father to take the initiative in organizing outings and visits for his partner; keeping active occupies her mind and is much better for both of you – and the baby – instead of hanging around the house feeling apprehensive.

PACKING YOUR HOSPITAL BAG
It's a good idea to have everything ready for the baby's arrival and your bag packed for hospital 3–4 weeks before the due date, so that you are prepared for any eventuality. Check with your midwife what the hospital supplies for you in the way of toiletries and other items, such as sanitary pads, and nappies, bedding and clothes for your baby. Your tour of the delivery ward (see p. 26) will help you decide what bulkier items you might need, such as extra pillows or cushions.

GETTING NEAR LABOUR

In the few days before labour begins properly, you may notice some signs that indicate you haven't got much longer to wait.
　　Feeling pre-menstrual You may experience similar feelings to those before your period, such as a low, nagging backache.
　　Braxton Hicks You may become more aware of the painless tightenings of the uterine wall. These are Braxton Hicks contractions, which can begin at around six months, and occur on and off during the last few weeks.
　　Mild diarrhoea You may have looser bowel movements as your system is affected by the increasing uterine activity.
　　Abdominal lightening There may be an easing of discomfort under your ribs – a feeling of lightening – as your baby's head engages in your pelvis. This may happen a week or two before the birth with a first baby, but just as often it does not happen until labour.
　　Burst of energy Many women experience a sudden burst of energy even if they have been very tired and sluggish for several weeks previously. You may find you want to rush around making sure everything is ready for your baby's homecoming; this is known as the "nesting instinct".
　　Irritability Understandably, you may become short-tempered and impatient, with a definite sense that it's time pregnancy was over!

THE STAGES OF LABOUR

Labour has three distinct stages. The first stage is when the uterine contractions pull the cervix open; second stage, when the baby is born; and third stage, when the placenta is delivered.

The first stage During the first stage of labour, contractions begin and are established, gradually becoming stronger and lasting longer; this stage can last up to 12 hours, or even longer with a first baby. First stage has three phases: the latent phase is the longest, lasting around eight hours. This is when the cervix is "taken up" and thins. Then there is the active phase, when the cervix is opened up wide; and finally the transitional phase, when the cervix reaches full dilatation, before pushing the baby out. You're most likely to need pain relief during the active phase, and you're likely to feel a burst of energy towards the end to take you through the second stage.

The second stage During the second stage of labour the baby leaves the uterus and is pushed through the birth canal into the outside world. This stage can take anything from a few minutes to two hours with a first baby, and can be exhausting.

The third stage The delivery of the placenta is the third and final stage of labour; it is the shortest stage and it's almost painless, although you may feel some cramping like a severe period pain. It happens within half an hour of the baby's birth, sooner if helped by an injection of syntometrine (see p. 46).

(see p. 46)

FATHER

Make sure you can always be contacted easily. If you've got a mobile phone, keep it turned on.

WHAT TO TAKE TO HOSPITAL

■ A change of clothes; labour wards are very hot.

■ Food and drink – hospital canteens rarely open at night.

■ Tape player and cassettes.

■ Camera or camcorder.

■ Phone card or change for a payphone, plus important numbers. (Do not use a mobile phone in the hospital.)

THINKING ABOUT PAIN RELIEF

It is sensible to consider options for pain relief before labour starts; discuss what is available a few weeks in advance with your midwife and put your wishes in a birth plan (see p. 27). Most people like the idea of a birth without the need for drugs, but it's as well to be prepared. When it comes to the reality of labour, you can't predict how you'll react, as everyone's pain threshold is different.

(see p. 27)

EPIDURAL

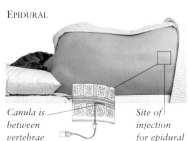

Canula is between vertebrae

Site of injection for epidural

EPIDURAL ANAESTHETIC
An anaesthetist injects anaesthetic into the spinal column through a catheter via a hollow needle (a canula); it numbs your uterus, vagina and vulva completely. A tube is attached to the needle and taped to your back so that the anaesthetic can be topped up.

GAS AND AIR (ENTONOX)
A mixture of oxygen and nitrous oxide is breathed in through a mask or mouthpiece during a contraction so that it deadens the pain at its height. You start using it as soon as you feel a contraction starting as it takes about 20 seconds to work. The baby is not affected.

TENS

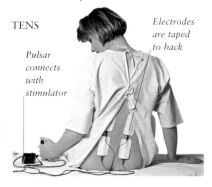

Pulsar connects with stimulator

Electrodes are taped to back

TENS
Transcutaneous electrical nerve stimulation (TENS) involves having electrodes taped to your back that connect to a stimulator. You give yourself small, safe amounts of electrical current to stimulate the production of endorphins, or natural painkillers.

PETHIDINE
A form of pain relief given by injection. Pethidine is quite strong, so you may feel sick or woozy afterwards. It can affect a baby's breathing at delivery (though this can be treated), and makes the baby drowsy, so it isn't given late in labour.

BIRTH POOL

Warm water is soothing

Water supports mother

BIRTH POOL
Many hospitals now have pools available for use during labour to help relieve the pain. Buoyancy helps reduce the pressure on the abdomen, making your contractions more efficient, and being in water enables you to move easily into different positions.

HOW LABOUR STARTS

Labour can start in a variety of ways, but once it's really under way, you will know about it. If you're unsure, you probably aren't quite in labour. There are various signs that labour is starting.

THE "SHOW"
This is a brownish/pink discharge that indicates that the mucus plug that has sealed the cervix during pregnancy has now come away in readiness for labour.

YOUR WATERS BREAK
Sometimes the amniotic sac ruptures before labour starts, causing fluid to leak slowly or in a gush from your vagina. This is painless. If your waters break, put on a clean sanitary pad and call your midwife or hospital delivery ward immediately for advice. Most doctors would prefer labour to start within 24 hours because of the risk of infection to the baby.

CONTRACTIONS START
The muscular tightenings of the uterus – contractions – gradually start to pull open the cervix. They last a few seconds to start with, and you may feel them as sharp cramping pains in the lower abdomen or as backache. If they're coming regularly about every 10–15 minutes, you're in labour.

42

WHAT HAPPENS IN LABOUR

WHEN YOU GO INTO LABOUR for the first time, it's natural to feel both excited and apprehensive. In spite of all the preparations you've made, for first-time parents labour is a journey into the unknown. Experiencing it together is something that you will always be able to share, regardless of what kind of labour it turns out to be.

KEEPING ACTIVE

When you realize you're in labour your first reaction may be to rush off to hospital. Try to resist this because the most important thing for a mother in early labour is to keep active. Moving around is a great help in getting and keeping labour established, and most people find it easier to cope with contractions if they're upright. If your partner isn't with you, telephone him so he can join you as soon as possible. While you're waiting, telephone a friend or relative, or see if someone can come round to keep you company until your partner arrives. The best thing is to potter around at home for as long as possible, trying to be normal; if you have a contraction just stop and breathe through it. You might like to have a shower or bath to relax you. However, it's best to avoid having a bath if your waters have already broken (see left), unless your midwife advises it.

EATING AND DRINKING

While you're still at home, try to eat and drink quite frequently in small quantities. Have high-energy snacks and warm drinks that will help to keep your strength up. Once you're in hospital this may be discouraged, and you probably won't feel like it anyway, but you'll need plenty of energy later.

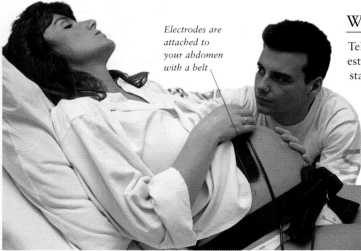

Electrodes are attached to your abdomen with a belt

WHEN TO GO TO HOSPITAL

Telephone the hospital when you think labour is established, but unless the hospital is far away, stay at home until contractions are coming every 5–10 minutes and lasting about a minute. However, bear in mind that you've got a journey ahead of you: don't wait until the idea of getting into a car is beginning to sound like agony. If your partner can't get home in time, don't try to drive yourself; call an ambulance or a taxi.

ELECTRONIC FOETAL MONITORING
When you arrive at hospital, your baby's heartbeat will be measured during contractions through electrodes attached to your abdomen.

WHEN YOU'RE IN HOSPITAL

It's now accepted that childbirth is not an illness and most delivery rooms are designed to be as homely as possible. You'll be assigned a midwife when you arrive, and she'll check how far the cervix has dilated, and measure your baby's heartrate, repeating these checks throughout your labour. You'll need to be near the equipment while your baby's heartrate is being monitored, then you can move around. Some medical interventions require constant monitoring so you'll have to stay on the bed.

MANAGING CONTRACTIONS

There are several ways of managing labour pains. Discuss the options with your midwife, including deciding when and if you want to use any pain relief (see p. 41). She'll try to accommodate your wishes and she'll support you both in finding ways of coping with contractions.

POSITIONS FOR LABOUR

Keeping upright as much as possible helps labour to progress as the contractions work with, not against, gravity. Standing or squatting supported by your partner allows you to control the pain and provides warmth and loving reassurance.

Squat between your partner's knees while he sits on a chair, taking your weight on his legs

Stand with knees bent, if necessary, letting your partner take your weight

STANDING UPRIGHT

SQUATTING SUPPORTED

COPING WITHOUT PAIN RELIEF

● Relax as much as possible, especially between contractions: concentrate on the out-breath as you exhale, and drop your shoulders.
● Keep moving about between contractions, then get into the position that feels right for you. These may include a supported squat, leaning against your partner, on all fours, or kneeling down and leaning forwards on a pillow placed on a chair.
● Try counting backwards from 100 through a contraction – the concentration needed to do this takes your mind off the pain. Keep your eyes open to externalize the pain; focus on something in the room such as a picture.
● Take sips of still mineral water from a sponge if your mouth is dry and ask your partner to massage or knead your back during a contraction.
● Don't be afraid to say – or shout – anything you like; no-one's going to hold it against you afterwards.

FATHER

You may feel that there's not much you can do, but just being there is a huge comfort. Trust your intuition and judgment as to what's needed, but ask for feedback too.

HOW YOU CAN HELP

■ Be loving and intimate with your partner: slow and gentle, quiet and reassuring.

■ Be there for her when she wants you, and give her space when she doesn't.

■ Be positive and never criticize; she needs lots of praise, encouragement and sympathy.

■ Offer practical help, such as a warm hot-water bottle if she's got backache, sprays of water or a cool flannel if she's too hot, and sips of water if her mouth is dry.

■ If your partner wants to go without pain relief, encourage her while it seems reasonable, but if she asks for it, don't put her off. She's the one who is in pain.

■ Talk to the midwife or doctor if you don't understand what's happening, or if you're worried. She's there to help both of you, but remember that she is a professional who has your partner's and your baby's best interests at heart. At the same time, don't let the hospital staff and their machines become your focus.

■ Keep your sense of humour; if your partner shouts – or swears – at you, seems to get angry or overwrought, take it in your stride. It's her way of coping with a very stressful situation. This is particularly likely to happen at the transition phase of the first stage of labour (see p. 41), so treat it as a positive step towards the birth – it's a sign that the second stage isn't far off.

43

WHO'S WHO AT THE BIRTH

For a normal vaginal delivery, you'll probably have just one midwife and an assistant, and possibly a paediatric nurse to look after the baby immediately after the birth. Sometimes, however, the delivery room may seem to be almost crowded with other people, and it's as well to be ready for this. Personnel present may include:

■ Your assigned midwife.

■ An assistant midwife and/or a paediatric nurse.

■ The obstetric doctor on duty.

■ An anaesthetist, if you have an epidural (see p. 41).

■ A paediatrician to check your baby's health if you have an epidural or any form of assisted birth (see p. 49).

■ Student doctors, midwives or nurses, if it's a teaching hospital. You'll be asked about this first, and you can refuse permission.

■ A paediatrician and midwife assigned to each baby if you are having a multiple birth.

THE BIRTH OF YOUR BABY

THE EARLY STAGES OF YOUR JOURNEY to parenthood are now complete: the cervix is open, and the birth canal is clear for your baby's progress to the outside world. Ahead of you is a shorter, but not necessarily easier, stage: that of pushing the baby out. But this is the culmination of all the hard work, and together at last you'll meet your new baby.

COPING WITH SECOND STAGE

As your baby is gradually pushed down your birth canal, you should try to use gravity as much as possible to help, so keep as upright as you can. Get into whatever position feels most comfortable – it may be sitting up on the bed, squatting on a mat with the support of your partner, leaning against a chair, being on all fours, or using a birthing stool – your partner and midwife can follow your lead. Between contractions use your breathing techniques; in particular, let your pelvic floor, rectum and anus relax.

CROWNING

Your midwife will tell you when your baby's head appears at the vaginal opening – this is called crowning. Listen to your midwife; she'll tell you when to push and when to relax. If you take your time and let your vagina stretch slowly, you may avoid a tear. Once the baby's head crowns your partner can show you by holding a mirror – this is a great encouragement because you know that your baby will soon be born.

BIRTH AT HOME

More and more women are giving birth at home, though birth in hospital remains the norm because it's difficult to predict how your labour will progress.

PRACTICAL PREPARATIONS
About a month before your due date the midwife will let you know what equipment you need readily available such as buckets, rubber gloves and polythene sheeting to cover furniture and carpets. She will provide all the medical equipment. Decide where in your home you want to have your baby and try to work out your expectations. You can then discuss these with your midwife and she'll be able to reassure you, dispel any misconceptions and help you to be realistic.

WHEN YOU'RE IN LABOUR
● Call the midwife, who will come as soon as possible. She will probably have an assistant with her.
● For pain relief, your midwife will only be able to provide gas and air and pethidine (obtained on

prescription beforehand), so you're likely to try drug-free ways of managing the pain first (see p. 43). You'll probably be better able to cope at home, anyway.
● You're more likely to feel in control of events as the medical staff are on your territory, and that's an important psychological difference for everyone.

IF THERE'S A PROBLEM
Talk through with your midwife beforehand when and why she'd recommend a move to hospital. If that were to happen, you'd go in an ambulance – and in most instances, the same midwives who'd attended you at home would continue looking after you once you arrived.

AFTER THE BIRTH
The midwife will stay for a couple of hours to make sure that you and your baby are comfortable and healthy, and will return later. You, your partner and your new baby can spend your first few hours as a family together in the comforting surroundings of your own home.

EPISIOTOMY

An episiotomy is a surgical cut in the perineal floor that helps to allow the baby's head to pass through. Given time, you may not need one, but if it's felt you should have one, the midwife or doctor will ask your permission to do this procedure as your baby's head crowns (see opposite). It's more common to have an episiotomy with a first baby because the vaginal opening may be less elastic and you are more likely to tear. Episiotomies are also performed if your baby is very large, is in the breech position or you need assistance with forceps or ventouse (see p. 49). If you haven't had an epidural, the pelvic floor muscles will be numbed first with an injection of local anaesthetic. Then the vaginal tissues, plus underlying muscle, are cut at the height of a contraction to extend the opening. The incision is stitched after the placenta has been delivered (see overleaf).

THE DELIVERY

The head is the widest part of your baby – it will slowly emerge, and the midwife will check that the cord isn't around the neck and clear fluid from your baby's mouth and throat. The midwife will ask you to pant, not push at this stage, then with the next contractions she will gently turn the baby so that the shoulders can be born one at a time and the rest of your baby's body will slide out; the pushing contractions stop immediately and you'll feel a wonderful sense of release. Your baby may or may not cry out; some babies whimper, some cry lustily, others begin breathing without any crying.

MEETING YOUR BABY

This is the moment for which you've waited nine months, when you can take your baby in your arms together for the first time, the moment that will make everything you've just gone through worthwhile. Your midwife will probably lay the baby on your tummy or give him to you to hold while the cord is clamped and cut; let your baby feel your skin, hold him close to your face and let him look up into yours. Share this moment – you're both his parents – and savour it; this is a meeting that will change both your lives forever. It is also the moment when you claim your new status as parents.

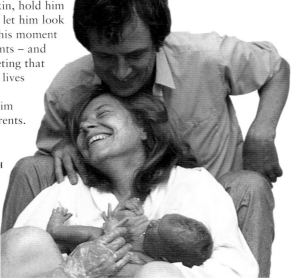

THE MOMENT OF BIRTH
You'll never forget the experience of holding your baby for the first time, immediately after he's emerged. It's so emotional that you may well find yourselves weeping with joy and relief.

FATHER

Helping your partner and watching your baby being born is an overwhelming experience for all fathers. The second stage is hard work for mothers, it's a real effort, but there are ways you can help your partner during this stage, so that you can feel as involved as possible.

HOW YOU CAN HELP

■ Help your partner to get into the position she feels is most appropriate, and support her there.

■ Talk to her and encourage her all the time, and keep in physical contact so she knows you're with her all the way.

■ If you can see your baby's head as it crowns, describe it to your partner or hold a mirror for her to see the head – this will be a huge encouragement to her. However, don't get in the midwife's way as she will need to be able to monitor the baby's progress second by second, and to check the birth of the head.

■ Announce that you have a son or a daughter, not just "it's a boy", or "it's a girl"; the words "son" and "daughter" express family feelings.

■ If the midwife agrees, clamp and cut your baby's cord yourself. It's a fantastic moment – the moment your baby really becomes an individual being.

■ If you feel like weeping, don't hold back. It's one of the most emotional moments of your life.

■ When the baby is born, share with your partner in the first minutes of your child's life.

■ By all means photograph or video your partner and baby, but don't do this to the exclusion of helping them. They are more important than anything else.

45

BONDING

Parent-infant bonding is sometimes misunderstood. Most newborn animals have an instinct to bond; more recently research has shown that human babies are similarly programmed.

WHAT HAPPENS AT BIRTH
Your baby can recognize your voice at birth and can focus on your face at 20–25cm (8–10in) away. You will also be hyper-sensitive to your baby in the minutes after birth. You can bond with your baby for life almost instantly, if you can be left alone together without interference – if this private time isn't offered, ask for it. However, don't worry if you don't bond at once – you might both just feel utterly exhausted after the delivery. Falling in love will have to wait.

AFTER THE BIRTH

THE FIRST HOUR OR SO after your baby's birth is a very precious time for all three of you – and it's a moment that most parents will always remember. Although there will be various medical and administrative procedures that still need to be carried out, you'll still have time to enjoy your baby and begin to get to know her together.

YOUR BABY AFTER DELIVERY

The midwife will check your baby's condition immediately after the birth by assessing her "Apgar score" (see opposite). Providing she is breathing without difficulty from the start, your baby will probably remain in your arms for the first minutes after birth. If she needs help to start breathing, she'll be put on the delivery room resuscitation table, which has an oxygen mask and a heater to keep the baby warm. Usually she'll soon be pink enough to be handed back to you, but in a few cases she may need to be taken to the Special Care Baby Unit for a while (see p. 58). Some time in the first couple of hours your baby will be weighed and measured and every part of her thoroughly examined by a midwife or paediatrician.

DELIVERY OF THE PLACENTA

The placenta is usually delivered with the help of an injection of a drug called syntometrine given as the baby's body emerges. The cord is cut and the midwife will then press gently on your abdomen and pull the cord slowly to draw out the placenta. Once the placenta is delivered the midwife will check to make sure that none has remained inside you where it could cause bleeding and infection. If you'd prefer the placenta to be delivered naturally, without syntometrine, it will take about half an hour and putting your baby to the breast will help the process.

HOW YOU WILL FEEL

Immediately after the birth, your body temperature drops a few degrees and you may shiver and shake quite violently as your thermostat re-sets. You'll need to be wrapped in a blanket, and possibly put on a pair of socks. If you are famished after labour, ask your midwife or partner for a small, easily digestible snack – a cup of tea and a piece of toast perhaps – and drink plenty if you want to. This will also help you to maintain the calories and fluids you need for breastfeeding.

GETTING TO KNOW YOUR BABY
Hold your baby close to your breast so that she can suckle if she wants to. This helps the bonding process and the breastfeeding hormones also encourage the uterus to contract.

IF YOU NEED STITCHES

The midwife will examine your perineum and assess whether or not you need stitches. Research shows that minor tears heal better on their own, so it's not necessarily true that any tear will inevitably mean stitches; however, an episiotomy (see p. 45) must be stitched. If you do need stitches, you'll probably have your legs put into stirrups, and you'll usually be given a local anaesthetic to deaden the pain. Depending on the length of the cut or tear, stitching will be done either by a senior midwife or the doctor on duty. You may be able to cuddle your baby while you're being stitched if you want to, but this is also a good chance for your partner to have time with his baby so that you both get a chance to bond individually with your new member of the family as early as possible after the birth.

THE FIRST BREASTFEED

Putting your baby to the breast within an hour of the delivery increases your chances of breastfeeding successfully; many women feel able to put their babies to the breast immediately after the birth, although not all babies want to suck then. Ask your midwife to help you get your baby to latch on, but don't worry if she doesn't want to suck immediately. It doesn't mean she isn't able to breastfeed, just that at this point she doesn't feel like sucking, or she may be tired. She may also be affected by painkillers used during labour, such as pethidine, which leave her rather drowsy and may take a few hours to wear off (see p. 41).

THE IMPORTANCE OF COLOSTRUM
You won't produce milk for three or four days after the birth (see p. 61), but it is very beneficial for your baby to have the high protein "pre-milk" called colostrum that is produced in your breasts at this time. It contains important antibodies from your body that protect a newborn baby from infections, plus a substance called lactoferrin, which acts like a natural antibody. Putting your baby to the breast also helps the uterus to contract, and if you've opted to deliver the placenta naturally (see opposite), suckling your baby will aid this because the same hormone that triggers the "let down" of milk in your breasts also acts on the uterine muscle.

THE APGAR SCORE

The Apgar score is a standard method of assessing the immediate condition of a newborn baby. At one minute and five minutes after the birth, the midwife or doctor does five checks on heartbeat, breathing, muscle tone, reflexes and skin colour, and gives them a score of 0, 1 or 2, with a total of 10. A score of 7 or over is normal, and a low first score improving to a normal second score is also fine. This may occur if you had a long second stage, or your baby has been affected by pethidine given during labour (see p. 41).

HOW THE SCORE WORKS
● Heartrate over 100 scores 2; below 100, 1; no heartbeat, 0.
● Regular breathing or crying scores 2; slow or irregular breathing scores 1; absence of breathing scores 0.
● If the baby is active (good muscle tone), the score is 2; if hands and feet only are moving the score is 1; if the baby is limp, the score is 0.
● Strong reflexes score 2; weak reflexes score 1; no reflexes score 0.
● Pink colouring scores 2; body pink but extremities blue scores 1; blue or pale colouring scores 0.

FATHER

After the birth, you may feel as emotionally exhausted as your partner, but it's important not to underestimate the physical effort of labour and birth on a woman.

HOW YOU CAN HELP
■ You will probably experience a wave of euphoria now that your baby is born, but if labour has been long and arduous your partner may be too exhausted to experience this same "buzz" immediately. It doesn't mean she isn't as excited and delighted as you are, but after a lengthy labour, it's not surprising if she finds it difficult to express immediate enthusiasm. Just hold her close and let her know how proud you are of her and of your new son or daughter. Stay with them both for as long as possible after the birth, including settling them in to the postnatal ward.

■ Congratulate your partner on her achievement, and let her know how much you appreciate her. But don't belittle your own contribution and the support you've been able to give. You may think you haven't really been much help – this is a common reaction for fathers who have seen their partners struggling through labour, particularly if it was long. However, most mothers will say how beneficial it was to have the emotional support and encouragement from their partner throughout labour and at the birth.

■ Hold your baby while your partner is being stitched, or checked; go into a quiet corner of the room and get to know your baby. Let her look into your eyes; if you hold her close so she's just 20–25cm (8–10in) from your face, she can see you and smell you, and she'll learn to recognize you from the very beginning (see p. 134).

47

MOTHER

It's understandable to feel disheartened if something happens that means you need an assisted delivery, or even an emergency Caesarean section (see p. 50) so that you're unable to experience the natural vaginal delivery that you'd been hoping for. Being prepared for the fact that intervention may be required can help to avoid too much heart-searching and disappointment after the birth.

COPING WITH A SPECIAL LABOUR
■ The medical staff will always tell you why a particular course of action is recommended, whether it's before labour or when labour is in progress. Don't think you're making a fuss by asking questions, or by asking for a repeat explanation: you have a right to know.

■ If you're in labour, it may be difficult to concentrate; ask your partner to make sure that all the reasons for certain procedures are clarified so that he can relay the information to you. Remember, unless you're actually unconscious, staff must specifically seek your permission to proceed; they won't accept your partner's opinion.

■ At the end of the day, the most important thing will be that your baby has been born safely. But that doesn't mean your feelings don't matter, and many women can't shake off the idea – however illogical – that they were in some way to blame that things didn't go to plan. If you find yourself in this position, talk it through afterwards: with your partner, with your midwives, to other health professionals or your family doctor. Having a baby can unleash deep emotions and you may need to work through them before you can move on to enjoy new motherhood fully.

SPECIAL LABOURS

IN THE PAST, WOMEN HAD TO RELY on nature alone to see their baby's birth through, and in many cases this unfortunately led to tragedy. Nowadays, however, modern obstetrics has given doctors many ways to intervene should labour prove difficult. Although some interventions may bring a small risk of complication, and one intervention may build on another, the risk is usually far outweighed by the benefit. If a particular procedure is suggested, ask the midwife or doctor to explain exactly why it's necessary, what the risks are, and what would happen if you waited a while before it was started.

WHEN LABOUR IS INDUCED

Sometimes labour may need to be induced, which means being started artificially. If you haven't gone into labour spontaneously by 42–43 weeks, or if there are worries about your own or your baby's health in the last few weeks of pregnancy, induction may be suggested. Similar procedures will be needed if your labour is not proceeding as it should.

HOW LABOUR MAY BE INDUCED
Induction is often introduced gradually, first with pessaries; then, if necessary, ARM (see below); finally, a syntocinon drip if things are going too slowly.
● You may be given vaginal pessaries containing prostaglandin, a hormone that should trigger labour.
● Your membranes may be ruptured artificially (ARM), which can either start or strengthen contractions.
● You may be given an artificial hormone (syntocinon) into a vein to induce contractions. Syntocinon contractions will probably be more immediately intense and painful than if labour had started naturally. A syntocinon drip is also used to speed up labour.

BREECH BIRTH

Instead of being born head first, in a breech birth, your baby is born buttocks first, usually followed by the legs and lastly the head. Breech babies frequently end up having to be delivered with the help of forceps or by Caesarean section for the baby's safety, although a natural breech delivery is occasionally possible with the help of an experienced midwife and obstetrician. A breech baby is almost always delivered in hospital; because of the likelihood of intervention you'll probably be offered an epidural, so that you're already anaesthetized if your doctor needs to apply forceps or do a Caesarean (see p. 50). You're more likely to have an episiotomy (see p. 45), because your baby's buttocks may not stretch the vagina enough to let the head out safely, or to allow forceps to be inserted to help lift the head out.

ASSISTANCE WITH FORCEPS OR VENTOUSE

Even if you have a normal vaginal delivery, there may be times when you need help, particularly in pushing the baby out during second stage. Depending on the circumstances, your hospital will provide assistance with forceps or ventouse (vacuum extraction). You'll need to have an episiotomy for either of these procedures.

Forceps The two blades of forceps cradle your baby's head, allowing it to be pulled safely through the birth canal without too much compression. However, forceps can normally only be used once the baby's head is engaged in the pelvic bones.

Ventouse, or vacuum, extraction This is a gentler procedure than using forceps and is used in similar circumstances. Your cervix has to be fully dilated but the head does not have to be in the birth canal. The vacuum plate leaves a bruise on your baby's head where the suction was applied, but this will fade within the first 2–3 weeks.

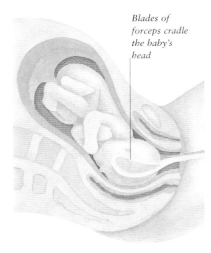

Blades of forceps cradle the baby's head

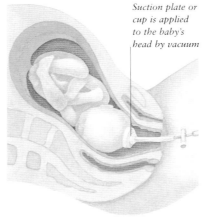

Suction plate or cup is applied to the baby's head by vacuum

FORCEPS DELIVERY
Forceps are instruments that look like the two halves of very large sugar-tongs. The blades are inserted one at a time and the baby is drawn out with a few gentle pulls during contractions.

VENTOUSE OR VACUUM EXTRACTION
With ventouse assistance, a small suction plate or cup is applied by vacuum to the lowest part of your baby's head. The doctor will gradually help your baby to be born by applying gentle traction.

IF YOU'RE HAVING TWINS

Twins or higher multiples are exciting for everyone, although you're bound to be apprehensive about their arrival. Medical interest in the birth is likely to be much greater if you're expecting more than one baby, and some intervention is more likely to be recommended. Often this becomes necessary, but there's no need to think it's inevitable: many twins, and even triplets, are born vaginally after a normal labour. But continuous electronic foetal monitoring is much more common, and, as with breech birth, you'll probably be offered an epidural because of the likelihood of intervention. This means it is in place in case there are problems with the delivery of the second twin and you have to have assistance with forceps or even a Caesarean. If one twin is known to be breech, you will probably be advised to have both delivered by elective Caesarean.

FATHER

A labour that doesn't go to plan can be very scary for you as well as for your partner. Be prepared for the fact that unexpected interventions may be necessary.

HOW YOU CAN HELP
■ Well before your baby is due, talk to your partner about what she feels about any special situation that may arise. Make sure you know her views and preferences for any eventuality. Bear in mind, however, that she may change her mind when it comes to the point.

■ Unless it's an absolute emergency, make sure that any interventions suggested are talked through properly with your partner, and either or both of you ask questions if it isn't clear. But remember that the final decision is your partner's – the health professionals must have her consent for any intervention.

■ If something is suggested that you know your partner is trying to avoid, try to buy time. For instance, if labour has slowed, suggest a change of position before procedures to accelerate labour are introduced.

■ If the medical team decide the labour needs monitoring with high tech equipment, try not to be distracted by it. Concentrate on your partner, not the technology.

■ Remember that if something unexpected occurs, and the medical team has to intervene, it's never your partner's fault. These things happen, and everyone will be working in the best interests of your partner and baby.

■ Whatever happens, talk about it afterwards, especially with your partner, but also with friends and, if necessary, health professionals. You'll have a lot of feelings to work through.

49

MOTHER

You're bound to feel apprehensive about the outcome if you have a Caesarean, and you may feel let down if you have an emergency Caesarean after going into labour spontaneously.

CONCERNS ABOUT CAESAREANS

■ You may worry that you won't be able to deliver a subsequent baby vaginally. However about 75 per cent of women who have a Caesarean can have a normal delivery next time.

■ If you have a general anaesthetic, you'll need a longer period of recovery, so it may be a little while before you feel close to your baby. You'll bond with your baby eventually, especially when you start breastfeeding, so don't worry if you feel a little distant to start with (see p. 46).

■ You'll only be left with a tiny scar on your "bikini line", usually hidden by your pubic hair.

WHY YOU MIGHT NEED A CAESAREAN

There are several reasons why you may require a Caesarean delivery, whether elective or emergency:

■ The baby's head is too large for your pelvis (disproportion).

■ Your baby is breech (bottom first).

■ Your baby takes up a cross-wise position (persistent horizontal lie).

■ You have a medical condition, such as pre-eclampsia or diabetes.

■ Any problems with the placenta.

■ Your labour is progressing too slowly or has stopped, which might cause foetal distress.

■ If there is foetal distress, even if labour hasn't slowed or stopped.

CAESAREAN SECTION

Nowadays, a significant number of babies are born surgically by Caesarean section. In many countries, Caesarean section is currently on the increase, partly because this procedure in expert hands may be safer than, say, a difficult forceps delivery. Sometimes, however, interventions earlier in labour, such as induction or epidural anaesthetic, may lead to a situation in which Caesarean section becomes more likely. If a Caesarean delivery is recommended – either before or during labour – your doctor is obliged to give you clear reasons why, even in an emergency. If it was something you had wanted to avoid, ask whether you could wait or if there is anything else you could try first.

ELECTIVE CAESAREAN

If a Caesarean operation is planned in advance it is known as "elective". This means the reason for it has become apparent before labour started – for example, your blood pressure may have shot up, or your pelvis is so small that delivery is likely to be difficult, or your baby is breech (see p. 48). Your obstetrician will probably discuss this with you 2–3 weeks before your due date, and a date will be booked for you to come in, so you'll know well in advance exactly when your baby is going to be born.

EMERGENCY CAESAREAN

An emergency (unplanned) Caesarean happens when events during labour make it preferable to vaginal delivery. For example, your baby may show distress (measured by heartrate and movements); the labour may not progress despite the use of drugs to speed things up; or your own condition may deteriorate. If you have not already had an epidural anaesthetic, the Caesarean will take place under general anaesthetic.

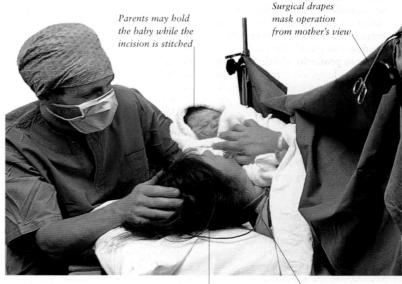

Parents may hold the baby while the incision is stitched

Surgical drapes mask operation from mother's view

DELIVERY OF THE BABY
If you have a Caesarean under epidural anaesthesia, you'll both be able to share your baby's first moments after delivery.

Mother is awake during operation

Catheter for continuous epidural anaesthesia

WHAT HAPPENS DURING THE OPERATION

Before a Caesarean, your pubic hair will be shaved and a catheter inserted into your bladder. You'll probably be given glucose via an intravenous drip.

The anaesthetic Most elective, and some emergency, Caesareans, are performed under epidural anaesthesia, because women recover more quickly afterwards. With an epidural, you'll be awake during the operation, but you won't feel anything, and your partner can be with you throughout. You won't be able to see anything because the operating team will be masked by a surgical sheet draped across your chest. However, an epidural takes about half an hour to take effect, so if there's an emergency and you haven't got one set up already, you'll be given a general anaesthetic instead. In this case, your partner won't usually be allowed into the operating theatre, but will be able to hold the baby afterwards while you recover.

The operation Your abdomen is opened through a small, low, horizontal incision along the line of the top of your pubic hair, and your baby delivered through a similar cut in the uterus. The amniotic fluid is drained off by suction before the baby is gently lifted out. You may feel some rather odd tugs and rummaging around in your insides as the operation proceeds. Your surgeon will tell you when the moment approaches that she can lift your baby from your uterus.

After the birth It takes about ten minutes to deliver the baby: you or your partner can then hold your baby while the placenta is removed and you are stitched. A baby born by Caesarean is likely to need help in starting to breathe, but a paediatrician will be on hand to help with this. Closing the wound can take as much as 45 minutes; depending on the hospital, the stitches may be self-absorbing or need to be removed a few days later.

SUDDEN BIRTH – THE FATHER'S ROLE

Far from needing a Caesarean, occasionally it happens that labour comes on with such speed that your partner could be overwhelmed by the desire to push before you have access to professional help, let alone getting to hospital! Although second stage can take a couple of hours, it may not, and babies have been known to be born after a couple of pushes. If this happens, neither of you need panic – babies who come quickly are almost always strong and vigorous and most emergency births are perfectly straightforward.

WHAT TO DO

• On no account leave your partner alone for more than a minute or two. Help her position herself where she feels most comfortable.

• Telephone the doctor or midwife and explain the situation. If it's difficult to get hold of them, call the emergency services and ask for an ambulance as soon as possible.

• Wash your hands well and have a heap of clean towels ready. Fold one and put it to one side for the baby. If you've got time, find some old sheets or plastic sheeting to cover the floor or furniture.

• Watch for the top of the baby's head at the vaginal opening. When it's visible, ask your partner to stop pushing and just pant. This will give the vagina a chance to stretch fully without tearing.

• Feel around the neck to see if the cord is looped round it. If it is, hook your finger under the cord and draw it over the baby's head.

• Hold the baby firmly as she emerges – she'll be slippery – and give her straight to her mother to hold. Wrap her immediately in the spare towel so she doesn't get cold.

• Don't touch the cord. If the placenta is delivered before medical help arrives, put it in a dish or plastic bowl so it can be checked by the midwife or doctor.

FATHER

Even an elective Caesarean delivery can be worrying, because it is quite a major operation. If it's an emergency, your partner may be feeling distressed, bewildered and helpless, but there's much you can do to smooth the way for her.

HOW YOU CAN HELP

■ If an emergency Caesarean is recommended, and your partner is finding it difficult to talk to the doctors, make sure you ask the clear question why. Although she has to give her permission, your partner may still not be quite clear afterwards why the operation was necessary, and it is important that you are able to help her understand the reasons.

■ Unless your partner wants a general anaesthetic or the operation is too urgent, see if it can be done under epidural anaesthesia. This means you can share the experience and meet your new baby together.

■ During the operation, sit by your partner's head and reassure her that all is well.

■ You don't have to watch what is going on; you'll both be shielded by the surgical drapes. But if you find the operation distressing or you feel faint – and many people do, even nurses – leave the room quickly. Don't hang on; you may cause further difficulties for the medical staff.

■ If the Caesarean is being done under general anaesthetic, your partner may not regain consciousness for an hour or more, and you'll probably be given your baby to hold. Cherish this time with your baby: father-child bonding can be at its best after a Caesarean section birth, because the early time you have together is so precious.

51

HOSPITAL ROUTINE

Some aspects of hospital routine can be tiresome, though you may enjoy talking to other mothers.

KEEPING YOUR BABY CLOSE
Almost all hospitals now expect babies to remain in their cots beside their mothers' beds at all times.

FOOD AND DRINK
The food may be bland, so ask your partner to bring fresh fruit as this will help prevent constipation. Drink plenty of water.

VISITS FROM STAFF
The midwives will check your stitches, lochia and uterus (see p. 60). They'll also give advice on cleaning your baby's umbilicus and on breastfeeding. At some point an obstetrician and paediatrician will check you and your baby, and a physiotherapist may visit to advise you on postnatal exercise.

FIRST DISCOMFORTS

You'll feel a little shaky in the first 24 hours, and there may be some specific discomforts, although these do pass quite quickly:

■ Your perineum will feel bruised and tender, especially if you had stitches. Have frequent salt baths, but don't stay in the bath too long as water can harm scar tissue and soften stitches.

■ You may find it difficult or even painful to pass urine. Take a jug of tepid water to the toilet to pour over your vulva as you pass urine.

■ A sore perineum plus stitches may deter you from opening your bowels. Support your vulva with a pad of tissues as you bear down.

■ Sitting upright can be awkward when your abdominal muscles are weak and your vulva and perineum are sore. Prop yourself with plenty of pillows and half sit and half lie on your side to reduce pressure.

THE FIRST DAY

Y OU HAVE BOTH been looking forward to this moment for the best part of a year; your baby is safely delivered and you've experienced a heady brew of strong emotion: relief, pride, elation, excitement and triumph. Now your baby is lying quietly in his cot by your bed and you both have a chance to take stock.

YOUR REACTIONS TO THE BIRTH

Unlikely as it may seem, this could be an awkward moment for you both. It could be passing through either or both of your minds that there is something missing. Where is the rush of love for your baby? It isn't a subject which gets much attention, but it is, nevertheless, a fact that large numbers of parents, quite possibly the majority, don't feel an overpowering attachment to their baby straight after the birth. Most highs, because of their intensity, are followed, not necessarily by a low, but by a diminution of emotion that leaves you feeling somewhat flat in comparison. Having a baby is no exception. It may have been a momentous event for you, but the hospital routine has to proceed as normal and, anyway, a hospital ward isn't conducive to the kind of closeness that you would like to feel for each other on this shared birthday, especially if you're both exhausted.

LOOKING FORWARD
When you go to the postnatal ward – and this may be two or three hours after the birth – the father goes back to an empty home and the mother is left wondering what her first night as the mother of a baby is going to be like. If it isn't quite what either of you envisaged, be philosophical. In a real sense, life with your baby will actually begin on the day you take him home.

IF YOU'VE HAD A CAESAREAN

A Caesarean section is major abdominal surgery and you'll feel quite sore once the anaesthetic wears off. As well as asking for pain relief, there are other ways of coping:

● Holding and feeding your baby may be difficult as pressure on your scar may be painful. Try laying him next to you on the bed (see p. 71) or supporting him on pillows – the so-called "football position" (see right).
● Mobility helps you recover so you'll be encouraged to get up as soon as possible. Support your wound as you walk.

Baby's body is raised and supported on a pillow

COMFORTABLE FEEDING
Put your baby on a pillow and tuck his body under your arm.

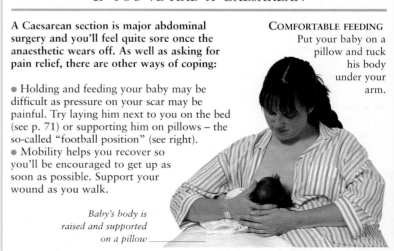

CONCERNS ABOUT YOUR NEWBORN BABY

YOUR CONCERN	WHAT IT IS AND HOW IT IS TREATED
BIRTHMARKS	Many babies have birthmarks, most of which fade within a few months, although some, such as the so-called strawberry mark, which is raised, may take much longer. The Mongolian blue spot, a blueish birthmark on the lower back of babies with dark skin tones, is sometimes mistaken for bruising.
MILK SPOTS	Tiny white spots on the bridge of the nose; they disappear after a few weeks.
URTICARIO NEONATORUM	A blotchy rash, a bit like a nettle rash. It only lasts a couple of days.
MECONIUM	At birth your baby's bowel contains a dark green sticky substance called meconium, which is usually passed into the nappy during the first 2–3 days.
JAUNDICE	Neonatal jaundice is quite common due to a baby's immature liver; it makes the skin yellowish and the urine dark. Your baby may be sleepy so he'll need to be wakened for feeds to ensure he has enough fluid. Persistent cases may be treated with ultra-violet light.
BREATHING	Babies snuffle and sneeze a lot, and get hiccups. They may even stop breathing for a second or two, but breathing soon becomes strong and regular.
LIP BLISTERS	Some babies develop a white sucking blister on the lips. It doesn't cause discomfort and will fade in a few days.
SCALP SWELLING	Some babies develop a swelling on the scalp due to bleeding under the skin during the birth. This is quite normal, but it does take a few weeks to disperse.

NEWBORN BABY CHECK

Your baby is given a top-to-toe check before you leave hospital.

VISION AND HEARING
The doctor will shine a light into your baby's eyes and note if they move on hearing her voice.

HEART AND LUNGS
She'll listen to your baby's heart and check his lungs and breathing.

ABILITY TO SUCK
She'll put her finger into your baby's mouth to check he can suck properly.

INTERNAL ORGANS
She'll gently feel his abdomen and check his anus.

SPINE
She'll pick him up and feel his spinal column to make sure the vertebrae are in place.

HIP MANIPULATION
She'll remove his nappy and manoeuvre his legs and hips to rule out the possibility of any congenital hip dislocation.

THE GUTHRIE TEST
On about the sixth day, your baby will have a tiny drop of blood taken from his heel to test for thyroid function, and for a rare disorder called phenylketonuria, which may cause mental retardation if it is undetected.

57

WHAT YOUR NEWBORN BABY CAN DO

SKILL	HOW TO STIMULATE YOUR BABY
SIGHT	He can see you clearly if your face is 20–25cm (8–10in) from his. He's wired to respond – his heartrate rises when he focuses on your face, so talk and smile. He'll react with body jerks and fish-feeding movements of his mouth – that's his first attempt at a conversation.
HEARING	His hearing is acute – he knows both your voices from having heard them in the womb and he'll respond instantly to pleasure in your voice. Start talking, singing, saying rhymes from the moment of birth and never stop – he wants to communicate with you.
MOVEMENT	He loves physical movement – after all he's been jogging and swaying in the womb for nine months – so carry him around as much as possible. Move his limbs gently while changing him, clap his hands gently, do gentle knee bends. But avoid sudden movements that startle him.

HOW A PRE-TERM BABY MAY LOOK

If your baby is born prematurely, she may not conform to the idealized picture you've had in your mind during your pregnancy:

■ Her skin will be loose, wrinkled and red because she hasn't had time to fill out with fat.

■ She'll be covered in downy hair called lanugo hair.

■ Her head will seem very large.

■ She's very thin and bony, especially her ribs and buttocks, with stick-like limbs.

■ Her breathing seems laboured and uneven.

■ Her movements may be jerky.

FEEDING SPECIAL CARE BABIES

In the early days your baby may need to be fed glucose intravenously, or have milk fed through a tube in her nose, but hopefully will soon be well enough to try sucking. Breast milk is especially good for a premature baby as your body will make milk that is suited to your baby's gestation, and you may need to express your milk in the early days and weeks so your baby can be tube-fed. Expressing can be time-consuming and difficult (see p. 72), but stick with it, it gets easier – and you'll know you're doing the very best for your baby by providing her with nourishment.

INTRODUCING BREASTFEEDING
When your baby is ready to try breastfeeding, don't expect her to suck immediately – it may take time and patience to get her used to it. Avoid bottles as far as possible if you intend eventually to breastfeed fully, as weaker babies can quickly get used to bottles and may then reject your nipple.

THE SPECIAL CARE BABY

IF YOUR BABY NEEDS some specialist care, you'll be understandably anxious, especially if it entails her spending some time away from the postnatal ward in the special care baby unit. However, it will only be done for the best of reasons – to increase your baby's chances of thriving as a normal, healthy baby.

WHY DO BABIES NEED SPECIAL CARE?

Although many people think special care only applies to premature births, in fact about one in ten babies need some sort of specialist attention, and by no means are they all born before term. There are several possible reasons.

Prematurity A baby born before 37 weeks is pre-term or premature, and may need close monitoring, as well as help with breathing and feeding.

Low birth weight Any baby who weighs 2.5kg (5lb 8oz) or less at birth is considered to have a low birth weight. Low birth weight babies may be either pre-term, or full term but "small for dates" (see p. 32), and may need to spend a short time in a special care unit.

A health risk A baby who may have had difficulties with breathing during the birth, or have picked up an infection, may need special attention for a while. Alternatively, there may be birth defects such as a "hole in the heart" that may have been diagnosed before or at the birth.

WHAT SPECIAL CARE MEANS
If your baby needs special care, her needs can be catered for in a special care baby unit (SCBU) or a special section of the unit called a neonatal intensive care unit (NICU). This may mean she has to be moved to a different hospital. If she was premature or of low birth weight, she could have difficulty with breathing, be prone to infections, unable to regulate temperature or feed properly. Without support, low blood sugar levels can cause brain damage and she may lack iron and calcium. For these reasons she may need the protection and constant monitoring of incubator care, with intravenous or tubal feeding (see left), until she catches up on growing and learns to feed and breathe without help.

GETTING THROUGH IT

Having a baby in special care is a bit like feeling you've lost a leg: something is missing; your baby is born, but isn't yet able to be where she should be – in your arms. If she was born early, you may feel cheated on having missed out on the end of your pregnancy. Another common reaction is to feel that your baby isn't really yours – while she's in the SCBU it may seem as though she belongs to the medical staff. Try to remind yourself that this is your child, and that soon she will be home where she belongs. Be as involved as possible in discussions about her condition and in her care, and try to look forward to the day when she'll be truly yours, and you can take her home.

HELPING TO CARE FOR YOUR BABY

All special care baby units welcome parents and actively encourage them to help with feeding, washing and nappy changing. There may be rooms where you can stay overnight from time to time, and many units provide space for a day or two before your baby is discharged so you can get used to the normal care routine of a small baby – this is particularly important if you had a multiple birth.

MAKING CONTACT

Just because your baby is in an incubator doesn't mean you can't touch, kiss and cuddle her. This sort of contact is vitally important because it actually helps your baby to develop and become strong. If it's a closed incubator, you can reach into her through hand-holes to play and fondle, and you should talk and sing to her as much as you can so that she hears your voice. Open special care cots enable you to stroke and fondle directly. All this will keep her contented and help her to thrive – love is an essential vitamin for premature babies. If it's practical, give your baby as much skin to skin contact as you can: when you hold your baby to your skin, her body temperature rises if she is cold, and then falls once she has warmed up. A successful experiment has also revealed that babies who are born prematurely thrive if they are nursed continuously between their mother's breasts – ask if you can try it. Skin to skin contact is essential for your baby, but it's essential for you, too, in fostering the bonding process. It will especially help you if you're nervous; you may feel this way because your baby is so small and you're finding it difficult to relate to her because she's in a special care unit.

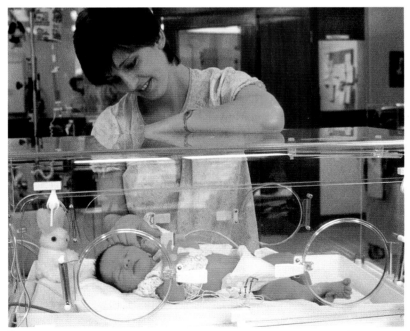

SPENDING TIME WITH YOUR BABY
It's important to spend as much time as possible in the special care baby unit with your baby. It will help to demystify the technology and help you bond with your baby.

COPING WITH THE TECHNOLOGY

Many parents are intimidated and frightened by special care technology with its tubes, computerized monitors, electronic displays and alarms. But the staff in the unit will be sympathetic about your concerns so share your feelings with them and ask if it's possible to see the ward psychologist together and get your feelings out in the open. It also helps to have some understanding of the functions of the equipment. These are some of the items that may be in use:

■ An incubator provides a warm, humid environment for the baby.

■ A ventilator takes over the baby's breathing, getting air into and out of the lungs.

■ A humidifier ensures air in the ventilator is warm and moist before it goes into the baby's lungs.

■ The apnoea alarm alerts the staff if a baby stops breathing.

■ The saturation monitor and blood gas analyzer measure levels of oxygen and carbon dioxide in the baby's blood.

■ The blood pressure gauge measures a baby's blood pressure.

■ A perspex head box may be used to provide extra oxygen when the baby is breathing without assistance.

■ The glucose monitor records the baby's glucose levels.

■ The ECG (electro-cardiogram) monitor measures heartrate.

■ The bilirubinometer measures the risk of jaundice.

■ A phototherapy lamp treats neonatal jaundice with ultra-violet light.

■ An eye shield would be used to cover a baby's eyes during phototherapy.

■ A heat shield keeps the baby warm in an open cot.

YOU AND YOUR BODY

I︎T TAKES A WOMAN'S BODY more than nine months to recover completely from pregnancy and childbirth, so go easy on yours. For the first week or so, you'll be as weak as water and unable to walk any distance or carry anything heavy. Even if you feel quite well, don't make the mistake of overdoing it, or you'll prolong your recovery period.

GETTING BACK TO NORMAL

The medical term for the immediate period of recovery after the birth of your baby is the puerperium. It's defined as the first four weeks, but most women are physically back to normal well before that, even if their emotional adjustment takes much longer. However, you may well be concerned about what is happening to your body during the first week or two after the birth, when changes are rapid but often accompanied by a certain amount of discomfort. When this is your first experience of childbirth, it's important to realize that vaginal discharge, painfully engorged breasts and unexpected abdominal cramps are quite normal!

HOW YOUR BODY RECOVERS

WHERE	WHAT YOU CAN DO TO HELP
CERVIX AND VAGINA	Because both were stretched during delivery, they will take at least 7–10 days to regain their former elasticity and close up. Doing your pelvic floor exercises (see p. 36) will help your vagina to tighten again. Start immediately after the birth.
PLACENTAL SITE (LOCHIS)	As the placental site heals, it bleeds for at least two weeks. This discharge (lochia) has three colour phases: red (4–5 days), pink to brown (6–8 days), yellow to white (7–10 days). If you over-exert yourself, you may start to bleed, making the lochia red and copious again, so let your doctor know and rest with your feet up.
UTERUS	Immediately after the birth, your uterus shrinks down to the size it was at about the fourth month of pregnancy. By about the tenth day it can no longer be felt in your abdomen – your midwife will check daily to make sure that it is shrinking normally. It takes about six weeks to revert to its normal pre-pregnant size.
OVULATION	If you're not breastfeeding, you may begin to ovulate within 6–14 weeks of the birth; menstruation will follow in anything between 8 and 16 weeks. Breastfeeding hormones can suppress menstruation so you may not have a period for months, but don't rely on breastfeeding as a contraceptive. Use contraception as soon as you resume penetrative sex (see p. 117).

POSTNATAL DISCOMFORTS

DISCOMFORT	HOW TO RELIEVE IT
COPING WITH STITCHES	Discomfort from stitches can last up to a couple of weeks. Don't stand for long periods and have daily salt baths to prevent infection. Dry stitches with a hairdryer rather than a towel. Keep a bottle of witch hazel in the fridge and apply cold on a sterile pad to soothe the stitches. Occasionally stitches may not dissolve and need to be removed by your midwife or doctor.
STRESS INCONTINENCE	Leaking urine when coughing, sneezing, taking exercise or even laughing is a common though embarrassing problem for many women after childbirth. It's the result of stretched and weakened perineal muscles, so once again it is important to concentrate on doing your pelvic floor exercises (see p. 36).
BREAST ENGORGEMENT	Three or four days after birth lactation begins; your breasts become engorged with milk, making them uncomfortably large, hard and tender. Relieve this by expressing, putting your baby to the breast as often as he wants, and having warm baths or laying hot flannels on your breasts. Always wear a supporting nursing bra.
AFTERPAINS	As your uterus shrinks back you may continue to experience quite severe cramps, similar to menstrual pain, especially during breastfeeding. This is due to the action of the hormone oxytocin, which controls the "let down" of milk in your breasts (see p. 70), and also causes the uterine muscles to contract (see p. 47).
HEADACHES	In a very few cases (less than one per cent), some women experience a severe headache after an epidural anaesthetic. It's caused by a minute puncture in the membrane of the spinal column, made when the needle was inserted. If you experience this sort of headache, you'll be advised to lie down flat and drink plenty of fluids, and you'll be given painkillers such as paracetamol until the tiny hole has healed and the headache lifts. This usually takes a couple of days.

POSTNATAL SEX

You can have non-penetrative sex whenever you both feel like it after the birth, but you'd be wise to abstain from penetrative sex until after the lochia has stopped (see p. 116). However, neither of you will probably feel like it for a while. Nature has seen to it that most men have a low sex drive for some time after the delivery of their baby, especially if they are present at the birth. Not surprisingly, low libido lasts longer in women who have just had babies. No-one who has vaginal bruises, painful stitches and enlarged, tender breasts finds it easy to feel sexy; your need for rest and recuperation is much more important. If you've had stitches, make sure your partner feels your scar when it's healed – he'll be more understanding and compassionate about sex after he's felt the extent of it (see p. 45).

AFTER A CAESAREAN

If you've had a Caesarean delivery you'll be monitored more closely while you're in the postnatal ward, and your stay in hospital will be longer than with a normal delivery. The doctors will want to be sure that both you and your baby are progressing well before you go home. Even so, your stay in hospital is likely only to be about five days.

REMOVAL OF STITCHES
Your stitches will be removed on the sixth or seventh day at home by your midwife or doctor. This may be uncomfortable, so practise your breathing techniques to help you through it.

TIME FOR RECOVERY
You may find that it's only when you get home that you realize how much you have been knocked back by a Caesarean. This won't last for long – most women are amazed at how quickly they bounce back – but don't expect to feel completely back to normal for at least a month after the Caesarean.

HELP IN THE HOME
You need to avoid exertion while the wound is healing so it's a good idea if your partner can arrange to take a little extra time off work to help, or to see if a friend or relation can stay for a while. You won't be able to do any heavy lifting, and will probably be warned not to drive a car for several weeks.

YOUR HEALING SCAR
At first your scar just needs to be kept dry and well ventilated, and you'll be able to bathe once the dressing is removed. If the wound becomes red or inflamed, consult your doctor as there may be a slight infection that can be treated with antibiotics. Your scar will feel less sore as the weeks go by, but may begin to itch as the pubic hair grows back. As the scar is on your "bikini line", it's a good idea to wear pants that come up to your waistline to avoid irritation.

61

BEFORE YOU EXERCISE

You can start the gentle programme of exercises given here at any time, but avoid vigorous exercise until the lochia has stopped (see p. 60).

WARMING UP
Professional athletes and dancers never embark on an exercise routine, competition or performance without warming up first – they know the damage they could do to their bodies without it. It's equally important for you when doing postnatal exercises. Warming up helps relieve tension and warms up muscles and joints so that they don't overstretch when you begin more demanding exercises. It also helps to avoid cramp and stiffness afterwards.

IF YOU'VE HAD A CAESAREAN
You can do pelvic floor exercises straight away, but don't attempt any other exercises until you've had your postnatal check.

TAKING CARE
Don't exercise if you feel exhausted or unwell, and be careful if you've had back trouble. Avoid sit ups or straight leg lifts.

62

RESUMING SPORT

Even if you were taking part in a regular sporting activity to a high level before you were pregnant, you should avoid strenuous aerobic exercise for at least nine months after the birth. Avoid anything that involves putting a strain on your abdominal muscles, and don't resume working out in the gym until your doctor advises it. Ask a qualified fitness trainer or sports instructor to give you a graded programme, take it very easy but don't expect to be back to your previous level of fitness or stamina for at least a year.

LOOKING AFTER YOUR BODY

Pregnancy and childbirth aren't illnesses, and your body is designed to recover naturally. However, this doesn't mean it couldn't do with a little help. Gone are the days when women were literally "confined" for several weeks, but you will need to conserve your energy during the first two or three weeks to help the healing process and to enable you to get breastfeeding successfully established (see p. 70). The fat laid down in your body during pregnancy specifically to provide the calories for breastfeeding will take a few weeks to be used up, but many women are surprised by how quickly they regain their pre-pregnancy shape and weight when they breastfeed.

POSTNATAL EXERCISES

Losing weight isn't the same as regaining muscle tone; you'll need to exercise the muscles in your abdomen and perineum to bring them back to normal. But finding the time and energy to do postnatal exercises may seem an impossible dream to you immediately after the birth. While you're in the postnatal ward you'll probably be visited by a physiotherapist within a day of the birth. She will explain exactly what has happened to your body and will show you the best way to start exercising. Your abdominal muscles will have stretched and parted to accommodate your growing baby; this muscle tone can be regained if you find ten minutes a day to do the simple exercises given here. Make sure you warm up properly first (see left).

GETTING STARTED
Start gently – your muscles and ligaments are still soft from the action of progesterone – and don't forget your pelvic floor muscles (see p. 36); just because you can't see them doesn't mean they aren't important.

HOW TO EXERCISE
Little and often is best; start with one or two repetitions of each, every day, then progress to ten. Remember to exhale on the effort, and inhale as you relax. Always stop if any exercise hurts.

CAT ARCHING

Feet are slightly apart

Hands are flat on floor

1 Kneel on all fours with knees and hands slightly apart. Make sure your back, head and neck are straight.

Arch lower back upwards

2 Tighten your buttocks and slowly arch your back upwards. Keep your arms straight but don't lock your elbows. This exercise is wonderful for relieving lower backache.

Head remains in line

Push up on arms without locking elbows

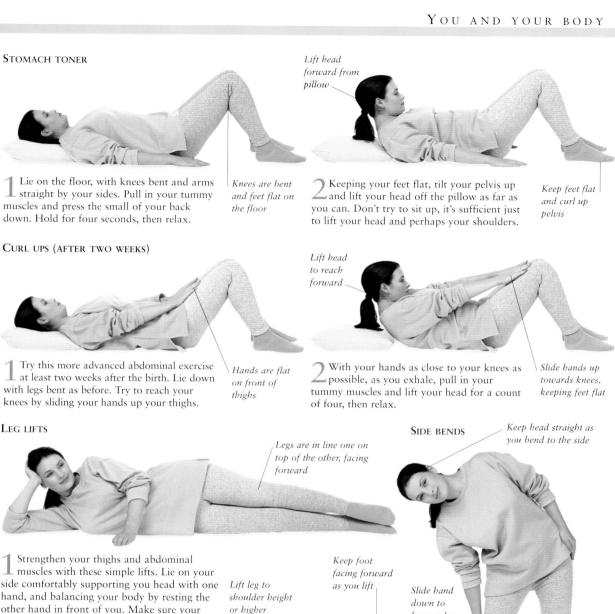

STOMACH TONER

Lift head forward from pillow

1 Lie on the floor, with knees bent and arms straight by your sides. Pull in your tummy muscles and press the small of your back down. Hold for four seconds, then relax.

Knees are bent and feet flat on the floor

2 Keeping your feet flat, tilt your pelvis up and lift your head off the pillow as far as you can. Don't try to sit up, it's sufficient just to lift your head and perhaps your shoulders.

Keep feet flat and curl up pelvis

CURL UPS (AFTER TWO WEEKS)

Lift head to reach forward

1 Try this more advanced abdominal exercise at least two weeks after the birth. Lie down with legs bent as before. Try to reach your knees by sliding your hands up your thighs.

Hands are flat on front of thighs

2 With your hands as close to your knees as possible, as you exhale, pull in your tummy muscles and lift your head for a count of four, then relax.

Slide hands up towards knees, keeping feet flat

63

LEG LIFTS

Legs are in line one on top of the other, facing forward

1 Strengthen your thighs and abdominal muscles with these simple lifts. Lie on your side comfortably supporting you head with one hand, and balancing your body by resting the other hand in front of you. Make sure your legs are in line with your hip and shoulder.

Lift leg to shoulder height or higher

Keep foot facing forward as you lift

Leg should remain straight without locking knee

2 Keeping your knee and foot facing to the front, lift your whole leg straight upwards to shoulder height, hold for a count of two and then lower. Do this a few times, then turn over and repeat with the other leg.

Keep lower leg flat on floor as other leg is lifted

Turn lower foot for balance if necessary

SIDE BENDS

Keep head straight as you bend to the side

Slide hand down to knee as leg is stretched

Stand with feet about 45cm (18in) apart

Stand with your feet apart and arms by your sides. Slowly bend sideways at the waist, stretching your leg outwards at the same time. Return to upright, and repeat with the other side.

CHAPTER FOUR

LOOKING AFTER YOUR
NEW BABY

Don't worry if you feel a bit clumsy to start with, every new parent is, largely because your new born baby is so tiny and you feel insecure about handling him. After a few days you'll gain in confidence and start to develop a routine.

Most babies need to feed every few hours and the smaller your baby the more often he'll want food. So don't expect unbroken nights and then you won't be disappointed. And most babies cry for a couple of hours every day. It's best to be philosophical about it, not take it personally and soothe your baby as best you can. The situation will improve with time and night-time crying usually stops at three months.

MOTHER

Your baby's first few months of life would be tiring for you even if you hadn't been through the rigours of labour and birth. Spoil yourself and make sure your own needs are satisfied: if you're happy and fulfilled you'll be better able to enjoy your baby.

HOW TO BE KIND TO YOURSELF
■ Rest with your baby. Use the time when your baby is asleep to catch up on your own sleep. It doesn't matter if you're still in your dressing gown at lunchtime. If she has her longest unbroken sleep period in the morning, take advantage of it, or rest in the afternoon when she does.

■ Share with your partner. If things are getting on top of you, he needs to know, for your sake and for your baby's – especially if he's out at work during the day. Equally, encourage him to look after the baby when he's at home; don't be over-protective and try to do everything yourself.

■ Ask for help. If you're feeling isolated, don't soldier on alone. Early offers of help may tail off because friends and family don't want to impose, but they will be glad to be asked, and their help and experience may prove invaluable to you.

■ Get out and about (see p. 114). Being tied to the house can make you feel cooped up and depressed, so try to get out as much as possible. It's helpful if you have friends locally who are also at home with young babies; you will probably have met like-minded parents at antenatal classes. Building a network of new parents enables you to share the good times as well as the worries, and, as your baby grows and becomes more sociable, she'll have a ready-made circle of friends with whom she can play.

THE FIRST WEEKS

AFTER THE MONTHS OF PREPARATION, the excitement of the birth, and following the many postnatal medical routines, you find yourselves back at home in a completely new situation – at last you are a family. Now you can get down to the serious business of learning how to care for your child as she grows and develops from a small and vulnerable baby who depends on you to meet her every need, into a social and communicative one-year-old who is very mobile and might even be walking. It's immensely rewarding but there's a lot to do, with no "trial period" to ease you in – it's a full-time commitment from the start.

FINDING A PATTERN

When you become a new parent, perhaps the most difficult thing to adjust to is the fluidity and unpredictability of your new lifestyle. Most people's lives have very distinct patterns, based on doing roughly the same things at roughly the same times, and they feel discomforted if this structure dissolves. Alternatively, you might be used to doing what you want exactly when you want to do it. But trying to impose this sort of orderliness on a young baby is the equivalent of spitting into the wind. If you can both relax and follow your baby's lead, a pattern of some sort will eventually emerge.

FOLLOWING YOUR BABY'S LEAD

Ignore anyone who tells you that you shouldn't pick up your crying baby because "she's only exercising her lungs" or "she'll cry herself back to sleep in a minute"; very young babies shouldn't have to wait. If a baby learns that she has to scream for ten minutes to receive attention, she is laying down a pattern of behaviour that you will not appreciate in the future. So-called "good" babies are either those who are contented because all their needs are met promptly, or those who have been taught by experience that their needs won't be met at once and have become apathetic. You cannot "spoil" a young baby except by imposing a regime that is governed by the clock – and by placing your needs before hers. This is what will lead to her becoming discontented and hard to pacify. Helping her to separate her needs from others' needs will come much later on in her development.

CHANGING YOUR PRIORITIES

If you're both following your baby's lead, you'll have to learn to be as relaxed as possible about things like meal-times and housework, even if you normally have a set routine and are houseproud. It's much more important for both of you to concentrate on becoming skilled and confident in the practical care of your baby. Initially, there may seem to be a lot to learn and you'll feel clumsy and nervous (everybody does), but you'll soon find that it becomes second nature, and you'll gradually develop a routine that allows you time to do chores at some point in your day.

COPING WITH THE NIGHT SHIFT

WHAT TO DO	HOW IT HELPS
PREPARE YOURSELVES FOR BROKEN NIGHTS	Many babies continue to wake once or twice during the night well beyond 12 months of age. If you're both prepared for this, you'll find it much easier to adjust.
SHARE THE BURDEN	Taking turns to get up is important. You may have followed the traditional pattern of father going to work, while mother stays at home, but remember looking after a baby is also a full-time job.
CHANGE YOUR SLEEP PATTERN	Broken nights are not necessarily sleepless nights. By developing a new sleep pattern, you'll find that you're able to wake, attend to your baby and then go back to sleep immediately.
KEEP YOUR BABY CLOSE	If your baby's cot is by the side of your bed, you don't have to disturb yourselves too much when she wakes for a feed. Put her back in her cot when you're ready to go back to sleep (see p. 86).
STAY TOGETHER	Sleeping separately could undermine your relationship as a couple and with your baby. Only sleep in separate rooms as a last resort, because of illness or extreme fatigue for example.
AVOID SLEEP DEPRIVATION	Long-term sleep deprivation can have serious consequences, so it's better that you both lose some sleep than for one parent alone to take all the burden and become completely exhausted.

IF YOU FEEL LOW

If either or both of you feels disillusioned or dissatisfied with what you imagined you would be experiencing at this time, you're not necessarily depressed, you're probably just out of sorts. This is natural: you're both tired. If the baby is fractious, the mother may feel that somehow it is her fault and she may also be suffering from the "baby blues" (see p. 112), while a new father may feel inadequate if he's unable to help as much as he'd like, because he's at work. Don't worry: you'll both soon begin to adjust to the new situation, but if negative feelings persist, talk to your doctor or health visitor. They'll help you realize that lots of people feel the same way, but will also be able to tell if you're suffering from the signs of actual postnatal depression, which is easy to treat if recognized early on (see p. 113).

REASSURE EACH OTHER

If you both start out in the knowledge that these first few months can seem like hard work, you'll be able to reassure each other that you're coping extremely well. If you accept the validity of each other's feelings, and hold on to the fact that any difficulties are temporary, you'll discover that parenthood really is as pleasurable as you expected.

FATHER

The first few weeks with your baby are important in helping you establish your new role as a father. The contribution you make while your baby is still small and vulnerable is important for the whole family.

HOW YOU CAN HELP

■ Support your partner. She will be very tired to start with as a result of going through labour and birth, and from the physical and emotional responsibility of breastfeeding. Provide her with the time and space to meet your baby's nutritional needs, and reassure her constantly that she's doing a difficult job well. Your support can make all the difference.

■ Find time to help. If you're back at work, your time will be limited during working hours, but relish the opportunity to do as much as you can for your partner and your baby when you're at home.

■ Give your baby love. Babies need as much love as they can get, and there's no difference between the love of a father and a mother. If your baby is being breastfed, then obviously she'll need her mother when she's hungry, but at all other times she'll benefit just as much from your closeness and attention. This closeness from you will mean that your baby learns to be secure with both of you, which will help her to settle and take the pressure off your partner.

■ Concentrate on building a relationship with your baby from the start. Your own feelings as a parent will be enormously enriched if you spend as much time as possible with her. Don't isolate yourself or just see yourself as the breadwinner. Being an equal partner in your baby's care will be rewarding and beneficial to you and to your family as a whole.

67

SAFETY MEASURES

You'll need to have a major overhaul of general safety equipment throughout your home. Before the birth instal smoke alarms, if you don't have them already, and before your baby becomes mobile instal:

- Covers for all electric sockets.
- Corner protectors for furniture.
- Locks and catches for video recorders, doors, cupboards and drawers (especially in the kitchen) and the refrigerator.
- A cooker guard.
- Retractable flex for electrical goods such as the kettle, iron and toaster.
- A stair gate at the top and bottom of stairs and across the kitchen door or opening.

EQUIPMENT

Providing for your new baby is exciting and rewarding, and you naturally want the best. However, as you set out to plan the nursery, do bear in mind that to start with your new arrival will need very little in the way of essentials.

THE BASICS

Manufacturers of nursery "hardware" have recognized that couples expecting their first child are among the biggest spenders around, but you don't need to break the bank to provide for your newborn baby if you stick to the basics shown here.

Lining should be washable

MOSES BASKET
Simple and lightweight for a newborn. You could make linings and trimmings yourself – use cotton fabric.

CHANGING MAT
Comfortable and practical to avoid mess when nappy changing and at bathtime.

Plastic cover can be sponged clean

BABY CHAIR
A rigid or bouncing baby chair with back support is useful for young babies before they can sit. Always place it on the floor.

Head rest *Flat base can be rested on a stand or firm surface*

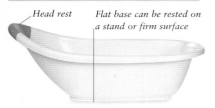

BABY BATH
A flat-based bath comes with a stand or can be rested on a firm surface; others fit over the big bath. For use in the first 3–4 months.

FULL-SIZE COT
When your baby outgrows his Moses basket, you'll need a cot. Choose one with two mattress positions and a drop-side to protect your back when lifting him.

Check cot bar gaps conform with safety standards

Removable tray so chair can be pushed to table for family meals

Safety harness

Check drop-side catches are secure in case your baby pulls them

Chair can be used separately

Base converts into toddler table

HIGH CHAIR
Foldaway designs take up less space, but rigid chairs may be more stable. The one shown is expensive, but it's a good investment because it can be taken apart to form a toddler's table and chair, when your baby is older.

Choose a firm, stable base

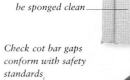

Look for adjustable mattress heights

OUT AND ABOUT

Your baby won't be walking until she's at least a year old, and even then she'll need transporting in a buggy or car seat for safety. It's worth looking ahead to future needs when you're thinking about buying any of these larger, more expensive items.

Changing bag holds all baby equipment

INFANT CAR SEAT
All babies under 10kg (22lb) should be put in a rear-facing seat in the car. Make sure it conforms to safety standards.

Car seat may be used as a carrier and seat outside the car

CHANGING BAG
Choose a bag to hold nappies, changing equipment and clothes, with space for bottles, baby food and toys when necessary.

SLING
There are several types of carrying sling suitable for young babies; try them on to see which is most comfortable A back-pack may be more comfortable once your baby can sit up.

PRAM AND BUGGY
A pram/buggy combination is ideal as it will last until your child is about three years old. Check ease of folding, and that the height of the handle doesn't make you stoop. A smaller, umbrella-type folding buggy may be preferable if you use the car a lot, although it's not suitable until your baby is six months old.

Carry cot can be removed

PRAM

BUGGY

Detachable sunshade

Seat should adjust to face forwards or backwards

Fixed wheelbase is firmer and easier to push

Integral shopping tray

Make sure foot brake is easy to use and secure

BUYING SECONDHAND

If there's a secondhand baby shop in your area, it's well worth a visit. Many nursery items get relatively light use, so there may be good bargains to be had. You can also try shopping at charity shops and car boot sales. However you should check all equipment carefully, and certain items should be avoided (see below).

GOOD SECONDHAND BUYS
■ Clothes, especially newborn baby clothes and outer wear.

■ Bedclothes (except duvets), but always wash before use.

■ Moses basket, but always buy a new mattress.

■ Plastic or wood toys only, but check carefully for cracks or splinters. Avoid anything that has metal or moving parts; even soft toys or dolls may contain hidden metal parts, for example, eyes, swivel heads and arms.

■ Large plastic items, such as sterilizing equipment.

POSSIBLE SECONDHAND BUYS
■ Pram or buggy, but check brakes, folding mechanism and all of the accessories before you commit yourself to buying.

■ Cot, but always buy a new mattress and check drop-side mechanism is safe.

■ Travel cot. Always check the folding mechanism and carrying case. Buy a new mattress if necessary.

■ High chair. Check that all screws are really secure and check crevices for food deposited by the previous user.

■ Safety items such as baby monitors or stair gates, but check that they work properly.

BAD SECONDHAND BUY
■ Never buy a secondhand car seat for your baby. It's too risky because the seat may have been weakened in an accident.

69

ADVANTAGES OF BREASTFEEDING

There are so many advantages to breastfeeding, both for your baby and for you. Here are some of them:

■ Bonds baby and mother closely.

■ Readily available, sterile and always at the correct temperature.

■ Easy for your baby to digest.

■ A perfect balance of protein, carbohydrate, fat, salt and other minerals, vitamins and iron.

■ Protects against infection.

■ May protect against allergies.

■ Breastfed babies have fewer nappy rashes and their stools are softer and inoffensive.

■ Helps burn off fat laid down in a mother's body during pregnancy.

70

YOU WILL NEED

2–3 NURSING BRAS
BREAST PADS
disposable or reusable

THE "LET-DOWN" REFLEX
When a baby suckles, nerves in the areola stimulate the pituitary gland in the brain to secrete oxytocin, which causes the breast to release ("let down") milk.

Pituitary gland secretes the hormone oxytocin

Nerves in areola signal to pituitary when baby sucks, so milk is released

BREASTFEEDING

THERE ARE NO DRAWBACKS to breastfeeding, only advantages. Breast milk is, by definition, the most suitable food for your baby, providing all her nutritional needs during her first six months. Although as a father you can't actually breastfeed, you can be involved in supporting your partner, knowing that this is beneficial to your baby.

GETTING STARTED

Some people have no difficulty with breastfeeding; but for many others it doesn't go smoothly in the beginning. Don't feel demoralized: follow the step by step guide opposite and discuss any problems with a midwife or breastfeeding counsellor, who will be happy to give advice at any time. Don't give up without consulting one of them first. Remember, your baby is learning too, so you have to be patient for her sake.

ENSURING A GOOD MILK SUPPLY

When you put your baby to the breast, the milk she drinks first – the foremilk – is thin, watery and thirst-quenching; the hindmilk that follows is richer in fat and protein, so your baby gets all her nutritional needs at one feed. To ensure that you provide a good milk supply make sure you are eating a good diet and drinking lots of fluids, especially in hot weather when your baby will be thirsty too. Feed on demand, when your baby is hungry; your body will automatically produce enough. If your baby feeds slowly in the first few days, you may have to express milk (see p. 72) in order for more to be produced. If your baby feeds often and hungrily, you will always keep pace, no matter how small your breasts are; don't believe old-wives' tales about small breasts not making enough milk – breast size is irrelevant. However, it is important for you to get plenty of rest between feeds, so your own metabolism can catch up. Many women find the mid-evening feed the most difficult as the milk supply is often lower because you are tired, and your baby may be fretful at this time of day. Plan ahead by resting in the afternoon if possible, preparing an evening meal earlier in the day, or better still, leaving it to your partner.

FREQUENCY OF FEEDS

Be prepared to feed often at the beginning – your newborn baby could feed ten or eleven times in 24 hours for the first few weeks. Feeding will take over your life to start with, but you'll find that your baby is contented, goes to sleep easily and by the time she's six to eight weeks, she'll be feeding more efficiently, and less often. Don't try to impose a rigid routine – your baby will be upset and the stress will affect your ability to feed. During the first few weeks, use alternate breasts for feeds, with ten to fifteen minutes per feed. This helps to balance the milk supply and avoids either breast becoming sore from over-long sucking. Many babies find one side easier than the other; if this happens with your baby, put her to the less favoured breast first.

SUCCESSFUL BREASTFEEDING

To establish successful breastfeeding, it's important to understand how your baby sucks. "Sucking" is really the wrong word; in fact she "smacks" the nipple between her tongue and the roof of her mouth. To do this properly she has to latch on properly (see below) with her gums firmly gripping the areola (this stimulates the let-down of milk – see opposite) and the nipple so far into her mouth that the milk is then squeezed right into her throat for her to swallow.

BREASTFEEDING POSITIONS

It's important to be in a comfortable position before you start feeding as you're likely to be there for 10–20 minutes. Whether sitting or lying, make sure your baby's whole body is angled towards you; she's more likely to latch on first time.

SITTING IN A CHAIR
Sit with both feet firmly on the ground. Support your back and arms with pillows and place a pillow on your lap to raise and support your baby if necessary.

Use both hands to bring your baby to the breast

71

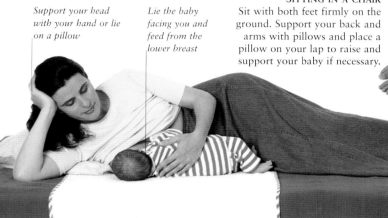

Support your head with your hand or lie on a pillow

Lie the baby facing you and feed from the lower breast

FEEDING WHILE LYING DOWN
This is a good position when you're tired or if you need to keep your baby's weight off a Caesarean wound. Lie on your side and lay your baby alongside you so she can reach your lower breast.

LATCHING ON AND RELEASING

1 Cradle your baby in the crook of your arm and use your other hand to bring her up to your breast. Line up your nipple with your baby's nose. As soon as she smells your milk, she'll open her mouth. While your baby is very young, you can gently stroke her cheek; when you do this, she'll turn towards your breast as a reflex action.

2 Your baby should "latch on" to your nipple at once. If not, support your breast with your hand and guide her on to it so that she has a mouthful of nipple.

Baby's gums should encircle the areola

3 A breastfeeding baby creates a strong vacuum on the breast, so when she has finished, you may need to release her grip on the nipple by gently easing your little finger into the corner of her mouth. Never pull your nipple away from your baby; this is a sure way to make it sore and sore nipples (see p. 73) may deter you from breastfeeding.

EXPRESSING MILK WITH A BREAST PUMP

Electric pumps apply a rhythmical suction to the breast, and are quite efficient at obtaining substantial amounts of milk. You can hire or borrow pumps from the hospital or one of the organizations that promote breastfeeding. Smaller hand or battery operated pumps work by holding the funnel over the breast and drawing the plunger in and out, or switching on, using an intermittent suction rhythm that avoids bruising the tender breast.

HAND PUMP
Many hand pumps incorporate a container that doubles as a feeding bottle.

EXPRESSING MILK

When you're breastfeeding you can express milk so your partner can feed your baby; it also helps to relieve overfull breasts in the first days. If your baby is in a special care baby unit (see p. 58), you can express milk to feed him. Few women find it easy to express milk, so don't be disheartened – it's a knack that takes a bit of learning. If you "leak" milk while feeding, place a breast shell against the other breast, and keep the milk in a sterile container.

EXPRESSING MILK BY HAND

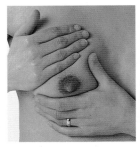  

1 Massage your breasts with flat hands, beginning at your ribs and working towards your areola, gradually going over the whole breast.

2 Then roll your fingers and thumb together below and above your areola so that you press on the wider milk ducts behind the nipple.

3 Collect the milk in a sterile bowl, transfer it to a sterile container and keep it in the refrigerator for a few hours. Freeze it for longer storage.

WHAT IF IT'S TWINS?

Don't be put off by people who say you can't breastfeed twins. Lots of mothers prove otherwise and, like all babies, twins benefit enormously from breast milk. Human breasts are quite capable of nourishing two babies, each of whom has the same need to bond with his parents, and you can feed them at the same time once breastfeeding is established.

GET ADVICE
Confidence is a crucial factor in breastfeeding twins. Try to talk to other mothers who've done it successfully – there are support groups to help you (see p. 163).

FEEDING TOGETHER
To feed your babies at the same time, lay them on their backs one under each arm with their heads forward, supported on pillows.

ONE AT A TIME TO START WITH
Concentrate on latching on with one baby at a time at first. Feeding singly may be easier in the early days, and gives you a chance to get to know each baby individually. However, this does take much longer than feeding together.

THERE'S PLENTY OF MILK
Breastfeeding is always controlled by demand, so your breasts will produce as much milk as your babies need. If one feeds more readily than the other, put the slower baby to the breast first; the stronger baby will stimulate more milk.

LOOK AFTER YOURSELF
Eat heartily, have plenty to drink and rest whenever you can. Although twins' practical needs are the same, there are two of them to look after, and you'll tire easily. Make sure you get as much help as you can.

BEING DETERMINED

Few women breastfeed without encountering problems at least once, and sometimes several times. So while you shouldn't necessarily expect to find it difficult, neither should you be surprised if you seem to have a run of problems. The important thing to bear in mind is that most breastfeeding difficulties can be put right – provided you have support and the commitment and confidence to continue.

SORE NIPPLES

Painful nipples are the most common reason for women giving up breastfeeding. However, there are ways to avoid them. Make sure your baby is properly latched on and never pull your baby off the nipple (see p. 71). Keep your nipples dry with disposable or cotton washable breast pads or clean cotton hankies. Don't use tissues as they will fall apart. Let them dry naturally at the end of each feed whenever possible. If they become cracked, calendula or camomile cream may be helpful. If your nipples become very sore, feed your baby before he is desperate as he will be calmer and treat you more gently. Try to get the milk flowing before the feed starts by expressing a little first.

BLOCKED DUCTS AND MASTITIS

A red, tender patch on your breast may be a sign of a blocked milk duct. You may even feel feverish. Take immediate action by feeding as frequently as possible, or express milk, particularly from the affected side. Massage any lumps gently as your baby feeds. See your doctor if there's no improvement within 24 hours, as you may need a mild antibiotic to clear any infection.

FATHER

Your support is essential when your partner begins breastfeeding, especially if she has any difficulties.

WHAT YOU CAN DO TO HELP
■ Be gently encouraging. This is not the time for a hint of criticism.

■ Don't leave your partner to feed the baby alone unless she asks you to – she could feel isolated and you'll feel neglected.

■ Your partner may like to express milk that you can give in a bottle at night. Undo your shirt and hold your baby against your skin to mimic breastfeeding (see p. 74).

■ Be aware that your partner's breasts may be tense, sore and very sensitive for the first few weeks of breastfeeding.

73

CONCERNS ABOUT BREASTFEEDING

YOUR CONCERN	WHAT YOU CAN DO
HOW LONG ON EACH BREAST	Your baby takes 80 per cent of the feed in the first five minutes, five minutes more and he's sucked out the creamy after-milk, so as a rough guide, expect him to spend about 10 minutes per breast. Breastfed babies are rarely underfed though they may only feed for a short time.
SLOW FEEDING	Many babies take a few days to get the hang of latching on and may be slow to feed. If this becomes a problem, seek advice. A baby who sucks a long time isn't necessarily feeding. He may just love sucking. If your baby has a tendency to fall asleep at the breast, let him take all he wants from one side, then offer the other breast first next time.
BABY'S WEIGHT GAIN	Don't weigh your baby before and after feeding. Weight gain in breastfed babies should always be calculated over a two to three week period, as they often gain unevenly. The very rare instances of underfeeding usually occur because the baby isn't properly latched on.
IF YOU'RE ILL	Common infections such as colds needn't interrupt breastfeeding. Stay in bed, and let your partner bring the baby to you just to feed. You could also express milk so your partner can feed your baby instead. If you need medication of any sort make sure your doctor knows you are breastfeeding as some medicines are not recommended for breastfeeding mothers. If you go to hospital, breastfeeding is usually still possible if you take your baby in with you.
BREASTFEEDING IN PUBLIC	Breastfeeding is the most convenient way to feed your baby, and you should be able to breastfeed anytime, anywhere. It's possible to feed discreetly if you use a nursing bra that undoes easily in front with one hand, and a big shawl or cardigan to screen yourself. A baggy T-shirt or sweatshirt also works – you can tuck your baby up underneath it.

STERILIZING AND PREPARING BOTTLES

Hygiene and correct formulation of feeds are important if you are bottle feeding as either could lead to health problems with your baby. To ensure your baby thrives and to avoid infection:

■ Buy equipment well in advance and practise cleaning bottles and placing them correctly in the sterilizing unit (see opposite), if you're using one.

■ Always wash your hands thoroughly before handling bottles and feeding your baby.

■ Always follow the manufacturer's instructions carefully when sterilizing. Any sterilizing chemical usually comes in the form of soluble tablets or concentrated liquid.

■ Bottles should be fully immersed in sterilizing fluid and left for at least two hours or according to the manufacturer's instructions.

■ With 6–7 feeds in 24 hours for the first few weeks you should change the sterilizing fluid twice a day. Later you can reduce this to once a day.

■ Make up batches of six bottles at a time and store them in the refrigerator. When all but two bottles have been used, make up some more.

■ Never add extra scoops of formula or sugar.

■ When a feed is over, pour away leftover milk, clean and rinse the bottle, cover it and place to one side until you are ready to sterilize it.

■ Never give a baby leftover milk from a bottle because it may be contaminated. Always use or make up a fresh bottle and keep a couple of cartons of ready-made formula for emergencies.

BOTTLE FEEDING

I'M NOT GOING TO PRETEND that bottle feeding is as good for your baby as breastfeeding, but I don't want you to feel guilty, either. If you're undecided, look back to the sections on breastfeeding so that you're aware of its positive advantages. Bottle feeding does, however, mean that both of you can share all of your baby's care equally.

FEEDING YOUR BABY

Either of you can bottle feed your baby, but bottle feeding really allows a father to come into his own. When you are giving your baby a bottle, you can mimic the closeness of breastfeeding by cradling her close in the crook of your arm. Hold her so her face is 20–25cm (8–10in) away from yours, in a position where she can make eye contact with you (see p. 57). If possible, open your shirt and hold her against your bare skin.

GIVING YOUR BABY A BOTTLE

Before you start, check also that the flow from the teat is neither too fast nor too slow – before giving the bottle, tip it up to make sure the teat produces a flow of several drops a second. Your baby may break naturally for a burp halfway through the feed, but it isn't necessary to force her to burp by rubbing her back; if she's still hungry she'll just get upset. If she seems comfortable, let her feed without a break until she's had enough.

If possible, hold your baby as close as possible to your bare skin

BOTTLE FEEDING YOUR BABY
Cradle your baby close enough to keep eye contact throughout, and talk to her while you feed. If necessary, put a pillow on your lap to raise her. She'll soon learn to associate the pleasure of feeding with the sight of your face.

Your baby will look at you while feeding if held close enough

MAKING UP A FEED

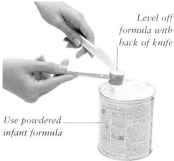

Level off formula with back of knife

Use powdered infant formula

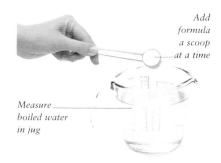

Add formula a scoop at a time

Measure boiled water in jug

1 Fill the scoop provided and level off the formula with the back of a knife. Do not pack the formula down.

2 Pour the required amount of boiled water into a measuring jug and add the formula a scoop at a time.

3 Stir the formula with a sterile spoon to make sure it is completely dissolved. Never add extra scoops of milk, it could be dangerous to your baby. Pour the milk into bottles through a sterilized funnel.

Formula dissolved in hot water

Fill bottles through funnel

Put enough for one feed in each bottle

Cover bottles until needed

Invert teat in bottle

4 Cover bottle immediately, keeping sterile teats inside the bottles ready for use. Allow to cool and store in the refrigerator until ready for use. Don't keep formula more than 24 hours.

Place bottle in bowl of hot water to reheat

75

5 When you are ready to feed, take the bottle from the refrigerator and warm the milk by placing it in a bowl of hot water. You can also cool hot milk by placing it in cold water.

TESTING THE MILK

Always check that the milk is not too hot or too cold before offering it to your baby by shaking a few drops on to your wrist. The milk should be blood temperature, which means it should feel neither hot nor cold against your skin.

Shake drops from bottle

Milk should not feel hot or cold on your wrist

KEEPING BOTTLES CLEAN

Scrupulous hygiene is essential if you are bottle feeding. Milk can be a rich breeding ground for the bacteria which cause diseases such as gastroenteritis, so you need to sterilize bottles, teats and all other equipment used for feeding until your baby is six months old. Clean bottles and teats thoroughly, using the method shown (right) before sterilizing.

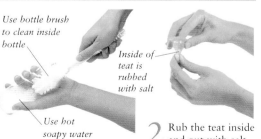

Use bottle brush to clean inside bottle

Inside of teat is rubbed with salt

Use hot soapy water

1 Scrub out each bottle with a bottle brush and hot, soapy water to remove all traces of milk, then rinse thoroughly in cold water.

2 Rub the teat inside and out with salt, paying attention to the inside rim and making sure that the holes are also clear. Then rinse in cold water.

CLEANING YOUR BABY

CLEANING GIRLS

Always clean your baby's vulva and anus from front to back to avoid spreading bacteria from the anus to your baby's vagina. Don't clean inside the labia; just rinse away faeces gently with damp cotton wool.

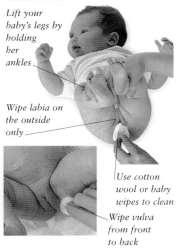

Lift your baby's legs by holding her ankles

Wipe labia on the outside only

Use cotton wool or baby wipes to clean

Wipe vulva from front to back

CLEANING BOYS

Cover a boy's penis with a tissue as you take off his nappy. Clean around the penis and scrotum with damp cotton wool; always wipe the anus from front to back. Don't try to pull back the foreskin as this remains fixed until your son is much older.

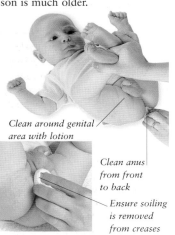

Clean around genital area with lotion

Clean anus from front to back

Ensure soiling is removed from creases

NAPPIES

Y OU'LL HAVE TO USE NAPPIES for at least two and a half years, until your baby gains full bladder and bowel control, so it's worth familiarizing yourself with the most efficient way to change your baby. Give some thought, too, to which type of nappy best suits your circumstances – there's certainly plenty of choice nowadays.

WHICH NAPPIES TO USE

There's a wide variety of disposable nappies available and you may be bewildered by the choice. If you want to use reusable nappies, there are several more modern alternatives to the traditional terry towelling square that requires safety pins (see opposite). Neither type is better than the other: unless you use a nappy laundry service, reusable nappies are a lot more trouble as they have to be washed and dried, while disposable nappies are more expensive, even taking into account the hidden costs of washing and drying reusables. There's been discussion about the adverse impact on the environment of disposable nappies both in their manufacture and disposal; reusable nappies are probably more ecologically sound in the long run.

NAPPIES FOR BOYS OR GIRLS

The most important feature when choosing nappies is to make sure they accommodate your baby boy and are comfortable for your baby girl. Some manufacturers of disposables have taken this into account: boys tend to wet the front of nappies so boys' disposables have extra padding in the front. Girls tend to wet the back of nappies more, and this is also accounted for in the design of girls' disposables.

NAPPIES, LINERS AND FASTENERS

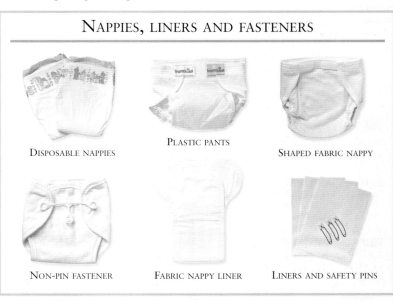

DISPOSABLE NAPPIES

PLASTIC PANTS

SHAPED FABRIC NAPPY

NON-PIN FASTENER

FABRIC NAPPY LINER

LINERS AND SAFETY PINS

CHANGING YOUR BABY'S NAPPY

Always change your baby on a firm flat surface, covered with a changing mat or towel. Protect your back by using a changing table of the correct height, or kneel beside the bed. Never leave your baby alone on the changing mat if it's on a surface above floor level. Even a newborn baby can wriggle off a mat, particularly if she's upset or angry. Collect together all the equipment you need before you start. Dispose of faeces in the toilet if possible; but don't flush disposable nappies or nappy liners down the toilet. Dispose of them in nappy sacks, preferably placing them in a covered bin.

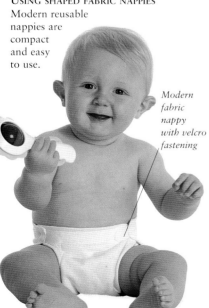

1 Remove the soiled nappy and clean carefully as shown opposite. Make sure all creases are clean and dry if you used water to clean. Slide the clean nappy under your baby, lifting her buttocks gently into position.

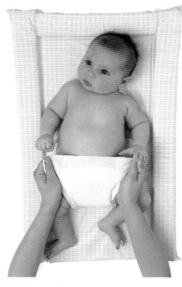

2 Using both hands, bring the front of the nappy up between your baby's legs, as high as it will go. Tuck in the corners securely around her waist, ready for fastening.

3 Holding the nappy in place with one hand, fix the adhesive tabs firmly on to the front flap of the nappy.

USING SHAPED FABRIC NAPPIES
Modern reusable nappies are compact and easy to use.

Modern fabric nappy with velcro fastening

77

NAPPY RASH

Nappy rash is preventable if you change your baby promptly, particularly after a bowel movement; bacteria in faeces breaks down the urine to release ammonia which ulcerates the skin. Use barrier cream only as a preventive measure. If your baby does become sore, leave his nappy off when possible, and apply nappy cream at every change. Check with your doctor if the rash persists for more than two to three days.

FABRIC NAPPIES

Traditional terry towelling squares are bulky, and can be uncomfortable for your baby when he's mobile. Modern reusables are usually shaped, and many types have strong velcro fastenings or you could use pinless fasteners, so you don't have to worry about using safety pins. If you're using these, it's a good idea to also use disposable or reusable liners (see box opposite) to avoid heavy soiling with faeces.

BATHING TIPS

To bath your baby as quickly and as safely as possible:

■ Wash or bath him in a room that is warm and draught free; it does not have to be the bathroom. Use a bucket to carry the water and to fill and empty the bath.

■ If you use a sponge and face cloth, make sure they are reserved strictly for your baby's use and wash them frequently.

■ Never poke about inside your baby's ears with a cotton bud as you could easily damage her delicate eardrum. Only remove ear wax that is visible at the opening.

YOU WILL NEED

COTTON WOOL
for face, eyes and nappy area
COOLED, BOILED WATER
for washing the eyes
BOWL OF WARM WATER
for washing face and body
SOFT TOWEL
for wrapping and drying
NAPPY CHANGING EQUIPMENT
(SEE P. 76)
CLEAN CLOTHES

78

KEEPING YOUR BABY CLEAN

VERY YOUNG BABIES don't get dirty, so they don't need frequent bathing – but bathtime does provide a perfect opportunity for cuddling and playing that infants come to relish. It also gives fathers a chance to spend time with their babies. Later, bathtime will be part of your baby's bedtime routine, a signal that it's time to wind down.

WHILE YOUR BABY IS YOUNG

Many parents are understandably nervous of bathing their newborn baby while she is still tiny and seems so vulnerable. It is, however, worth remembering that a baby is quite resilient provided she's handled gently but firmly, so try to be as confident as possible. You'll be shown the safest and easiest methods for bathing your baby a few days after the birth by a midwife at the hospital or when she visits you at home. As with all aspects of caring for your baby, bathing her will soon become second nature once you have given yourselves time to get used to it. The first few times, your baby may get quite distressed when she is being bathed, so don't feel you have to bath her every day. Thorough cleansing using the "topping and tailing" method outlined below is quite sufficient.

TOPPING AND TAILING

"Topping and tailing" means cleaning your baby thoroughly by washing her face, hands and nappy area, without undressing her completely. You can do this most days as part of your baby's nappy changing and dressing routine and then just give her a bath every two or three days instead. This will save you time and be less distressing for your baby.

1 Undress your baby on a changing mat or towel. Leave her vest on or wrap her in a towel. Gently wipe her face, ears and neck folds with cotton wool moistened in warm water. Pat her dry, making sure that you have dried thoroughly between her neck folds.

Wash face with small pieces of damp cotton wool

Use separate pieces of cotton wool for each eye to avoid cross infection

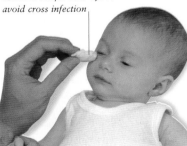

2 Take two more clean pieces of cotton wool and moisten them with cooled boiled water. Using separate pieces of cotton wool for each stroke, to avoid the risk of cross infection, carefully wipe your baby's eyes from the inner corner outwards.

3 Take off her nappy and clean the nappy area (see p. 76), then wipe with cotton wool moistened in warm water, especially around the folds in your baby's thighs. Wash the genital area front to back. Pat dry, put on a fresh nappy, then dress her in clean clothes.

Clean from front to back

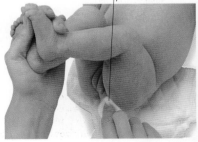

BATHING YOUR BABY

Choose a bathtime that suits you and your baby; it doesn't always have to be in the evening, especially if your baby tends to be fretful at that time of day. However, if you're working parents, bathing your baby in the evening is often a good way for you to spend time with her; you can even have a bath with her when she's older (see p. 81) to make it more fun! Make sure you've got all of the items you need within easy reach to make the task quicker and easier.

Look at your baby and talk to him

Support your baby's head and shoulders

> **YOU WILL NEED**
> ───────────
> BABY BATH
> TWO TOWELS
> BABY BATH SOLUTION
> COTTON WOOL
> *for face, eyes and nappy area*
> COOLED BOILED WATER
> *for washing the eyes*
> NAPPY CHANGING EQUIPMENT
> CLEAN CLOTHES

1 Fill the bath 5–8cm (2–3in) deep, putting cold in first. Test the temperature with your elbow or wrist; it should only feel warm.

4 Holding your baby in the bath and supporting his head with one arm, gently wash his body with your free hand, and encourage him to kick and splash in the water.

Make sure his head is dry as most heat is lost through the head

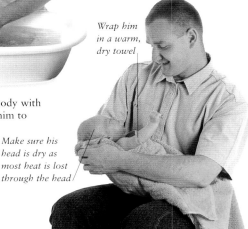

Wrap him in a warm, dry towel

79

Add baby bath solution to bath water

Gently wash his hair and scalp

Place the bath on a flat, secure surface

2 Undress your baby down to his vest and wash his face and neck (see opposite). Wrap him firmly in a towel, then, holding him under your arm and supporting his head over the bath, gently wash and rinse his hair with water from the bath. Pat his hair dry with a towel.

Support your baby's head and shoulders with your right hand

5 To get your baby out of the bath, raise his head and shoulders with one hand and slide your free hand under his bottom as before, then lift him on to the dry towel. Wrap him up immediately so he doesn't get cold. Pat him dry all over, paying particular attention to the folds of his neck, bottom, thighs and under his arms, then put on his nappy and dress him.

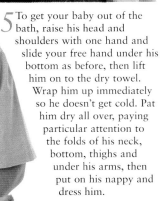

3 Leave a dry towel ready for after the bath. Unwrap the first towel, remove the nappy and lift your baby into the bath, supporting his head and shoulders firmly with one hand, and his bottom and legs with your other hand.

Support your baby's legs and buttocks with your left hand and arm as you lower him into the bath

BATHING AN OLDER BABY

SAFETY FIRST

When you use the big bath, bear in mind that your baby could drown in just a few inches of water (see p. 103). Take the following precautions to avoid accidents:

■ Have all equipment on the floor beside the bath and change your baby there. It is safer than carrying a wet slippery baby to a chair.

■ Put a non-slip mat in the bath.

■ Kneel on the floor to support your baby, and to prevent straining your back.

■ Never leave your baby alone in the bath, even when he can sit up.

80

YOU WILL NEED

NON-SLIP BATH MAT
SPONGE OR FLANNEL
BABY BATH SOLUTION
SHAMPOO
FACE SHIELD
to protect his eyes from shampoo
TOWEL
NAPPY AND CLEAN CLOTHES

O NCE YOUR BABY is three to four months old and has good head control, you could start using the big bath. Once he has got used to it, he will appreciate the extra room to play in the water. The same principles apply – keep your baby warm before and after the bath, do not over-fill the bath and check that the water is not too hot.

USING THE BIG BATH

Making the transition from the baby bath to the big bath can cause some babies distress, while others love it. It's a good idea to begin by putting the baby bath into the big bath the first few times so that the change is gradual and less frightening. Once your baby has got used to it and can sit up in the bath by himself, he'll begin to look forward to it as part of his routine, and enjoy bathtime games and water play (see opposite). You'll find bathtime can become a riotous affair with lots of shouts and splashing, but the problems may come when you want to get him out! It's advisable to make bathtime a part of your baby's overall bedtime routine (see p. 87) so that it acts as a clear signal to him that the day is over.

Pouring games will amuse your baby

THE BIG BATH
Kneel or sit beside the bath so that you're at your baby's level; wear an apron to protect yourself from splashes.

Sit your baby on a non-slip bath mat

GIVING YOUR BABY A TOWEL BATH

Cleaning your baby by towel bathing him is a halfway house between topping and tailing (see p. 78) and a proper bath. It is a useful method if your baby isn't feeling well or if he gets distressed when he's having a bath. It is also much quicker and more convenient for you, for those times when he needs a thorough wash but you're short of time; for example, after an enthusiastic self-feeding session (see p. 95).

TOP HALF FIRST
● Collect the same equipment as for topping and tailing (see p. 78).
● Undress him to the nappy and wrap his lower half in a towel. Wash his face, neck and upper body and pat dry.

Wash top half with lower body wrapped in towel

LOWER HALF
● Put a clean vest on your baby or wrap him in the towel. Remove the nappy, then wash his legs and feet, followed by his nappy area.
● Dry your baby thoroughly all over, then put on a clean nappy and dress him in clean clothes.

Cover top half with vest or towel while sponging lower body

MAKING BATHTIME FUN

Older babies really enjoy bathtime and it's an excellent time to catch up on your baby's developing personality and skills if you aren't able to be with him during the day. Bathtime is a wonderful opportunity for creative play and you can use it to help stimulate his development in a variety of ways. Babies love the freedom to sit in the warm water and you'll find that your baby will be endlessly fascinated by filling, pouring and splashing water. This really is learning through play – your baby is finding out about the properties of water and other liquids. Help him to do this by:

● Using simple household items like plastic cups and jugs or spoons and sieves to show your baby what holds water and what doesn't, and how water can be poured and stirred.

● Introducing floating toys such as boats or traditional bath ducks that your baby will enjoy handling.

● Having fun with your baby by taking him into the bath with you; have a lovely skin to skin soak together. Keep the water at an even temperature with a slow trickle from the tap – you should be lying with your head at the opposite end from the taps.

HAIRWASHING

Even though your baby may love his bath, hairwashing may continue to be a problem if he hates having water poured on to his head or over his face, especially if it goes in his eyes. Don't worry; this is very common. Take your time in getting your baby used to water on his head and face; make a game of it by dripping tiny amounts over his head from time to time. Until he's more confident, you can simply sponge his hair clean or wipe it with a face cloth.

Some babies love having water on their faces and don't even mind it in their eyes. If your baby likes water, you can use the bath shower attachment or a cup to rinse his hair and make a game of it. But even the mildest baby shampoo will sting your baby's eyes a little, so it is advisable to use a face shield to keep the soap and water out of his eyes until he's old enough to keep them shut or to hold his head back for you. Dry his hair with a towel and brush it with a soft brush.

TROUBLE-FREE HAIRWASHING
Use a simple face shield to keep water and shampoo away from your baby's face and eyes. Pour water gently so there's no danger of it splashing back.

FATHER

Your baby will grow to love bathtime, particularly if it is his special time with you. Encourage this bonding by handling him with confidence; the more often you do it, the less nervous he (and you) will be. Giving a bath is a positive way of contributing to your baby's care, and he'll know you're an equal partner in his life with his mother.

MAKE THE MOST OF BATHTIME

■ When you have a bath with your baby, lay him on your chest half in and half out of the water. Smile and talk to him all the time as you clean him.

■ Splash water gently over his body carefully, avoiding his face. This way your baby will learn to enjoy, and be unafraid of, water.

■ Allow plenty of time; a bath is not much fun for either of you if you have to rush. Remember, sharing a bath with your baby is also a good and enjoyable way for you to wind down after a stressful day at work.

81

Use a face shield to prevent shampoo from stinging eyes during hairwashing

Your baby will enjoy playing in the bath

DRESSING YOUR BABY

BABIES GROW OUT OF CLOTHES very quickly in the early months so don't spend a lot of money on first-size babywear. Many of the presents you will be given for your baby will be tiny outfits that will only fit your child for the first few weeks, so you should concentrate on buying a few practical, simple items for the first four months.

CHOOSING CLOTHES

You could be changing your baby's clothes several times a day to begin with, so choose clothes that are simple to put on and take off, and quick to wash and dry:

■ Choose roomy garments, with loose elastic at the cuffs.

■ Make sure fastenings are easy – snap fasteners are better than buttons. Avoid ribbons as they may be difficult to undo.

■ Avoid pure wool which may irritate skin. Choose non-irritating fabrics, such as cotton.

■ Only get machine-washable, colour-fast clothing.

■ Always look for labels that indicate clothes are inflammable.

■ Your baby's fingers and nails may get caught on open weaves.

■ Clothes can safely be bought second-hand, but check for inflammability, shrinkage and condition of fastenings.

■ Nightdresses are useful for newborns; they're quick to put on and allow easy access to the nappy.

■ Buy adequate protective clothing to avoid sun damage (see p. 98).

82

HOW TO DRESS AND UNDRESS YOUR BABY

Many parents are nervous of dressing their very young baby, particularly when it involves handling her "wobbly" head with its soft fontanelle (see p. 53). Always lay her down on her back on a changing mat or towel to dress and undress her; it's safer and you will both feel more secure. Although your baby doesn't know day from night, nightdresses may be easier to use when she's tiny. By the time she's three or four months old, she will have developed some head control, and you can safely dress and undress her on your lap, if you haven't had the confidence to do so previously.

PUTTING ON YOUR BABY'S VEST

Vests are probably the most awkward items of clothing to put on a tiny baby, because they have to be put on over her head, which is the biggest yet least manageable part of her body. Most vests are now designed with wide, "envelope" necks or shoulder fastenings to make it easier for you to slide the vest over her head.

Slide vest over your baby's head gently but quickly

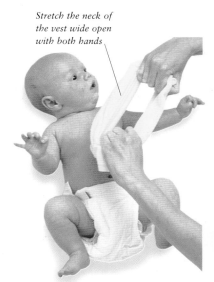

Stretch the neck of the vest wide open with both hands

YOU WILL NEED

BASICS FOR A NEW BABY
6–8 VESTS OR BODY SUITS
6–8 STRETCH SUITS
2–3 CARDIGANS
2–3 PAIRS OF SOCKS
PROTECTIVE CLOTHING AND SUNHAT FOR SUN PROTECTION
1 BLANKET OR SHAWL

USEFUL EXTRAS
2 PAIRS OF SCRATCH MITTENS
2 NIGHTDRESSES
ALL-IN-ONE PRAM SUIT

1 Lay your baby on a flat, firm surface on her back. Stretch the neck opening of the vest or body suit as wide open as you can with both hands.

2 Slide the vest over your baby's head, gently lifting her head up to bring it over to the back of her neck.

3 Widen each sleeve or armhole with your fingers and bring your baby's arms through, fist first, one at a time. Draw the vest down over her body.

PUTTING ON A STRETCH SUIT

Stretch suits are a very practical and economical item of clothing for you to buy for your baby. They're particularly useful at first because they allow freedom of movement, easy access to the nappy area, keep your baby warm but not too hot, and they are simple to put on even the tiniest baby. They are ideal for all-day use for the first 3–4 months and can also be used as sleep wear when your baby is older. To put on a stretch suit, follow the steps illustrated here; to take it off, reverse all the steps, beginning by undoing all the fastenings.

Hold your baby's head and bottom to lift her

1 Undo all the fastenings of the stretch suit and lay it on a flat surface. Then, lay your baby on top of the suit so that her neck lines up with the neck of the suit.

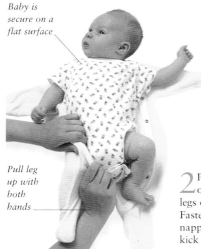

Baby is secure on a flat surface

Pull leg up with both hands

2 Put your baby's legs one at a time into the legs of the suit feet first. Fasten the suit under the nappy area so she can't kick her way out again.

Hold baby's wrist with one hand to guide it into sleeve

3 To put her arms in, roll back one arm of the stretch suit, holding it open with one hand. Then guide your baby's arm, fist first, into the arm of the suit and roll the sleeve up into place. Repeat with the other arm.

Fold back sleeve if too long

PRACTICAL CLOTHES FOR OLDER BABIES

Once your baby is sitting up, and especially when she becomes mobile, clothes have to be robust and comfortable, as well as machine-washable. Look for:

■ Bigger sizes, especially with outdoor clothes, so movement isn't restricted and she doesn't grow out of them too quickly.

■ Clothes that have easy access to the nappy area, such as dungarees or all-in-one suits with snap fasteners, or tights.

■ Lightweight clothing to protect your baby's skin from the sun. Use a wide-brimmed sunhat and shirts with sleeves and collars.

■ Soft boots or socks with non-slip soles when she starts to pull herself up to stand.

83

DRESSING OLDER BABIES

Once your baby can sit up, you'll find he's a lot easier to dress. But he may also wriggle and protest when you want to put on his clothes, so hold him firmly while you dress him. You could make a game of it to keep him occupied.

Name parts of clothing (sleeve, sock, zip) as you put them on

For safety, hold your baby firmly on your lap while you dress him

MOTHER

If you find you are trying to encourage your baby to sleep as much as possible, ask yourself for whose benefit you're doing it.

DOES YOUR BABY NEED TO SLEEP?
Trying to get your baby to sleep when he doesn't need to is pointless; even if you would like a break, you're going to feel more frustrated when your baby doesn't drop off. He's longing for your company, so talk and play with him instead; put him in a baby chair so that he can watch what you're doing. Research has shown that even young babies are very receptive to interaction with their parents, and with increased stimulation overall, your baby is much more likely to sleep more soundly and for longer.

YOU NEED REST TOO
You may find you're becoming overwrought if you're suffering from lack of sleep. Being over-tired builds resentment, makes you irritable and liable to get things out of proportion. If you're exhausted, express breast milk (see p. 72) and ask your partner to take on the night-time feeds for a couple of days so that you can get some rest. If you're really desperate, ask a relative or friend to come and help for a day or two. That way you can catch up on sleep in the daytime.

YOU WILL NEED

FOR THE FIRST 3 MONTHS

4 SMALL CELLULAR COT BLANKETS
as cotton is better than wool

6 FLAT COTTON TOP SHEETS

6 FITTED COTTON
MATTRESS SHEETS

SPARE MATTRESS (OPTIONAL)

PORTABLE MOSES BASKET, CRADLE
OR CARRY COT (SEE P. 68)

WHEN YOUR BABY SLEEPS

SLEEP IS IMPORTANT to babies, and to parents. Young babies spend a large proportion – up to 14 hours – of any 24-hour period asleep but, unfortunately, this doesn't often coincide with their parents' sleeping pattern, because it takes a few months for babies to learn the difference between night and day. However, if your baby is tired, he will sleep, no matter where he is or whether it's light, dark, noisy or quiet.

HOW BABIES SLEEP

The way babies fall asleep differs from adults; adults can crash suddenly, whereas babies sleep lightly for about 20 minutes, then go through a transitional stage before reaching deep sleep. Nothing will wake them, until they've had enough sleep. This means that babies who are simply "put down" will not necessarily go to sleep peacefully. You may need to nurse your baby to sleep for quite a while, so try to be patient, particularly if you are trying to get him back to sleep at night, when you are longing to go back to bed.

USE A MOSES BASKET
While your baby is small, put him to bed in a Moses basket or carry cot. You can then keep him in the room where you are most of the time, while he sleeps.

WHERE SHOULD A BABY SLEEP?
Where a baby sleeps isn't important to him to start with. He won't automatically fall asleep when put into a darkened bedroom; light doesn't bother him at all. He's much more likely to be disturbed by being too hot or too cold. Your baby will be happiest going to sleep hearing your voices and the household noises that he is used to in the background so, from the start, be kind to yourselves and the baby by letting him sleep in a Moses basket or carry cot placed in whichever room you happen to be.

USING A BABY MONITOR
If you leave your baby in another room, set up a baby monitor so you can hear him as soon as he wakes. Bear in mind that your baby may feel disturbed by the silence when you leave the room, and this could make him more fretful; leave the door open so he can hear you moving around the house – unless you have a cat which may climb into the cot. Avoid going back into the room once your baby is asleep; your smell could wake him, so resist the temptation to check him too frequently.

ENCOURAGING LONGER SLEEP PERIODS AT NIGHT

A young baby requires nourishment and calories at regular intervals, so he'll wake for a feed when his body tells him he needs it. The way to encourage your baby to sleep for a stretch (four, then rising to five or six, hours) during the night is to make sure he's taken in sufficient calories to last that long. This means feeding him whenever he shows he's hungry during the day. As he steadily gains weight, he can go longer between feeds and by about six weeks he could be sleeping for at least one period of about six hours – hopefully during the night. When he wakes for a night feed make as little fuss as possible: feed him in bed; if he needs changing, do it gently and quickly in a dim light. Don't make this a time for chatting and games and he'll begin to learn that waking at night doesn't bring any special privileges.

RESCUE PACKAGE FOR A SLEEPLESS BABY

Night after night of broken sleep is wearing for parents, and a young baby who perhaps only "catnaps" during the day makes it hard to catch up. Use this checklist of strategies to reduce unnecessary fatigue.

Be aware of background noise Don't shield your baby from the sounds of your home, such as the telephone, vacuum cleaner and washing machine. They won't disturb his sleep; in fact some babies are soothed by the rhythmic noise of household appliances!

Keep him close to you At night, put your baby's cot next to your bed so that you can take him into your bed to feed him. Then put him back in his cot afterwards with minimum disturbance.

Play music Babies respond well to soothing music (classical is best). Keep certain pieces for when your baby shows signs of tiredness.

Carry him in a sling Rhythmic movement can hasten sleep, but your baby may wake up when you stop moving. Carry him around in a sling when you are in the house, whenever possible. As well as being relaxed by the constant movement, your baby will be comforted by your body and your smell if he is this close to you.

Give him plenty of fresh air Fresh air is said to tire babies out. In fact, it's likely to be the stimulation they receive from the sounds and sights that bombard them when they're outside, or simply the movement of trees or branches, that makes them sleepy. Getting out of the house will also benefit you, particularly in the first months.

PUTTING YOUR BABY TO BED
Lay your baby down to sleep on his back, supporting his head and body with both hands. Make sure you don't let him become too hot (see overleaf).

85

FATHER

Understanding the way your baby's sleep patterns work will help you to tune into his and your partner's needs, particularly during the night.

BEING REALISTIC
You need to be realistic about how much time your new baby will sleep – I'm afraid it's probably less than you think. He spends 50–80 per cent of the time in light sleep, when he wakes very easily. His sleep cycle – light, deep, light – is shorter than an adult's sleep cycle, so he's vulnerable to waking each time he passes from one sleep state to another. Your baby isn't waking to spite you; he's programmed to wake up for all kinds of reasons – when he's wet, hot, cold, unwell – because his survival depends on it. It may be a comfort to realize that light sleep is likely to make your baby more intelligent because the brain remains active and it enhances brain development.

HAVING A SLEEP ROUTINE
Your baby has to be deeply asleep before he'll settle so try a tranquillizing sleep routine – gentle rocking, quiet songs and talking. He's deeply asleep when his eyelids don't twitch and his limbs feel limp. Lay him down and gently pat his shoulder at about 60 beats a minute for a few minutes.

GETTING HOME LATE
If you find you're getting home from work and your baby is asleep, ask your partner if it's possible for your baby to nap in the afternoon so that he's awake when you arrive. Be patient if this isn't possible to bring about; it's not your partner's fault. Try getting up earlier and spending time with your baby before work.

SAFE SLEEPING

The way babies are put to bed has been shown to have a bearing on Sudden Infant Death Syndrome – or what is more commonly known as "cot death". Recently the number of babies dying has halved thanks to a campaign to inform parents about safe sleeping:

■ Stop smoking – and NEVER let anyone else smoke in the same room as your baby. Preferably don't allow anyone to smoke in your home at all.

■ Always lay your baby on her back to sleep so that her breathing is unimpeded and she can lose heat from her front, face and head.

■ Don't let your baby get too hot, as she isn't very efficient at controlling her temperature. If the air temperature feels hot to you, it's very hot for her.

■ Don't increase the amount of bedding when your baby is unwell.

■ Never over-wrap your baby. Cover her with a cotton sheet and cellular blankets according to room temperature (see right).

■ If your cot is a big one, lay her in the "feet-to-foot" position at the end of the cot so that she cannot wriggle down under the blankets and become too hot (see below).

FEET TO FOOT
Lay a baby under six months with her feet touching the foot of a full-size cot, even if it means her head is halfway down the mattress.

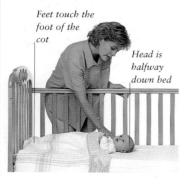

Feet touch the foot of the cot

Head is halfway down bed

WAKEFUL BABIES

Most babies develop a routine of sleeping perhaps for two hours in the morning and again in the afternoon, but there are always exceptions. While wakeful babies can be trying, they reward you in the end as they're usually very bright and affectionate, so don't be downhearted. Your baby is wakeful because she loves you and craves your friendship; she doesn't mean to starve you of sleep, she just wants to learn and be sociable. Every minute spent awake with you, she'll be forging new links with the world and developing many skills. Think about this, too, when she's awake during the day; if she isn't tired, why should she sleep? From her point of view, it's much better for her to stay with you, so don't be surprised if she cries when you leave her.

WHAT YOU CAN TRY
● Keep her temperature even; touch her skin to check that she isn't too cold or hot, add or remove blankets if necessary (see below). Check the room temperature; a temperature of about 18°C (65°F) is comfortable.
● Change her nappy if it's wet or soiled and soothe the nappy area with a bland nappy cream (zinc oxide), if necessary.
● Use a rocking cradle or push her rhythmically in her pram.
● Play her a tape of the human heartbeat, the sound she heard in the womb.
● Play her music you listened to during pregnancy, or an old-fashioned musical box with a simple repetitive melody can be really effective.
● Play her a tape of you and your partner quietly talking.
● Put the cot on alternate sides of the bed each night so that you can take it in turns to see to her. Talk to her and rock her; you don't need to pick her up.
● If she's obviously reluctant to sleep, get her up and put her in her baby chair where she can see you.
● Hang a mobile over her cot so she's got something interesting to watch when she wakes up. A mobile that plays music is ideal.
● Fix a "baby gym", with different noises and textures, across her cot or attach it to the bars so she can reach for it when she's bored.

BLANKETS AND BEDDING

The traditional practice of swaddling – wrapping infants fairly tightly with a sheet or blanket in their cots – is tied to a mythological notion of reproducing the conditions they had in the womb. In fact, they were free to move their limbs then and they should now. Swaddling can be harmful if it makes your baby too hot (see left), so simply use enough bedding to keep her comfortably warm (see below). When your baby is under 12 months, don't give her a pillow, and avoid quilts or duvets, baby nests, sheepskins or cot bumpers because they also prevent loss of heat.

WHAT BEDDING TO USE ACCORDING TO THE TEMPERATURE

TEMPERATURE	WHAT TO USE
15°C (60°F)	A sheet and four blankets.
18°C (65°F)	A sheet and three blankets.
21°C (70°F)	A sheet and two blankets.
24°C (75°F)	A sheet and one blanket.
27°C (80°F)	A sheet only.

SLEEP AND YOUR OLDER BABY

As your baby grows, her sleep pattern will gradually change; she will begin to stay awake and alert for longer periods during the day, even after feeds. When she's being stimulated with play and talk from you, she'll start needing longer periods of sleep to recharge her energy levels. The introduction of solid food may also mean that she settles better. The trick is to persuade her that these longer sleep periods should be at night, to align with your own.

ESTABLISHING A BEDTIME ROUTINE

Your baby may well get upset at bedtime – she could be anxious about being separated from you (see p. 140), or she may simply want to continue playing, so establishing a bedtime routine is essential to build her confidence and to help her learn that there is a time when playtime has to stop. Set up your own routine at a time to suit all of you – if you're working you may want it to be a little later than other parents, so that you can have time with your baby when you get home – but try not to vary the routine, whatever time you do it. A suggested routine might be as follows:

● Give her the final meal of the day – preferably not her main meal (see p. 95).
● Give her a bath without too much romping, and change her into bedclothes.
● Spend a quiet time in your baby's room; sing gentle songs, or read a story (depending on your baby's age and stage of development).
● Give her the last breastfeed (unless your baby still wakes at night).
● Lay her in her cot, with any comforter or security object she has become attached to, turn the dimmer switch down low, then sit quietly with her for a minute or two.
● Go out of the room quietly, saying good night, and leaving the door open.

THE BEDTIME ROUTINE
Allow time for quiet play with your baby, with books and toys. Remove hard objects when you lay her down.

Talk, sing or tell stories quietly as part of the bedtime routine

Let your baby play in her cot for a while before sleep

Musical mobile is both soothing and interesting

YOU WILL NEED

FOR 3–12 MONTHS
4 CELLULAR COT BLANKETS
6 FLAT COTTON TOP SHEETS
6 FITTED COTTON BOTTOM SHEETS
FULL-SIZE COT (SEE P. 68)
NURSERY EXTRAS
DIMMER SWITCH FOR THE NURSERY LIGHT
BABY MONITOR
COT TOYS (SEE BELOW)
TAPE DECK FOR SOOTHING MUSIC

DAYTIME NAPS FOR YOUR OLDER BABY

As babies grow older they sleep less and less, but up to 12 months your baby may continue to nap during the morning and afternoon; right up to the age of three many toddlers still like to rest some time during the day:

■ To help your baby relax and drop off, always put her in her favourite place, which may not necessarily be her room, and make sure she has with her any special comforter or security object. Play calming music, let her have toys and books in the cot, and keep her within earshot so she can hear you bustling about. If she calls out to you, it's probably only for reassurance, so calmly call back.

■ If your baby doesn't want to sleep, that's all right; just make it a quiet time when she can sit in her cot and play happily alone. But never let your baby cry for longer than a few minutes without going to see her or picking her up. If your baby is unhappy, that defeats the purpose of a nap.

■ If your baby falls asleep in the car, or her pram, never wake her suddenly from her sleep; like you, she'll need time to adjust.

■ Never leave your baby asleep alone in the car or in her pram outside a shop; this could be dangerous.

87

WHAT MAKES A NEWBORN CRY

The circumstances of your baby's birth may affect the amount he cries. It helps if you understand the possible underlying causes of a fretful baby's behaviour. Try not to become impatient with him as it will be out of his control, but he will begin to settle as he gets older. Your baby may cry more:

■ If you had a general anaesthetic during labour.

■ If you had a forceps delivery.

■ If he was born after a long labour, after which babies tend to sleep in short bursts.

■ If he is a boy. Boys may cry more than girls in new situations. Try not to make the mistake of some parents of boys who have been known to attend to them less, in the mistaken belief that it will "toughen them up".

WHEN YOUR BABY CRIES

ALL YOUNG BABIES CRY at some time during the day. Whether it's a subdued grizzle or a full-throated roar, a baby's cries are his only means of communicating his needs. Sometimes his cry will signal some obvious discomfort – hunger, a soiled nappy, boredom, tiredness – and at other times it will be difficult to pinpoint the reasons, but over the weeks you will learn the best way to respond to him. Having said that, there is no doubt that a persistently fretful baby can be a strain for parents, so it's worth thinking about the underlying causes. Look upon crying as conversation rather than an irritant designed to upset you.

RESPONDING TO YOUR BABY'S CRIES

Research shows definitively that babies do better if you respond promptly when they cry. It's a mistake to think of a baby as "good" if he doesn't cry much and one who does as "naughty", because a baby's cries have nothing to do with good or bad behaviour. Although constant crying can be difficult to cope with, it is necessary because responding to your baby's cries is a crucial part of bonding – your attitude to your baby in the first few weeks forms the blueprint for your future relationship with him, and for all the relationships he goes on to form later in life. He'll learn kindness and sympathy from you, which is why you should always answer his cry, whatever anyone else tells you. A loved baby will be secure and when the time comes he will be able to take separations in his stride if he's learned that you will answer his needs. A baby who is left to cry is more likely to grow up clingy and attention-seeking because he's learned that he has to work harder to make you respond to him.

GIVING YOUR BABY ATTENTION
All babies thrive on the company of their parents, and will cry because they miss the comfort of your presence. Try to give your baby as much contact as you can.

Picking up your baby and distracting him will often stop him from crying

WHY YOU SHOULD RESPOND PROMPTLY
● Your baby is longing to communicate with you, but his repertoire is limited to start with. Crying is the only way he can convey his feelings so don't just ignore him.
● Your baby will develop good communication skills and outgoing, friendly behaviour.
● It will make him secure and self-confident.
● It will not "spoil" your baby or teach him "bad habits"; you cannot spoil a baby this way, only love him.

WHAT HAPPENS IF YOU DON'T RESPOND
● Not responding to your baby's cries is a form of rejection, and your baby will soon sense this.
● If you don't respond, he will cry for longer, continuing until he gets the attention that he needs.
● He will be driven to create a pattern of frequent crying.

WHAT TO DO WHEN YOUR BABY CRIES

PROBLEM	DESCRIPTION	WHAT YOU SHOULD DO
HUNGER	If your baby has been asleep for two or three hours and begins to cry insistently, he is probably ready for a feed.	Give him a feed. If he cries afterwards, he may not have had enough so offer more. If it's very hot, offer him a drink of water.
DISCOMFORT	A cold, wet or soiled nappy could be uncomfortable enough to cause your baby to cry. Your baby may also be too hot or too cold.	Check and change the nappy if necessary. Treat nappy rash (see p. 77). Check bedding and air temperature (see p. 86).
INSECURITY	A jerky movement, bright light or sudden noise can startle a young baby. Many babies are also upset by being undressed and bathed.	Cuddle your baby to promote security. Handle your baby as gently and firmly as possible when dressing or bathing.
FATIGUE	Your baby will cry when he is tired, and may become quite upset when over-tired, which can make it doubly difficult to soothe him.	Create a soothing bedtime ritual (see p. 87) of rocking or stroking when you lay him in his cot, or push him in his pram.
BOREDOM	As your baby grows, he is more aware of people and cries because he wants company.	Cuddle him; at 4–6 weeks, sit him in a baby chair where he can see and hear you.
PAIN	Your baby may have earache, abdominal pain or persistent nappy rash.	Contact your doctor if he's hard to soothe, off his feed or appears unwell (see p. 100).

PERSISTENT CRYING

Some young babies have prolonged bouts of crying, which typically occur in the late afternoon and evening, and can last for anything between two and four hours. Babies often begin this pattern of persistent crying at about three weeks of age, and will usually have grown out of it by about three months. This pattern of crying has become known as "colic", because as the baby becomes increasingly upset and difficult to soothe, he may often pull his legs up and arch his back as if experiencing abdominal pain. In fact it is probably misleading to give it any special name, because there doesn't seem to be any known cause for this pattern.

GETTING THROUGH IT
A baby who is persistently fretful may cry readily at other times, not just in the evening. However, the evening pattern of crying can be a particular strain for parents, especially if one or both of you has been working during the day. It may be that your baby senses and reacts to your tiredness at this time. Although this crying pattern may only last three months, this period can seem never-ending to new parents who have to deal with their baby's distress day after day. Trying some of the suggestions for soothing your baby given above and overleaf should help you through this difficult time.

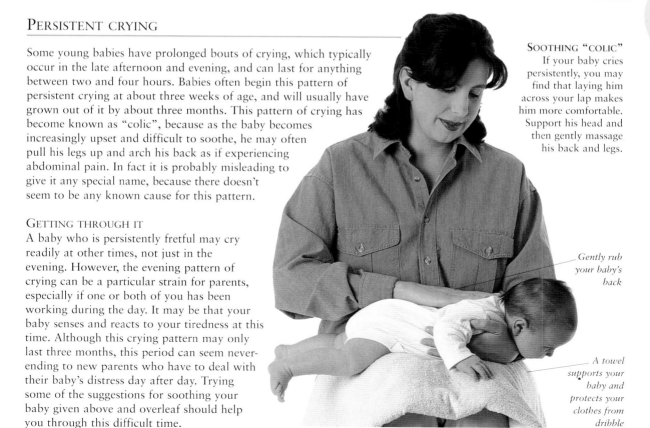

SOOTHING "COLIC"
If your baby cries persistently, you may find that laying him across your lap makes him more comfortable. Support his head and then gently massage his back and legs.

Gently rub your baby's back

A towel supports your baby and protects your clothes from dribble

SOOTHING YOUR CRYING BABY

LAY YOUR BABY ON YOUR CHEST

Lie on the bed or sofa, well supported by cushions. Lay your baby on your chest and gently rub her back. It will relax both of you. You can also provide skin contact by opening your shirt and laying your baby's face against your chest.

Hearing your heartbeat comforts your baby

USE A DUMMY

Encourage your baby to find her thumb or use a dummy or pacifier. There is no stigma attached to a baby sucking a dummy, but make sure it is sterilized and never sweeten it with honey or juice. However, it may only be a temporary relief so it's probably better to look for the underlying cause of the crying, keeping the dummy as a last resort.

Sucking a dummy or thumb helps a fretful baby

HOLD UPRIGHT

Bring your baby up against your shoulder and gently rub her back. (Put a cloth on your shoulder to protect it from any regurgitated milk.) Walk around, gently singing or talking to your baby.

A cloth protects your clothes

Support your baby firmly when you hold her upright

90

Cover your baby, but make sure she's not too hot or too cold (see p. 86)

Rocking often helps a baby to sleep

CARRY IN A SLING

Put the baby in a sling and carry her around with you. If you're a working father and your partner has been at home with the baby all day, take the initiative: let your partner rest and while you prepare the evening meal, carry your baby in a sling.

A sling keeps your baby close so she feels secure

COMFORT WITH MOVEMENT

Most babies are soothed by regular movement: it was what they were used to in the womb. Put your baby in a rocking cradle (make sure it conforms to safety standards) or in her pram and gently rock her backwards and forwards while you sit and watch television or eat a meal.

ACCEPTING HELP FROM OTHERS

Sometimes a crying baby can make parents who are already tired from broken nights feel quite desperate: this is the time to seek help. Don't ever feel that you are failing as parents if you accept assistance; countless other parents will have felt as frustrated and exhausted as you because their babies have cried a lot and have been difficult to soothe. Jump at the chance if your baby's grandparents or other friends or relations offer to look after your baby for a while so you can get out on your own for a couple of hours' break, or enjoy some unbroken sleep. If they don't offer any help, don't be afraid to ask them. There's no need to feel guilty – they will be glad to have the chance to relieve you and it will help you to get things back into perspective. It's a great help, too, to talk to health or baby care professionals, who are there to support you.

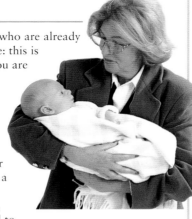

HELPFUL GRANDPARENTS
Grandparents know that you need a break and enjoy developing their own relationship with the baby.

COMFORTING YOUR OLDER BABY

As your baby grows and becomes more aware of her surroundings, her pattern of crying will change because it's not the only way she can communicate with you now. Her reasons for crying will also be easier for you to both predict and interpret. You'll begin to distinguish between frustration, hunger, pain or loneliness. Even when your baby is beginning to become more mobile and independent, the best way to comfort her if she's unhappy is with your company, hugs and cuddles.

COMFORTERS

Towards their first birthday, many babies will have become attached to a particular comforter – a favourite soft toy, a cloth or blanket – that probably helps them sleep and that may be grabbed when they're feeling a bit insecure and upset. Other babies become attached to a dummy or suck their thumbs (see opposite). This is perfectly normal and there's no point in distressing your baby by removing a comforter on the grounds that it is a "bad habit"; it isn't. As your baby's confidence and independence develop after her first birthday, she'll gradually become less dependent on her comforter, although it may take a year or so. It's a good idea to have some spares in case the main one needs a wash.

TEETHING AND CRYING

Your baby's teeth will normally start to come through from about six months (see p. 132) so she'll dribble a lot and her gums will occasionally be sore. Your baby may become rather grizzly when she's teething and it's usually quite obvious if she's uncomfortable; she'll want to chew a lot and may have a hot, red area on her cheek. However, it isn't a good idea always to blame persistent crying on "teething", when in fact your baby may be bored (see right), or even unwell (see p. 100).

TROUBLESHOOTING

As your older baby learns to communicate by other means, she'll start to cry to communicate emotions and pain. There are lots of reasons why she may cry.

SHE'S BORED
The older your baby gets the longer she spends awake, so she can become bored more easily. You baby may cry from boredom if left alone, unable to hear your voice and with nothing to look at or play with. You are her favourite playmate so keep her in the same room as you where she can see you and you can talk to her, and don't leave her for long periods alone in her cot if she's crying. Some babies do play happily in their cots for a short while after waking, so leave toys and books within reach.

SHE'S FRUSTRATED
As your baby grows her desire to do things outstrips her ability to do them; she gets frustrated and often starts to cry as a result. She may also cry if you don't let her have something she wants. Change her toys frequently – her attention span is still short. Find time to play with her (see p. 152).

SHE'S FRIGHTENED
At about six months your baby will cry when she's separated from you and she'll be nervous of other people, even when she knows them well. Right from the start, get her used to seeing you leave the room and come back in again. This way she'll gradually learn that she can trust you always to return to her. Make sure she meets lots of other people before she reaches this stage and learns that even if you leave her with someone else for a while, that you always come back.

SHE'S ILL OR HAS HURT HERSELF
If your baby hurts herself, you'll know at once from her cry, but it may be more difficult to tell when she's ill. See pages 100–103 for what you should do if your baby is ill or has an accident.

91

MASSAGE TIPS

Babies love massage as much as you do; it's a good way to calm an unsettled baby because it feels nice to him. It's also an expression of love and your baby knows it. It has the added advantage of relaxing you as you do it – you've got to be calm yourself to communicate physically with your baby. Always prepare yourself carefully for massage:

■ Make sure the room is really warm. Lay your baby on a soft blanket or towel.

■ Play favourite music or the taped recording of a heartbeat. Talk in a low, gentle voice or sing a song quietly.

■ Although massaging your baby's skin directly is best, many younger babies don't like being undressed. If your baby is one of these, dress him in a cotton vest or similar garment, through which you can easily feel his body.

■ Work around his body, massaging both sides with slow even strokes simultaneously. Keep your face close to your baby's and look into his eyes as you massage him. This is very potent for both of you.

TOUCH AND MASSAGE

B EING TOUCHED IS IMPORTANT to all young animals – including humans – it's an essential part of the bonding process that helps young creatures to thrive. It's been shown that premature babies gain more weight on lambswool blankets than cotton ones because it feels as if they're being stroked when they move and they're more contented.

THE IMPORTANCE OF TOUCH

Your baby is born sociable and he craves physical affection. This is best communicated through touch, cuddles, being gently held, kissed and nuzzled. It's important, therefore, that you're both completely free with your physical affection from the start. Your baby longs to be close to you and to be carried, and he will cry less and be more easily comforted if you carry him. Remember also that being carried in a sling close to your body feels like being cuddled to a baby (see p. 90), and allows you to do other things at the same time. Small babies are much stronger than you think so be firm, but avoid sudden jerky movements – your baby may think he's falling and he'll be startled rather than comforted. As your baby gets older you can be more robust with him; he'll enjoy tickling and rolling about on the floor with you, but don't overdo it if he becomes at all distressed – and don't blame him if he pulls your hair or scratches you: under a year he won't know that it hurts.

GIVING A MASSAGE

NECK AND SHOULDERS
Using fingers and thumbs, gently massage your baby's neck from his ears to his shoulders and from his chin to his chest. Then stroke his shoulders from his neck outwards.

Use gentle pressure with finger and thumb

ARMS
Lay your baby on his back and hold his arms up one at a time. Stroke down each arm using your fingertips, first from wrist to elbow, then from elbow to shoulder. (You may discover he's ticklish!) Then gently squeeze all along his arm, starting from the top.

CHEST AND ABDOMEN
Gently stroke down your baby's chest following the line of his ribs. You can use one hand and then the other in a continuous stroking movement, but don't press too hard. Massage his abdomen in a circular motion with one hand, working outwards from the navel. Talk and sing softly to him all the time.

Your baby will
concentrate on
your touch

Your hand
will make him
feel secure

HEAD
Using both hands, lightly massage the
crown of your baby's head using a
circular motion, then stroke down the
sides of his face. With your fingertips,
massage his forehead and cheeks,
working from the centre outwards. This
is particularly calming for a fretful baby.

Stroke
both
sides of
his
head

Talk to your baby
and encourage him to
look at you

FEET AND TOES
Rub your baby's ankles and feet,
stroking from heel to toe, and then
concentrate on each toe individually.
Your baby may kick his legs and curl
his toes while you're doing this. If he's
less than three months old show him
his toes – it will help him realize they
are part of himself (see p. 137).

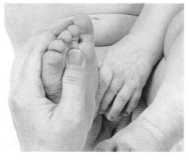

LEGS
Massage your baby's legs one at a
time. Place your free hand on his
tummy, then gently squeeze his leg
from the thigh down to the ankle.

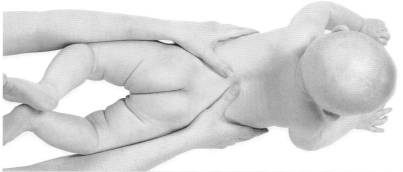

PHYSICAL AFFECTION

As children grow up, they need
the reassuring and loving embrace
of caring parents more, not less
as many parents think. And there's
no place for Victorian ideas of
"stiff upper lip" or statements like
"boys don't cry", any more than
"girls shouldn't be tomboys".
Boys do cry, and should be
encouraged to give vent to their
emotions as much as
girls. Indeed, it is
known that a child's
ability to achieve some
kind of emotional stability is more
or less determined before the age
of 12 months – a sobering
thought, but nonetheless true.

EMOTIONAL FEEDBACK
The mechanism by which a child
comes to master his emotions is by
getting sympathetic feedback from
adults that mirrors the emotions
he's feeling. If your baby holds out
a hurt hand, what helps most –
as any parent knows – is lots of
sympathy, "kissing better" and
cuddles. A child doesn't grow out
of the need for physical affection
because these positive signs of
parents' care are necessary for
emotional growth. If you deprive
a child of physical affection, you
deprive him of an essential
"growth vitamin".

YOUR BABY NEEDS YOU BOTH
This applies equally to both
parents, and continues throughout
babyhood, childhood and, in some
cases, into adolescence. And
nothing should be allowed to
discourage loving parents – even
hesitant fathers – from doing what
their child needs them to do.

93

BACK
Once you've massaged your baby on his
front, gently turn him over on to his
tummy and massage his back. Using both
hands, run your palms down his back
from under his arms to his buttocks,
pressing gently against his spine with
your thumbs. Talk to him all the time, as
he can't see your face in this position.

WEANING

MANY PARENTS VIEW weaning with trepidation; it seems such a huge step and there are so many pressures from outside sources – when to start, what to give and how much to give. But it needn't feel so daunting if you try to see the introduction of solid foods to your baby's diet as encouraging her independence rather than as an obstacle. Think positively and remember that all babies are longing to do things for themselves. When she starts to feed herself, it will encourage her self-confidence, and give her a chance to show off and receive praise from you. In such a frame of mind you'll both take early mishaps in your stride.

INTRODUCING SOLIDS

Weaning is rarely a problem from the baby's point of view, but some babies take longer than others to get used to having solid food as well as their normal milk feeds. It really doesn't matter – until six months milk is enough for many babies' complete nutritional needs. However, after that time they will need the extra calories, vitamins and minerals in solid food, as there won't be enough for them in milk alone (look at the weaning chart opposite for a suggested pattern of feeding).

When you introduce first solids, choose a feed when you know she's usually alert and awake – for instance, at midday, halfway through her milk feed. Sit your baby on your lap or in her baby chair and offer tiny amounts at first on the tip of a sterilized plastic spoon. Don't force it into her mouth; brush her upper lip with the spoon and let her suck it off. She might splutter and dribble a bit the first few times, but keep trying.

GIVING THE FIRST FEED
Hold her firmly on your lap and tilt her head back as you offer the spoon.

WATER OR JUICE

Remember milk is a food, it isn't a drink, and so from the moment mixed feeding is introduced, your baby will also need another fluid to drink from a bottle or cup. Offer cooled boiled water alone or with a few drops of pure unsweetened fruit juice added. Look carefully at labels to make sure there isn't hidden added sugar (such as fructose) listed. Start with 15ml of fluids between feeds, increasing gradually according to your baby's needs.

SUGGESTED WEANING SCHEDULE FROM FOUR MONTHS

FEEDS	WEEK 1	WEEK 3	WEEK 6
1ST FEED	Milk feed.	Milk feed.	Milk feed.
2ND FEED	Half milk feed. 1–2 tsps cereal. Finish milk feed.	Half milk feed. 1–2 tsps cereal. Finish milk feed.	3–4 tsps cereal. Milk feed.
3RD FEED	Milk feed.	Half milk feed. 1–2 tsps pureed fruit or veg. Finish milk feed.	2–3 tsps pureed chicken and veg. 2–3 tsps pureed fruit. Water or dilute juice.
4TH FEED	Milk feed.	Milk feed.	2–3 tsps pureed fruit or veg. Milk feed.
5TH FEED	Milk feed.	Milk feed.	Milk feed.

TROUBLE-FREE MEAL-TIMES

Just as it was important not to get hung up about how much milk your baby drank when you were establishing breastfeeding, try not to worry now about how much she is eating, or indeed about how much is going on the floor! It's going to be messy – until the age of five or six all children are messy eaters – so be philosophical and clear up afterwards. As long as meal-times are happy and relaxed, don't worry and don't allow them to become battlefields. You can never win – your baby simply refuses to eat (you can't force her) and the battle is lost. She's cute enough to learn that it's a weapon she can use to manipulate you, so don't join in the struggle.

ENOUGH TO EAT?
Even if you think your baby isn't taking enough food, she is. Don't make the mistake of forcing adult standards on her. Think of a balanced diet in terms of what you offer your baby over a period of time, such as a week, and make sure it has variety; accept that there's bound to be a certain amount of waste. Don't worry about fads either; she's eating what her body needs.

STARTING SELF-FEEDING

Self-feeding is an important step to your baby's independence, so be patient with her:

■ Use shaped plastic bibs that catch a lot of the spilled food, and put a large plastic sheet under the high chair so that you don't have to wash the entire floor every time.

■ Give your baby her own spoon and offer food that is of a stiff consistency, such as mashed potato or other pureed vegetables, in a non-spill bowl. Never mind that she gets very little at first, she'll have a lot of fun, which is how meal-times should be. While you're eating, have a spare spoon handy so that you can feed her, if needed.

■ Even if she finds a spoon difficult, she'll love feeding herself with finger foods (see p. 97). Finger foods are very useful in keeping your baby occupied when the meal isn't quite ready.

■ Above all be flexible; if one food doesn't suit just try another – no single food is essential. Don't spend ages on preparation, you'll only be resentful if your baby throws it on the floor.

■ Introduce a trainer cup with a spout for drinks as soon as your baby can manage it. Some breastfed babies never accept a bottle at all, going straight to a cup for juice and continuing to get all their milk from the breast. Others prefer a bottle for juice and may take time to get used to a cup.

RELAXED SELF-FEEDING
While your baby feeds himself, have your own spoon to feed him at the same time.

Use a non-slip plastic bowl to avoid any mishaps

FOODS TO GIVE

As well as making sure your baby has a balanced diet, vary it so that he learns to like different tastes and textures. You should include:

■ Fruit and vegetables: wash them thoroughly in cold running water, and peel potatoes, carrots, apples and peaches to avoid the risk of pesticide residues. Aim to give some vitamin C at each meal, whether as fruit, vegetables or juice, as it helps your baby's body to absorb iron.

■ Milk: from six months you can use full-fat cow's milk in cooking and to mix foods such as mashed potato. From one year, it can be used as a drink.

■ Meat and fish: try to offer at least one serving every day of lean meat or boneless fish.

■ Plenty of protein in the form of low fibre foods such as cheese or tofu, if you're giving your baby a vegetarian diet.

FOODS TO AVOID

Don't worry too much, but do take some sensible precautions:

■ Don't give foods containing wheat flour or gluten before your baby is six months old as he may find them difficult to digest.

■ Don't add sugar or salt – the former encourages bad habits and bad teeth, and the latter is too much for your young baby's kidneys to cope with.

■ Avoid giving your baby soft-boiled eggs until he is about one year old.

■ Very high-fibre breakfast cereals have little place in your baby's diet as they are too difficult to digest.

■ Avoid cheese made with unpasteurized milk until your baby is at least two years old.

BEST FOOD FOR YOUR BABY

To GROW AND DEVELOP WELL, babies need as varied a diet as your income will allow; research shows that babies who are offered a wide menu to choose from invariably choose a healthy diet and accept varied tastes. On the other hand, if they're only given fast foods and sweet things, they'll inevitably want chips and ketchup with everything.

WHAT YOUR BABY NEEDS

To provide for your baby's healthy nutrition, he needs complex carbohydrate from such things as sugar-free cereal, wholemeal bread, potatoes and other vegetables, rice and pasta; protein from lean white meat, fish and pulses such as beans, and, after he's about six months, eggs and cheese; and the vitamins and minerals contained in fresh fruit and vegetables. He needs some fat, but he should be able to get enough for his nutritional needs from the other foods you give him, especially milk. Avoid the "empty" calories of sweet foods like biscuits and sugary cereal: look at the food pyramid chart below to see the proportions of each type of food your baby needs for healthy growth and development.

THE FOOD PYRAMID

Once your baby is used to a variety of tastes, you can plan his diet to include a combination of foods from each group. The "pyramid" of foods shown illustrates the rough proportions of each type that you should try to give to your baby.

Too much sugar is bad for teeth and may lead to obesity

Low fibre foods provide protein for vegetarians

Fresh fruit is an important source of vitamins and minerals

Give least of fats, oils and sugars.

Give a little more of proteins: meat, fish, eggs, cheese and pulses.

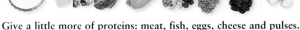

Give your baby fresh fruit and vegetables as part of his daily diet.

Give most of complex carbohydrate: bread, rice, pasta, porridge oats, potatoes (not fried or roast).

JOINING FAMILY MEALS

As soon as your baby is sitting in his high chair he can join you at the table for meals. The sooner you can include your baby in this, the sooner your baby will learn by example what is and isn't acceptable behaviour at the table. Some suggested menus are given in the chart below.

SUGGESTED MENUS FOR AN OLDER BABY

TIME	DAY 1	DAY 2	DAY 3
BREAKFAST	Rice cakes Chopped hard-boiled egg Milk	Mashed banana Wholemeal toast fingers Milk	Cottage cheese or yogurt Wholemeal toast Milk
LUNCH	Vegetable or chicken casserole Stewed apple Diluted fruit juice	Mashed potato and cheese Pear slices Diluted fruit juice	Strained lentils and mixed vegetables Banana and yogurt Diluted fruit juice
TEA	Toast fingers Peeled peach slices Milk	Rice cakes Peeled apple pieces Milk	Rusks Peeled seedless grapes Milk
SUPPER	Cauliflower cheese Semolina and fruit puree Diluted fruit juice	Pasta with sauce Yogurt and fruit puree Diluted fruit juice	Tuna, mashed potato, courgettes Rice pudding Diluted fruit juice

MAKE MEAL-TIMES FUN

It's frustrating to find that good food is being thrown on the floor or wiped over the high chair, but remember that your baby will eat if he's hungry. If he starts to throw food about, he's probably bored with eating because he's had enough so he's moving on to experiment with the textures instead. Try tempting your older baby to try new tastes with fun food such as the examples given here, and he'll learn to see meal-times as enjoyable occasions.

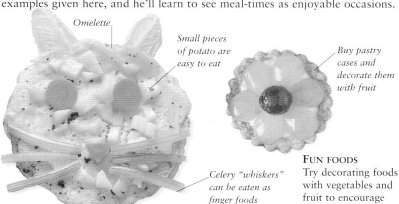

Omelette

Small pieces of potato are easy to eat

Buy pastry cases and decorate them with fruit

Celery "whiskers" can be eaten as finger foods

FUN FOODS
Try decorating foods with vegetables and fruit to encourage healthy eating.

FOOD HYGIENE

Bacterial infections picked up from badly prepared food can be dangerous for babies and children so be careful with hygiene.

■ Always wash your hands thoroughly before handling any food and after you have handled raw meat.

■ Store raw meat away from other foods in the refrigerator and keep fish in the coldest part.

■ Clean the spout holes of your baby's feeding cup regularly.

■ Always throw away leftover baby food. To avoid waste, prepare very small amounts and freeze in individual containers.

■ Don't reheat cooked baby food unless you're able to bring it to the boil, and cook it thoroughly for at least five minutes to kill bacteria.

■ If you're using a microwave, follow the manufacturer's instructions exactly for times. Stir the food thoroughly to ensure the heat is evenly distributed.

97

FINGER FOODS

Once your baby is about six months, he'll want to try feeding himself so give him easy-to-hold finger foods. Don't give him very small things and don't leave him alone. Try:

■ Any fresh fruit that's easy to hold, such as a banana or peach: remember to peel and remove pips.

■ Vegetables, particularly carrots, cut into a shape that's easy to grasp. Don't cut them too small.

■ Pieces of dry, sugar-free cereal.

■ Wholemeal bread or rusks (without grains), toast fingers, bread sticks or rice cakes.

■ Cooked pasta shapes.

BABY-FRIENDLY ACTIVITIES

There are lots of activities on offer for new parents and their babies, so there's no need to feel cut off:

■ Coffee mornings and parent and toddler groups (see p. 118).

■ Music groups for babies from six months. Again, the community centre may be able to help here.

■ Swimming – once your baby is immunized. Ask at your local pool about parent and baby sessions.

■ Baby movement classes may be run at leisure centres, for babies from six months of age.

■ Baby massage classes, probably run by a natural health centre or local yoga teacher.

PROTECTION FROM THE SUN

Babies have very little skin pigment so they have much less protection than adults from the sun's ultraviolet rays. Being exposed to direct sunlight can lead to skin damage and skin cancer later in life. To protect your baby:

■ Use sunscreen of at least factor 15 in addition to the natural protection of clothes and shade. Twenty minutes before going out, apply the lotion to your baby's face, neck, ears, back of hands and feet – not all over her body.

■ In very hot weather, avoid taking your baby out in the sun between 11am and 1pm.

■ Dress her in a wide-brimmed hat and protective clothing, such as a shirt with sleeves and a collar.

■ Be aware that your baby is still at risk on cloudy days.

■ Make sure the pram or buggy has a protective hood or umbrella to shade your baby.

OUT AND ABOUT

TRY TO GET OUT AND ABOUT with your baby as soon as you feel up to it – it helps her to get used to travel, new places and people. It's also good for you – it keeps you in touch with the world outside your home, and gives you a change of scene away from the sometimes claustrophobic world of nappies and baby paraphernalia.

FIRST OUTINGS

The first few outings that involve more than pushing the pram around to the local shops may seem daunting, and you'll probably be a bit nervous and unsure about how your baby will react. Keep calm and try to relax – your baby will pick up on any anxieties you have. You'll soon become a family of seasoned travellers – the easiest time to be out and about with your baby is while she's small and portable. Make the most of it because when she's toddling and needing constant supervision, the range of outings will become more limited for a while. Don't be too ambitious on your first outings – go to your local park, perhaps, or for coffee at a friend's house. Make sure you're confident about being away from home with your baby before you opt for something further afield. Travel at off-peak times when there's less congestion, especially if you're travelling by bus or train.

Hat, especially in hot weather
Changing mat
Nappies
Small toys
Large bag
Change of clothes
Baby wipes
Nappy cream
Bottle, if used
Tissues
Cotton wool
Toy for amusement
Bib
Bowl and spoon

YOUR TRAVEL BAG
You'll need a bag large enough for everything you need for your baby. Include sunscreen of at least factor 15 to protect your baby against sun damage (see box left).

GOING SHOPPING

There's no need to leave your baby at home when you go shopping as most supermarkets and department stores now provide facilities to help parents with babies (see chart opposite). Shopping malls can be more difficult if they are on more than one level, but most have lifts as well as escalators. When you are in the supermarket:

● Always use a supermarket trolley that is appropriate to your baby's size and weight and strap her into the seat with a harness. Be aware that she may try to grab items off the shelves.

● Shopping tends to make children hungry and therefore fretful. Avoid this by taking a snack and drink with you. These will provide refreshment for your baby and also keep her occupied.

● Use any creche facilities that are available.

SHOPPING WITH YOUR BABY

FACILITY	WHAT TO LOOK FOR
PARKING SPACES	Some stores have dedicated parent and baby parking spaces close to the entrance.
WIDER CHECK-OUTS	Good supermarkets have at least two wider than average check-outs to accommodate prams.
SPECIAL DISCOUNTS	Some stores offer discounts for parents with a baby under 12 months.
BABY CARE	Supervized creches are available at some stores, as long as you're there to be called if necessary.
CHANGING AND FEEDING	Many stores have a baby changing area in their toilets, and some have a room where you can breastfeed – but if you're happy just to sit out of the way to feed your baby, don't feel you have to do it in private. Just ask an assistant.

TRAVELLING BY CAR

Rear-facing car seats (see p. 69) make travelling by car with a young baby relatively trouble-free, but your car seat must be correctly fitted. These seats can be put in the front or back seats; however, don't use a rear-facing seat in the front passenger seat if you have an air-bag. Correct fitting is equally important when your baby graduates to a fixed seat in the back. Most babies are lulled to sleep by the movement of a car, but a hungry baby will wake and become upset. If you're on your own, find a safe place to park and feed her; it's better than trying to drive on with a screaming baby, which will make you both become tense. Keep a few nappies, wipes and nappy sacks in the car for emergencies. The sun can be a problem for babies, so use a detachable blind on your car window to provide shade.

HOLIDAYS

If you're going away with a very young baby, you may feel more comfortable not going abroad in case you need medical help. Having said this, small babies – especially breastfed ones – often travel abroad very well, but it's sensible to take out adequate medical insurance. Whatever the age of your baby, when you're away you should:
● Check how far you'll be from a doctor's surgery, medical centre or hospital.
● Make sure the cot in your holiday accommodation conforms with safety standards – the tour operator, travel agent or Tourist Information Office should be able to reassure you on this. Alternatively, take your own travel cot – modern designs are safe and compact.
● Always make sure your baby is adequately protected from the sun (see box opposite): use adequate sunscreen lotion, dress your baby in protective clothing and keep her in the shade.

Planning ahead is the secret to trouble-free travel by any form of public transport:

■ If you're travelling alone, make sure you can manage everything yourself – although you may hope for offers of help, people are not always as thoughtful to parents with babies as you may wish.

■ Allow plenty of time to reach the station or airport to avoid the extra stress of worrying about missing a train or aeroplane.

■ On an aeroplane, feed your baby on take-off and landing as sucking reduces the risk of earache caused by changing air pressure.

■ If you're flying long-haul, try to book a seat with a bassinet so that your baby can sleep in mid-flight.

■ A portable car seat is invaluable, though for air travel you may have to pay for an extra seat on busy flights if you want to use one just for your baby.

99

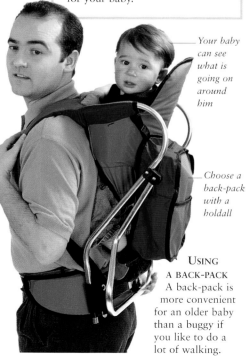

Your baby can see what is going on around him

Choose a back-pack with a holdall

USING A BACK-PACK
A back-pack is more convenient for an older baby than a buggy if you like to do a lot of walking.

MEDICATION

The doctor may prescribe a medicine such as liquid paracetamol or an antibiotic for your baby if he has a high temperature or infection. Give him the medicine in his mouth using a sterile dropper or medicine spoon. Always give the dosage that is recommended by the doctor or as instructed on the bottle.

TAKING YOUR BABY'S TEMPERATURE

A raised temperature usually means your baby is fighting off an infection. Take his temperature with a digital or mercury thermometer by holding it firmly under his bare armpit for three minutes. Bear in mind that the temperature measured in the armpit is about 0.6°C (1°F) less than the actual body temperature. Alternatively, you can use a temperature strip, although these are less accurate. Don't use a thermometer in your child's mouth until he's at least seven years old.

Make sure the bulb is in contact with the skin

CHECKING THE TEMPERATURE
Place the thermometer under your baby's bare armpit and hold his arm across his chest to hold it in place.

CARING FOR YOUR SICK BABY

ALL PARENTS WORRY if their child is ill; it's even more distressing when it's a baby as he's unable to tell you how he's feeling. If you suspect that your baby isn't well, don't hesitate to get medical advice. You're the best judge of when your baby is off-colour because you know and understand his moods and personality.

NURSING YOUR BABY

When babies are ill they are often grizzly and fretful, probably waking more frequently at night and needing constant attention and cuddles. However a very ill baby will become listless and unresponsive. If your baby has a cold, it might make feeding difficult as he won't be able to breathe properly through his nose. Be patient and let him come up for air when feeding, but if this becomes a real problem ask your doctor or pharmacist for nose drops.

RECOGNIZING A FEVER
The best way to recognize a fever is to lay your hand on your baby's brow. If his skin is hot, red and clammy he has a fever. When the temperature is very high, he may also shiver.

LOWERING TEMPERATURE
If your baby has a very high fever, you should lower it to prevent overheating. Remove all his clothing, lie him on a towel and sponge him down with tepid (not cold) water. Don't let him get too cold. If he's over three months, you may also give him liquid paracetamol (see above left).

TEPID SPONGING
To cool down your baby, apply tepid water with a sponge or cloth to his face and body.

Soak a soft cloth or sponge in tepid water, squeeze it out then dab it over your baby

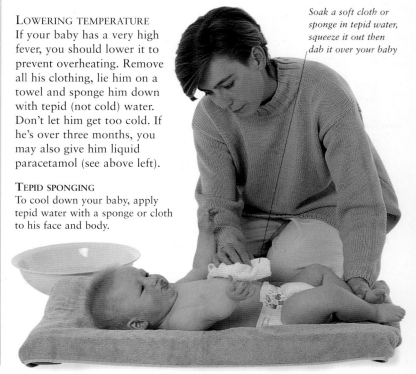

PREVENTING DEHYDRATION

Dehydration in babies under 12 months can be dangerous, and steps must be taken to replace lost fluids, sugar and salt. Signs of dehydration in babies are general listlessness and a sunken fontanelle (the soft area of skin on the top of the skull). Your baby may also wet his nappy less frequently. When your baby has a temperature, or when the weather is hot, make sure he doesn't become dehydrated by offering the breast more frequently or giving him cooled boiled water in a bottle or on a sterile spoon.

If your baby suffers from vomiting and diarrhoea for more than 24 hours, always consult your doctor. If you are bottle feeding, stop milk feeds for 24 hours and give rehydration solution (this is available from your doctor or pharmacist) by bottle. If you're breastfeeding, give rehydration fluid in a bottle, if possible, before the feed. If your baby won't take a bottle, you will need to breastfeed more often to maintain fluid intake.

Mild diarrhoea can sometimes occur when you introduce new types of solid food (see p. 94) – if you suspect this is happening, stop giving your baby that particular food and then try again after a couple of weeks.

RECOGNIZING AN ILLNESS

AILMENT	WHEN TO CALL THE DOCTOR
HIGH OR LOW TEMPERATURE	• If your baby's temperature rises above 38°C (100°F) and he's obviously ill, or if it rises above 39.4°C (103°F), when he doesn't seem ill. • When your baby's temperature goes up and down. • If your baby is unusually quiet and limp and his skin is cold, though his hands and feet are pink (see p. 103).
BREATHING DIFFICULTIES	• If your baby's breathing becomes difficult. • The rate of breathing speeds up and you notice his ribs being drawn sharply in with each breath.
LOSS OF APPETITE	• If your baby is under six months and refuses to feed either at the breast or from a bottle. • If your older baby refuses food when he is normally a good eater.
VOMITING	• If your baby is burping up whole feeds or the vomiting is violent, prolonged or excessive, it can cause rapid dehydration and medical help should be sought straight away. However, all babies regurgitate a little milk from time to time after feeds.
DIARRHOEA	• If the stools are watery, possibly greenish in colour, foul smelling, and are abnormally frequent. • If diarrhoea is accompanied by a raised temperature, you should always consult a doctor.
RASHES	• If you notice an unusual rash it can be a sign of infection, especially if it's accompanied by a raised temperature, or it might be an allergic reaction. Your baby's doctor will want to examine the rash. • One type of rash caused by meningitis is very serious and should be treated as an emergency (see above right).

MENINGITIS

This is an inflammation of the membranes that cover the brain, resulting from an infection. Viral meningitis is relatively mild; bacterial meningitis is life-threatening and requires immediate action. The main symptoms can develop over a matter of hours.

SYMPTOMS
In a baby under 12 months the main symptoms are general irritability, a slightly tense and bulging fontanelle (see p. 56), fever and a rash consisting of flat, pink or purple spots that don't disappear when you press them. There may also be listlessness, vomiting, loss of appetite and pain in the eyes from light.

WHAT TO DO
Press a glass to your baby's skin to see if the rash remains visible through it. If you think your baby has meningitis, get him to a hospital immediately.

101

FEBRILE CONVULSIONS

These occur in children (mainly aged from six months to five years) if there is a rapid increase in temperature due to an infection. The sudden rise causes the brain cells to discharge impulses to muscles which contract jerkily. It does not mean there is an underlying brain defect. The symptoms can be frightening to witness, but febrile convulsions are relatively common and rarely serious. The risk of epilepsy developing is very small.

SYMPTOMS
Loss of consciousness and uncontrollable twitching of the arms and legs. There may also be frothing at the mouth and the eyes may roll back.

WHAT TO DO
Clear a space and sponge your baby down to lower his temperature (see opposite). Call a doctor.

EMERGENCY FIRST AID

FIRST-AID MATERIALS

In preparation for an accident or emergency, keep a box of first-aid materials in your home. Make sure that any carers, such as a baby-sitter, know where this is kept. It should include the following:

■ Adhesive plasters.
■ Sterile dressings – do not open these until you need to use them.
■ Bandages.
■ Cotton wool.
■ Scissors and tweezers.
■ Adhesive tape or safety pins.

Y OU NEED TO KNOW what to do if your baby is seriously injured or ill. The following is not a substitute for proper first-aid training, but you should familiarize yourself with the techniques and information detailed here so that you know what action to take in an emergency. Although it may be difficult, always try to stay as calm as possible.

AN UNCONSCIOUS BABY

If your baby does not respond when you gently shake her shoulders or pick her up, she is unconscious. She may have stopped breathing, which will mean no oxygen is reaching her brain and her heartbeat may have slowed down or stopped altogether. You need to act quickly to open your baby's airway and resuscitate her if necessary (see below).

Calling an ambulance If you have a helper, ask him or her to call an ambulance. If not, resuscitating your baby for one minute before you call for help could save her life. When you call an ambulance, take your baby to the telephone with you; give the controller as much information as you can.

102

WHAT TO DO IF YOUR BABY IS UNCONSCIOUS

If you think that your baby is unconscious, act as quickly as possible. Look, listen and feel for breathing so that you can decide on the best course of action, and then follow the relevant procedure outlined below.

IF SHE IS BREATHING

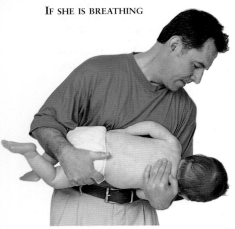

IF SHE IS NOT BREATHING

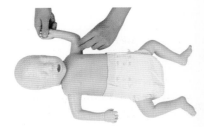

PULSE CHECK
● Place two fingers on your baby's inner arm to find the pulse.
● Watch for other signs of recovery.

MAINTAINING AN OPEN AIRWAY
If your baby is unconscious, there is a chance that she could choke on her tongue or vomit. To prevent this happening, cradle your baby with her head lower than her chest, as shown above, so that her airway remains open. While you're waiting for help, keep checking her breathing and pulse (see right); if either or both are absent, follow the procedure for not breathing (see right).

MOUTH-TO-MOUTH VENTILATION
● Place one finger under your baby's chin, and your other hand on her head, and tilt her head back to open her airway.
● Keeping the airway open, remove any *obvious* obstruction from her mouth.
● Seal your lips tightly around her mouth and nose and breathe into her lungs until her chest rises. Then remove your lips and let her chest fall back.
● Continue to do this for one minute, aiming at one complete breath every three seconds.
● Check the pulse (see right). If it is very slow (under 60 beats per minute) or absent, begin resuscitation by alternating chest compressions (see right) with artificial ventilation.

CHEST COMPRESSIONS
● If the pulse is absent or slow, position your index finger in the centre of the nipple line on the lower breastbone.
● Place the next two fingers on the lower breastbone, just below the nipple line and press down sharply to a depth of 2cm (1in) (five times in three seconds).
● Give one mouth-to-mouth ventilation (see left). Continue cycle for one minute.

CHAPTER FIVE

ADJUSTING TO BEING
A PARENT

Life is never the same after a baby.
There are many adjustments to make to your
lifestyle and to your relationship in the
transition from loving couple to loving family.
It's rarely straightforward at first. This tiny
stranger makes demands that put a strain on
both of you and you'll find you may have to
make a superhuman effort to stay
understanding and friendly to each other.
Looking after each other by keeping the
channels of communication open is important
and will make it that much easier to adapt to
your new role of parent.

HELPING EACH OTHER

MOTHER

If you've been at home with your baby for a few months while your partner is at work, you may begin to feel that you know your baby better than he does; at the same time you may feel resentful that you don't get enough help from him. Think about how your attitudes may affect your partner.

SUPPORTING YOUR PARTNER

■ Resist the tendency to think that your partner isn't as "good" as you are at caring for your baby. His role is vital and by encouraging him to get involved with the baby care and share the workload, you'll all benefit.

■ If your partner is tired after work, be patient. Let him wind down, then encourage him to spend time with your baby as a way of relaxing, not as a chore. Bathing the baby is often a good way for him to look after the baby and wind down at the same time (see p. 81).

■ Try to keep communicating. Tell him about your day with the baby. If it's been difficult, don't bottle it up resentfully, but, equally, don't convey it accusingly as if it's his fault.

BUILDING YOUR SELF-ESTEEM

■ Be proud of your achievements. As the main carer, you should justifiably take pride in the upbringing of your baby.

■ Stay in contact with work colleagues so that you can keep in touch with career developments and gossip! That way it's less of a shock when you return.

■ Make sure you have some time away from the baby, on your own and with your partner (see p. 114).

YOU BOTH WELCOME YOUR BABY. His presence is a shared joy that cements your relationship. However, new parenthood is a testing role, when both of you are faced with a new set of priorities and when expectations come up against hard realities. So spare a thought for each other's needs, as well as those of your baby.

THE INITIAL IMPACT OF THE BABY

As first-time parents you may seriously underestimate the amount of work and disruption caring for a baby entails and the extent to which this affects your relationship. Many couples are shocked to find that rather than bringing them closer together, their baby can bring to light differences that drive them apart. This is normal and very much part of your growth into parenthood, when you begin to lay the foundations of your new parental relationship with your baby and with each other.

DIFFERENT PATTERNS OF BONDING

While two-thirds of mothers bond with their babies almost immediately or within a few days, many fathers admit that intense paternal feelings take much longer to develop. Many mothers are overwhelmed by the depth of their feelings for their baby. Unfortunately, some fathers view this as an obsession, to which they are not sympathetic, and they resent being excluded from their partner's affection and attention. A man whose partner breastfeeds, often feels excused from nurturing as a consequence, driving a wedge between himself and his baby. Fathers who are involved in their baby's daily care, will strengthen their paternal bond in the early weeks and close the gap between how fathers and mothers feel differently about their baby.

SHARING THE CARE
Your baby needs the protection and love of both his parents. Sharing his daily care will help you and your partner to really understand each other's needs and feelings.

DEFUSING AREAS OF CONFLICT

WHAT TO DO	HOW IT HELPS
DISCUSS WHO DOES WHAT	You probably both have views about what roles men and women should play; this can be a powerful hidden agenda. Discuss how you feel and be prepared to have your views challenged.
TALK ABOUT YOUR EXPECTATIONS	Disappointed expectations may produce disillusionment so it's best to give and take in those areas where your views diverge, even though you won't escape hard choices.
LISTEN TO EACH OTHER	Try to talk openly about your feelings and think about how to express them. Do this in a way that avoids accusation, sarcasm or belittling your partner. Give "I" rather than "you" messages.
RESOLVE CONFLICT IMMEDIATELY	Resolve conflict by determining the cause and coming to a mutually agreed solution. A common area of conflict is when you have differing views on division of labour (see below).
PUT YOUR FAMILY FIRST	Self-denial isn't a very popular concept these days, but if you're to turn your trio into a family you'll each need to forego some individual pleasures in the interest of building that family.
LEARN TO COPE WITH STRESS	Reactions to stress differ from person to person. Try to evolve together a pattern of "stress management" for difficult periods, to minimize any possible damage to your relationship.

DIVISION OF LABOUR

By far the biggest bone of contention between new parents is how they should share caring for the baby and the workload that goes with it. Only about one in twelve fathers takes on a full 50 per cent of the load (even allowing for work commitments). Even when some mothers return to full-time work, they frequently have to shoulder more than half – and in some cases virtually all – the baby care and running of the home outside working hours. Some fathers help with the fun and rewarding tasks, such as bathtime and bedtime stories, but may be less enthusiastic about changing nappies, washing clothes and getting up in the middle of the night. They may also be more reluctant to make lifestyle changes and sacrifices, such as giving up a hobby or spending time with friends. This attitude is inappropriate: parenting is a partnership and a father must make sure he doesn't miss out on invaluable time with his baby.

AN EQUAL RESPONSIBILITY

Find ways of sharing the drudgery and the delights of caring for your baby. Look positively at your baby's development and how you can stimulate and enjoy it together (see p. 126). You and your partner should think of parenthood as one of the most demanding jobs you can have, and reinforce each other's equal responsibility to succeed in this new role.

FATHER

If you're at work and your partner is at home looking after the baby, try to see things from her point of view. Although you'll miss your new family when you're at work, you'll have the usual challenges and friendships of working life to stimulate you during the day. Your partner may well be missing these if she's stopped work to look after your baby and she may be finding the change in lifestyle difficult.

SUPPORTING YOUR PARTNER

■ Telephone her at different times of the day – several times a week. If you're near enough, go home for lunch every now and then.

■ Let her know what time you're going to be home and stick to it. She'll need a break in the evenings and this is valuable time for you to spend with your baby.

■ Share the ups and the downs. If you've had a rotten day at work, talk to her about it, but listen to her and be sympathetic if she's also had a bad day.

■ Make sure she has time out to relax away from the baby and to see her friends (see p. 114).

BECOMING MORE INVOLVED

■ If your partner is at home with the baby most of the time, don't think that she's the only one who can care for him. Your role in caring for your baby is vital and will be very rewarding for you.

■ Talk through what happened during the day and find out what milestones your baby may have reached – then spend time with your baby so that you can experience them for yourself.

■ Try to use your weekends and days off to have extended time with your baby. Continue caring for him just as you did when he was first born.

LEARNING TO COPE

MINIMIZING STRESS

Most family arguments occur at stressful times. Early in the morning when you're only half awake and feel you have to do too many things too quickly, you can become clumsy and irritable. If you're in full-time work, it's easy and natural to bring the stress home with you, making it more difficult to cope with the demands being made on you at home. It's at times like these that you and your partner need to work together to help each other; if you take out your stresses on each other or on the baby it will probably only make matters worse:

■ Try to find ways of relaxing with each other and by yourselves (see p. 114).

■ Try to be honest about how you're feeling to help prevent any misunderstandings.

■ Don't try to do too many things at once: you'll only get frustrated and over-tired.

■ Try not to bring work home with you – physically or mentally.

NEGATIVE FEELINGS

You may experience a cocktail of emotions that conflict with your ideas of what it's proper to feel. Having negative thoughts towards your baby because she's kept you up all night or because she's crying is normal. There's no point in refusing to accept how you feel; it doesn't make you wicked. It's abnormal, however, to use violence as a way of expressing yourself; if your temper is really being pushed to the limit, talk to someone or take time away before you do something you'll regret.

CARING FOR A BABY tests all parents. If you get upset, angry, argue with your partner, or if you can't comfort your baby, you may feel that you have in some way failed, but you haven't. Getting through these times is part of being a parent; you'll learn from every occasion and be a better parent and partner for having come through it.

DEALING WITH ANGER

It's paradoxical that some of our strongest negative feelings are directed towards those we love most. On closer examination, of course, this is easily explained: the extent to which we are hurt, angered, disappointed or disillusioned by others is an index of how strongly we feel about the people concerned. You're probably never going to feel more strongly about anybody than about your children. Your love for them will not be diminished by the fact that you're sometimes angered or disappointed by them, but at such times you'll be wracked by conflicting emotions, especially when you're dealing with a baby.

WHY ANGER IS NORMAL

If your baby cries for long periods or sleeps only for brief intervals, you're bound to feel concerned and worried. If this worry is then compounded by a feeling of impotence, it often expresses itself as anger. You may sometimes be seized by acute feelings of helplessness, guilt and inadequacy when nothing you do seems to pacify your baby. At such times it's difficult not to feel victimized and the worry can often quickly escalate to resentment and then anger. You may also feel angry that nothing you do seems to work, and resentful that you're left with little time or energy for your own needs. You both have to accept that these feelings are very natural.

BREAKING THE CIRCLE OF NEGATIVITY

The knowledge that your tension and frustration can be communicated to your baby will only increase your anxiety, which will in turn make the baby feel more insecure. It's very easy to become locked into a vicious circle of negativity. Your baby will express this in the only way she knows, by crying, and her crying will further unnerve you. This circle must be broken.

Talk to someone Telephone someone in whom you can confide; just getting your feelings out in the open will help to put everything into perspective. Talking to other parents in the same situation is often useful – you'll realize that how you feel is very normal. You should also talk to your partner, but remember he or she may also be feeling exasperated; try to talk to each other when you're able to go out without the baby or when the baby is asleep. If none of the above is possible, speak to your health visitor or doctor.

A change of scene If you're alone with your baby during the day, get out of the house. The change of scene will help to relax you and being driven in a car, wheeled in a pram or walked in a sling can often soothe a baby. In the short term, if you feel yourself being engulfed by anger, leave the room or put the baby in another room until you feel calmer. When your baby is older, make sure you have adequate time away (see p. 114).

IF YOUR BABY IS DIFFICULT TO LOVE

Just like both of you, your baby has her own personality. She may be happy and smiling all the time, or she may be reserved and seemingly unsociable. She may be independent and not very affectionate, or clingy and easily upset. Remember, your baby doesn't choose to behave in a certain way to spite you – it's just how she's made. As with all relationships, you need to keep the communication channels open with your baby. You have to get to know what makes her tick and accept that you're not going to have an easy relationship with her all the time.

MAINTAINING AFFECTION

Some babies don't like to be handled or cuddled very much; others go through phases of being unsociable. If a baby does not want attention, she will tend to stiffen her body and cry when you hold her. Most babies will become more sociable with time, but if you're particularly worried, seek advice from your health visitor. Try to do the following:

● Accept that babies are sometimes just difficult and don't blame yourself.

● Don't thrust unwelcome attention on her – it may make matters worse.

● If your baby is more affectionate with your partner, be grateful! Don't take this personally; babies often go through periods when they prefer or cling to one partner and this will pass with time.

● Remember, your baby will respond to you so make sure you're smiling and being affectionate towards her.

WHEN YOUR BABY MISSES YOU

If you have invested time in your baby and bonded closely, you'll have created a feeling of rightness when you're together that is shattering when you're apart. An upheaval such as returning to work, the preferred parent being away for a period of time or the introduction of a childminder may make your baby unsettled. This is most likely to reveal itself in her being fretful, fussy, needing more cuddles than usual and a change in her eating and sleeping patterns. If your baby appears to be genuinely unhappy, reassess the situation; for example, it could be that she's unhappy with her childminder. To help your baby when you're away from home:

● Telephone frequently.

● Ask your partner or childminder to talk about you to your baby.

● Leave an item of your clothing for your baby to hold.

● Tape yourself singing and talking to your baby.

● Leave photos of yourself.

KEEP IN TOUCH

A baby will love to hold the telephone, hear Mummy's voice and "talk" to her when she's away.

A FRETFUL BABY

Very few parents escape a period during which their baby is consistently fretful and demanding for no apparent reason. This inability to communicate what is wrong can be very frustrating for both of you and your baby.

WHY SHE MAY BE FRETFUL

■ Your baby may not be receiving as much stimulation as she needs. Babies who can sit up and who would like to explore their environment, but who can't yet crawl can become particularly frustrated.

■ If your baby is teething, she may be experiencing discomfort or even pain (see p. 132).

■ If you're particularly stressed, your baby may be picking up your heightened tension.

GETTING THROUGH IT

■ Remember, you haven't produced a monster – your baby's behaviour is normal. Much of your frustration stems from her inability to communicate. This is part of the human condition and not a failing in her or you.

■ The fact that your baby is going through a bad patch doesn't mean that you're inadequate: difficult periods are experienced by the majority of parents.

■ If you accept your feelings rather than getting angry with yourself, you'll find it easier to retain an overall positive attitude. This will help you to resolve your difficulties.

■ If you can share your negative feelings with each other, or with a friend, without shame or blame, it will help you to keep things in perspective.

■ There are particular ways that a crying baby can be comforted: try some of the suggestions outlined on pages 88 to 91.

111

HELPING EACH OTHER

In the days following the birth, when "baby blues" may be rife, you'll both need to pull together to be able to support each other. This can range from working as a team as you share the day-to-day care of your baby, to just listening and being there for each other.

WHAT FATHERS CAN DO
■ Encourage your partner to talk about the things that are getting her down. Give her lots of "I care" messages and as much attention and affection as possible.

■ Tell her you love her often to boost her self-esteem – she may dislike her body and feel she's unattractive; tell her that she's beautiful to you.

■ Take her shopping specifically for clothes and flatter her until she regains her pre-pregnant figure. Be patient and tell her she looks good. Don't push her to lose weight.

■ Encourage her to join a mother and baby support group and make it easy for her to go.

■ Encourage people to visit if that's what she wants, but, if not, help to maintain her privacy.

WHAT MOTHERS CAN DO
■ If you've got the blues, try your best not to take out your tensions on your partner. Try to express how you're feeling rather than blaming or arguing. If you need a cuddle, tell your partner – remember, he's not a mind reader.

■ Remember that your partner also has some big adjustments to make. He may be finding it difficult too.

■ Make sure your partner has time with the baby; it will create problems if he feels left out.

■ Try to limit the number of people that visit. It may make your partner feel like an outsider if your house is crowded with female friends and relatives cooing over your baby.

FEELING LOW

IT'S CERTAINLY TRUE that nothing can prepare you for caring for a new baby. The physical and emotional upheaval is bound to have an impact; quite often when most mothers think they're going to be happiest, they often feel very low – the "baby blues". In most instances this only lasts a few days but, sadly, in others, these feelings can continue for months due to a condition known as postnatal depression. It's important for a father to be aware of the symptoms and recognize the difference between the normal "blues" and real depression so that he knows how to help and when to seek medical advice.

BABY BLUES

The "baby blues" are mood swings caused by hormonal changes. In all likelihood this period of feeling low one minute and euphoric the next won't last beyond the first week, but you'll still need a lot of support to get through it. Maybe the "baby blues" are a natural sign to those around you that you need time and space to come to terms with being a mother. That's certainly how a concerned partner, relative or friend should deal with it: although you'll find that because your hormones are all over the place, you'll also cry when someone's nice to you!

WHY YOU GET THE BLUES
Your hormones, progesterone and oestrogen, will have been high during pregnancy. After you have had your baby, these hormone levels drop and your body may find it difficult to adjust. This can have a marked effect on your emotions. With this, and the fact that you're probably completely exhausted from the labour and lack of sleep, it's not at all surprising that you may not be feeling on top of the world.

WHAT YOU CAN DO
● Give yourself time: accept that you'll feel like this for a short time and that what you're going through is incredibly common.
● Accept offers of help and don't try to do everything yourself.
● Try to talk about your feelings and have a good cry if it helps.
● Tell your partner you need a lot of love and affection, but remember this is a time of upheaval and change for him, too.

WHEN FATHERS GET THE BLUES

Most fathers feel an anticlimax after the birth. There are the extra responsibilities and sudden changes in lifestyle. If your partner is feeling low, you'll be called on to be a tower of strength, which can be a huge strain. Try to think of the first few months as a period of rapid change that is testing for both of you; when you come through it, you'll both emerge closer than you were before. If you get really unhappy, talk things over with your health visitor, doctor or a close friend.

Postnatal depression (PND)

If symptoms that started out as the common "baby blues" don't go away and, in fact, start to become worse, you could be suffering from postnatal depression. This is a temporary and treatable condition that varies from woman to woman. It can develop slowly and not become obvious until several weeks after the baby's birth, but if it's diagnosed and addressed early enough, there's a good chance of a fast cure. Health visitors are trained to recognize the symptoms and treatment ranges from something as simple as talking to a friend, health visitor or doctor about how you feel, to taking medication, such as anti-depressants, for more severe cases.

Why postnatal depression happens

There are many reasons why postnatal depression occurs. It depends on you as a person, your personal circumstances and the way your baby behaves. Research shows that the following risk factors may make you more susceptible to postnatal depression:

- If you enjoyed a senior position at work or high-flying career before the birth, it can be difficult to adjust to the status change.
- If you already have difficulties in your relationship, the baby may make them worse; this in itself may lead to disillusionment and low self-esteem.
- If you had an unexpected difficult birth experience (see p. 48), you could easily feel demoralized and feel that you've, in some way, failed.
- If you've had depression in the past.
- A very demanding, sleepless baby can trigger postnatal depression from sheer exhaustion.
- If you have particularly difficult living conditions and no support network, this can exacerbate postnatal depression.
- If you've bottled up your emotions and not sought help early on.

Seeking help

Many women are too embarrassed to admit how they feel, fearing that it will appear that they have somehow failed. Talking about how you feel is the most important thing you can do; once you accept that you're not "mad" and that there are things you can do to help yourself, you are one step on the road to recovery. Once you seek help you'll be guided to:

- Understand how you feel and learn to express this.
- Learn to prioritize and go with the flow.
- Devote more time to yourself and find ways to relax.
- Visit the health visitor more regularly and seek support.
- Begin taking medication if your postnatal depression is very extreme.

What fathers can do

You may feel helpless because you don't understand postnatal depression. Remember, it's temporary and treatable, so try to be patient. You can be a huge help if you make an effort to understand and do the following:

- Talk and listen to your partner. Never tell her to pull herself together – she can't. Don't assume she'll snap out of it – she won't.
- Mother the mother: encourage her to rest and eat and drink properly.
- Encourage her to be with the baby as much as she wants so that she can take things slowly and gradually work out how the baby will fit in.
- Make sure she's not alone too much as she'll fear isolation.
- Go to see the doctor first for advice as your partner may refuse to accept that she's ill. The doctor may arrange to visit her informally at home.

PND SIGNS TO LOOK OUT FOR

The signs and symptoms of postnatal depression will vary from woman to woman, but include:

- Anxiety: in particular, a mother may worry about her baby and refuse to be parted from him.
- Irrational fears, for example about being left alone.
- Loss of appetite.
- Insomnia.
- Fatigue.
- Lack of concern with appearance.
- Making mountains out of molehills.
- Withdrawal from social contact.
- Feeling negative and inadequate.
- Growing feelings of despondency and helplessness.

113

POSTNATAL PSYCHOSIS

Postnatal – or puerperal – psychosis, is the rarest and most serious form of postnatal depression. It affects about one in 1,000 women and usually occurs in the first three months after the birth. This illness should not be underestimated, but it is curable. Urgent medical help should be sought and hospitalization will be necessary. Where possible, the mother and baby should be kept together. The symptoms the mother may have include:

- Sleeping all day.
- Crying for long periods.
- Being tense and anxious.
- Being manically jolly and behaving oddly.
- Being paranoid and hallucinating.
- Thinking about harming herself and the baby.

MOTHER

It's vitally important, for the sake of all your relationships, that your partner also has time out. He needs his own time with the baby, time alone with you and a chance to relax away from the workplace and home.

HOW TO HELP YOUR PARTNER
■ Encourage him to have an occasional night out with friends or time to continue a hobby, even if he's been out of the house all day. It's good for anyone who works to reduce the pressure this way, as long as it doesn't take over his life to the exclusion of you and your baby.

■ Make the most of your time at home with your partner. He may feel left out, so make the effort to make him feel special, particularly when the baby is asleep.

114

HOW THE BABY GAINS

Spending short periods of time away from your baby can make you a better parent, so don't feel guilty about leaving her every now and then. You should see leaving her occasionally as something positive for the following reasons:

■ You'll appreciate your baby more when you see her again.

■ A break will help you feel relaxed and rested, which will mean you'll be able to cope better and the baby will benefit from this.

■ It's good for her to get used to you going out (she'll soon learn that you always come back), and being with others will stop her becoming too dependent on you.

■ Your baby will learn the seeds of confidence and develop her social skills by having to relate to others.

TIME OUT

BEING A NEW PARENT is undoubtedly a tiring and time-consuming experience. Finding five minutes peace and quiet may seem impossible to begin with, but it's essential that your routine includes time out for you and your partner – individually and together. It will be good for your relationship and good for your baby.

TIME TO YOURSELF

Making time for yourself is not a luxury, it's a necessity. You both need time when you're not being parents or partners, but are just being yourselves. To ensure that you have time away from your baby you'll need to be well organized and divide your life into areas: baby, partner, work and you. That doesn't mean you should put yourself last. Having time to yourself should be high on your list of priorities, especially if you're feeling tired or stressed. Otherwise, you may become unhappy, which will be upsetting for everyone, including your baby, and not what you expected at all.

MAKE TIME FOR YOURSELF
● If you're the primary carer, incorporated into your daily timetable should be at least half an hour devoted entirely to yourself, when you can have a soak in the bath, read a magazine or just have a friend to visit.
● When your baby is asleep, take the opportunity to rest; if you're feeling tired, having a catnap is more important than cleaning the house. Don't be hard on yourself – it's okay to sleep in the middle of the day, especially if you're having to get up during the night.
● Time away doesn't only mean half an hour away from your baby when she's asleep; it means time away from the home environment. If you arrange to see a friend, suggest that you visit her or meet her somewhere – if you're at home you are more likely to become involved with your baby.
● Arrange a "baby swap" with other parents: they look after your baby alongside their own on a particular day or evening, and then you do the same for them. Ask friends and relatives to help out, if they live nearby.
● Find out if the local leisure centre or gym has a creche – and use it!

BE FLEXIBLE WITH YOUR DAILY ROUTINE
You can roughly plan your day, but don't be too regimented and inflexible. The needs of a young baby change all the time and if your baby wakes up unexpectedly you may not be able to have the half an hour you wanted. Try to be relaxed about it and take a break later in the day.

ACCEPT HELP FROM OTHERS
It will be much easier to make space for yourself if you learn to accept offers of help. Don't be stoic and don't feel you're somehow a failure because you let someone else look after your baby. Just say yes, gracefully, and then do your own thing – you deserve it. It's very normal to feel strange about leaving your baby to begin with, but this will pass with time once you have learned to trust your helpers. Your baby will also benefit in many ways by not only being with you all the time (see left).

SPENDING TIME TOGETHER AS A COUPLE

An important part of keeping the communication channels open with your partner is to find time when you can be alone together. Doing this is possible, but may require planning. It will seem odd to book a time to see your partner, but if you try to be spontaneous about it, you'll always find an excuse or decide that your baby is more important. Sometimes it may only be possible to spend time together in the house, but try to find times when someone else can look after your baby so that you both have the opportunity to go out and have uninterrupted time.

AT HOME
● Try to continue any rituals you had before your baby was born, such as having a drink together in the evening, sharing a bath or just doing the crossword. Try not to talk about your baby all the time.
● Cuddle up together for half an hour on the sofa; this precious time together will help you to keep some semblance of normality and act as a reminder that you're still a couple, as well as being parents.

GOING OUT
● Don't turn down invitations and, if possible, try not to take your baby with you all the time (although it may be easier to do so in the first 6–8 weeks). Find a reliable babysitter and, if you're breastfeeding, express milk (see p. 72) so that you don't have to cut your evening short.
● When your baby is a bit older, find people you can rely on – such as grandparents – to look after her for a longer period of time so that you can take the opportunity to have a weekend away together.
● Continue hobbies you enjoyed together before the baby was born, such as playing sports (see p. 62). If you can't find a baby-sitter, go swimming as this is something you can all enjoy together (see p. 119).

GRANDPARENTS

Your baby's grandparents can loom large in your life both positively and negatively. If they respect your privacy, and your right to bring up your children your way, grandparents are unquestionably the best friends, helpers and supporters you and your baby will have.

MAKING THE MOST OF THEIR HELP
Grandparents are the people most likely to encourage you to have time off, not least because they'll want to spend some time with their grandchild. Make the most of this. Let them be a part of your baby's life and have their own relationship with her – the bond between grandparents and grandchild can be priceless for your child and for them. It is, however, important to get the balance right, not least because you don't want to fall out with the people who are your best helpers:
● Don't let bossy parents or parents-in-law take over, pop around every five minutes or turn up uninvited. If they live nearby, try to get into a routine that suits everyone, for example, choose a particular day of the week for them to look after your baby.
● Be clear from the outset about how you want to bring up your baby to prevent any misunderstandings later on. Make sure that when grandparents look after your baby they do things the way you like them done, and not the way they think best.

♂ FATHER

If you're not used to domestic work, looking after a baby will come as a bit of a shock. It should, however, give you a better understanding of how your partner feels and how important it is for her to have some time off.

HOW TO HELP YOUR PARTNER
■ Take your baby out shopping with you or just for a walk in the pram at weekends to give your partner some space.

■ Be fair to your partner: if she has stayed in looking after the baby while you've been out with your friends, make sure you offer to do the same for her.

■ Share the cooking, even if you have been at work. Make a habit of treating yourselves to a take-away occasionally so that neither of you has to cook.

115

BABY-SITTERS

Use a baby-sitter who has experience with babies and young children, and preferably one who is recommended by friends. Don't ask a person under 16 years old to look after your baby in case a problem arises that he or she may be too inexperienced to handle. When you go out the baby-sitter will need:

■ Telephone numbers for you and a relative or neighbour.

■ The location of the first-aid kit (see p. 102) and an explanation of how to use the baby monitor.

■ An idea of your baby's routine and what to do if she wakes up.

■ Feeding equipment and details of what your baby should be fed.

■ Nappy changing equipment and a change of clothes.

SEX AND PARENTHOOD

MOTHER

Your life has gone through a big change and it will take time to adapt. Given your new responsibilities and possible physical discomforts (see below right), having intercourse is unlikely to be a high priority.

YOUR BODY IMAGE
You may feel unattractive if you have stretch marks and feel bloated, but your partner is likely to be less bothered about these things than you think. However, you do have to start liking yourself again before you can give and receive pleasure from sex. Do consider exercising (see p. 62); if nothing else, it will make you feel better about yourself. If you're breastfeeding, you may be uncomfortable about your partner touching your breasts. Tell him – he may share your feelings.

YOUR BABY
You're likely to be completely preoccupied with your baby and having sex may be the last thing you want to think about. This is normal, but once you decide to resume sex try to put the baby to the back of your mind. It's pointless to assume you're going to be interrupted every time.

YOUR PARTNER
Don't put up with discomfort, even pain, because you mistakenly feel dutiful. Your main duty is to your baby and, although your partner needs to feel loved, you don't have to show that by having uncomfortable sex. Remember, however, that although you are preoccupied and fulfilled by your baby, your partner may not be to the same extent. Explain to him how you feel and how it affects your attitude to sex.

YOUR SEXUAL RELATIONSHIP with your partner will, for a short time, be one of the many aspects of your partnership that has to adapt. The last thing either of you will want, while you're caring for your new baby, is for this to become an issue. So try to talk openly to each other about your sexual needs and expectations.

YOUR FEELINGS ABOUT SEX

Don't just have sex because you think it's what your partner wants and don't expect to have sex after a certain time. It's normal to feel sexually different now that you're in the dual contradictory role of being a parent and a lover. You may even feel guilty about wanting or thinking about sex because you feel you should be looking after and thinking about your baby. Don't take sexual rejection personally. Talk to each other and try to understand the reasons for wanting or not wanting to resume intercourse. Sex can only become a problem if you let it, and it should be easily resolved if you keep talking to each other about how you feel.

How sex can help Looking after a baby can cause tensions and problems: having intercourse at the right time, when you're both ready for it, may be just what you need to bring you closer again, reaffirming your desire and affection for each other.

PHYSICAL CONSIDERATIONS

Nowadays, the general advice is that you can resume sex whenever you both feel ready (unless you have been advised to wait for any particular reason), but there could well be physical problems that will deter you from resuming sex in the first few weeks after the birth.

Vaginal discomfort It's normal to feel too sore and tender to resume penetrative sex. The vagina will be bruised, making sex painful even if the childbirth was free of intervention. If you had an episiotomy (see p. 45), you may not be able to tolerate anything rubbing against the site for many months. In addition, the glands that normally lubricate the vagina will not function effectively because of hormonal changes, so it's advisable to use a lubricating cream which is available from your pharmacist.

The lochia (see p. 60) Don't resume penetrative sex until this discharge has stopped, which will not be until at least three weeks.

Breastfeeding Your breasts may leak milk during intercourse, especially when you orgasm, which can be a shock unless you're both prepared for it.

Tiredness Given the choice between having sex or sleeping, most new parents would choose the latter. Until you have more of a routine, and have found ways to have time to yourselves, it's difficult to resume a normal sex life. Try to be understanding if either one of you is too tired for sex.

Libido It appears that the sex drive in both new parents is much lower than normal and it returns slowly over a matter of months.

Caesarean Although you won't have any vaginal discomfort, a Caesarean is major abdominal surgery. You're likely to feel very tender for around six weeks and should wait to resume sex until you're fully recovered.

116

CONTRACEPTION

The last thing you're likely to want when you're looking after a newborn baby is to find that you're immediately going to be parents all over again! So do start thinking about contraception as soon as you can after the baby is born. The midwife or family planning adviser will ask you about contraception before you're discharged from hospital and you will also be asked about this at your six-week check (see p. 60). You can become pregnant if your periods have not started and you can be fertile as early as three weeks after the birth of your baby.

Breastfeeding Although breastfeeding does reduce fertility, you have to be breastfeeding very regularly (at least every four hours and for some women, more frequently) to prevent ovulation occurring. Breastfeeding is not a contraceptive: don't rely on it.

METHODS OF CONTRACEPTION

TYPE	ADVICE
PILL	Those containing oestrogen are not prescribed for women who are breastfeeding because they reduce milk production.
MINI-PILL	These only contain progestogen which does not inhibit milk production, but they may worsen any postnatal depression (see p. 113) by inhibiting the natural production of progesterone. The mini-pill must be taken at the same time each day.
CONDOM (MALE AND FEMALE)	These should be used with a contraceptive gel for comfort and security. A female condom may cause discomfort if you're bruised and sore after childbirth.
IUD (INTER-UTERINE DEVICE) AND DIAPHRAGM	Your cervix may have enlarged and won't return to its normal size for 2–3 months. If you used an IUD or diaphragm before you were pregnant, you'll need a new one. Some doctors will fit this at the six-week check (see p. 60), although others prefer to wait a bit longer.

HAVING SEX

Without it being an automatic prelude to sex, you should both feel that you can engage in physical contact whenever you feel like it. It's important that you continue to enjoy sex and find what is right for both of you – talk about your preferences and be open to trying new things.

Foreplay It's good to build up your sex drive through foreplay: touch and caress, massage each other with aromatic oils or take a bath together.

Non-penetrative sex For the first few times, maybe quite soon after the birth, try bringing each other to orgasm through gentle manual and oral sex. Consider being experimental: for example, try sex toys such as a vibrator.

Comfortable positions Once you feel confident enough to try penetrative sex, experiment with different positions to find the ones that put least pressure on the sore areas. Stop at any time if the mother feels discomfort.

FATHER

It's quite natural to have a low sex drive (see below) for a short time after the baby is born. It's often a good thing, because it allows you to concentrate all your energies on your baby. However, many men do want to resume sexual activity sooner than their partners feel ready to do so.

REASONS FOR A LOW SEX DRIVE
■ Being too tired and preoccupied with the baby.

■ Having witnessed the birth.

■ The baby sharing a bedroom with you and your partner.

■ Feeling that your partner's body (especially her breasts) belongs to the baby and finding it difficult to think of her sexually.

■ Being frightened of physically hurting your partner.

UNDERSTANDING YOUR PARTNER
■ Start being closer and more affectionate gradually and you'll soon begin to see your partner as your lover and not just as the mother of your baby.

■ Don't expect too much from your partner too soon. Sex will be much less enjoyable for you if she's not ready or comfortable enough to participate fully.

■ Remember, from the moment of birth your partner's ear is attuned to the baby's cry (and yours may be, too). This means that she may find it difficult to relax when she's having sex. Be understanding and try to find a time when you can be alone without your baby (see p. 114).

■ If your partner cuddles you or you are just being affectionate with each other, don't read it as an open invitation to have sex. If you do, it will only upset her, disappoint you and probably cause an argument.

117

YOUR NEW WORLD

PLAYGROUPS AND CRECHES

Playgroups and creches range from informal arrangements between several parents to professionally organized sessions, where a trained superviser, with the help of member parents, offers a wide variety of play-based activities:

■ The playgroup acts as an information exchange centre, giving you a chance to meet other parents, and your baby an opportunity to make friends with other children and adults.

■ A child of two and a half can be left at a playgroup for a couple of hours, but many also have a mother and baby group attached to them where parents can go along with their babies. You must, however, stay with your baby because the playgroup won't have the resources to look after her.

■ Many shopping centres, leisure centres and supermarkets have creches where babies and children can be left for a couple of hours. You must, however, stay in the vicinity in case you're needed.

BEING A PARENT will become the core not only of how you see yourself, but of how others view you. Your obligations to your baby will take precedence over any other and, whatever your other responsibilities, being a parent is the first role you assume every morning and it can't be shaken off at the end of the day. This shift in priorities can take some getting used to, especially if you have, until this point, lived a very independent and career-driven life. To avoid isolation you need to join forces with other parents and use the facilities designed to help make caring for a baby easier and more fun.

OTHER PARENTS AND CHILDREN

Being a parent will extend your range of friends to include those who have children. As well as counteracting the demoralizing effect of mid-morning and early-afternoon isolation that can be the curse of solitary child care, making friends with other parents benefits you in many ways:

● It gives you the opportunity to mix with other people who are equally focused on being a parent.

● It's a good way to introduce your baby to relationships outside the family, which helps to develop her social skills.

● Parenting is a learning process: you'll be breaking new ground every day and be able to exchange tips with the friends you've made.

● You'll have people who understand the difficulties you're going through because they're going through them too.

Your babies will enjoy interacting with each other

MEETING PEOPLE
Forming friendships with other parents and their babies can be hugely beneficial to you and your baby.

HOW TO MEET PEOPLE
A good way to make friends who have children is to stay in touch with some of the parents you met while pregnant, particularly if you live in a rural area where there may be fewer activities. Swap telephone numbers at antenatal classes or in the maternity ward, and don't think twice about getting in touch. If you have a spring or summer baby, you'll probably meet people in the park or playground. However, if your baby is born in the winter, find out about activities from your health visitor or local library.

WHEN PARENTHOOD IS NOT ENOUGH

It used to be thought that motherhood and domesticity were satisfying ways for a woman to spend her most creative and active years; the same would rarely be thought of a man. But nowadays many women would be far from fulfilled by simply being a parent. Some who have tried to do it, because they believe that it is the best start they could give their child, have found the experience quite limiting, especially when they don't have the support network of the extended family.

LEARNING TO ADAPT

In a society where the worth and freedom of the individual, the opportunity for self-development, and an obligation to be oneself are constantly cited as legitimate goals, it's not surprising that most people are ill-prepared for the narrowing of horizons that comes with caring for a baby. You and your partner simply won't have as much of yourselves left over as before and this doesn't sit easily with the kind of ambitions bred by modern society.

Finding fulfilment Women who want to take an active part in the wider world, and have been educated and trained to do so, can hardly be expected to substitute an intimate relationship with the washing machine for the stimulation and satisfaction they derived from their work. The thousand joys of nurturing babies and children don't, for some women, wholly compensate for the loss of a fulfilling life outside the home because the joys are not the same. You can't make up for a lack of vitamin A by taking large doses of vitamin B. It goes without saying that full-time parenthood is a worthwhile career for a person who is happy in it, but anyone who hankers for more out of life than pure domesticity need never feel ashamed. Just because you have interests beyond day-to-day child care does not mean you don't love your baby and it will not harm her.

Avoiding isolation Many people decide to become parents with the view that it will be a temporary – never total – denial of their needs and ambitions. This is why it is important – and, ultimately, in the baby's best interest – that you do not feel trapped by your parenting role. What most of us understand as isolation is the absence of other people and for those who spend their days caring for children, this means other adults. However wonderful the communication between you and your baby, it's important to have the stimulation of adult interaction, which is why it's essential that you get out there and meet people.

WORKING FROM HOME

To make the transition to being a parent easier and less of a shock to the system, some women try to keep some of their old self by working from home. The information technology revolution has made this possible for more women than ever before, but it's not as easy as it sounds, especially if it's attempted too early on:

● You must have a routine with your baby in order to do justice to your work and to make sure you don't end up working in the evenings.

● It's important to make sure you're not just dividing your time between work and your baby; you must still have time for yourself to rest, relax and spend time with your partner.

● It's likely that you'll still need to organize some form of proper child care (see p. 150) and this could mean that you miss out on precious time with your baby in her early months.

ACTIVITIES AT HOME

It's unrealistic to be out of the house all the time, especially in the winter months. Team up with other parents and each take it in turn to host social activities at home. This is also a good way for your baby to get used to strangers coming into the home. Some suggestions are:

■ Coffee morning: this is a good and cheap activity, giving you the chance to chat as your babies play.

■ Lunch party: provide simple snack food as it's not realistic for everyone to sit down to a meal and baby watch at the same time. Ask friends to bring a contribution (especially for their babies) or just take it in turns to host lunch.

■ Home-selling party: this is a good way to be sociable and earn some money. It involves presenting and taking orders for products, such as household goods or books and earning commission on what is sold. Before embarking on this, always check that the company you're working for is reputable.

119

LEISURE CENTRES

A good way of getting out is to join a leisure centre. Find one that has creche facilities (see opposite) so that you can take your baby with you – some have a "soft room" where your baby can play safely. Most swimming pools offer parent-and-baby sessions and your baby, equipped with suitable buoyancy aids, will enjoy dabbling with you in a heated pool as soon as she can hold her head up confidently (at about four months). She should also have had her first vaccinations (see p. 162). Remember, you should avoid high-intensity exercise for the first nine months and while breastfeeding.

ACCEPTING HELP

Most couples struggle to bring up a baby without help, so as a single parent don't think you have to do it all yourself, and don't let pride come before your baby's welfare. You need to know that at given points in the week you'll have some guaranteed respite and it's good for your baby to interact with other people:

■ Try to build up a small network of people on whom you can rely.

■ If you have several helpers, spread their time with your baby throughout the week.

■ If possible, ask a relative or friend who is not working to stay once a week so that you're guaranteed a good night's sleep, especially if you're working.

■ Seek the help of voluntary organizations (see p. 163) if you don't have a network of people on whom you can rely.

■ Make sure you're getting all your financial benefits and any maintenance payments from the absent parent, if applicable.

■ If you know other single mothers, "baby swap" with them so that you both get a chance for some time to yourselves.

■ Don't be embarrassed or too proud to accept gifts – people would probably have given you these even if you weren't single.

NEGATIVE REACTIONS

There will be people who judge you, and your ability to bring up your baby – especially if you have chosen to have a baby outside of a committed relationship. Dealing with this can have a positive effect: many single parents become determined to prove that they are just as capable of raising a happy and contented child. However, criticism can also put pressures on single parents, making them feel that to ask for help is equal to admitting failure. It isn't, so do try to resist this.

SINGLE PARENTS

BEING A SINGLE PARENT, you won't have the luxury of a partner to share the day-to-day care of your baby or the joys of watching him develop. Without a good support network, it can be physically and emotionally exhausting, but the knowledge that you've done it alone can also be hugely rewarding for you and beneficial to your baby.

SINGLE PARENT BY CHOICE?

If you've chosen to be a single mother, you may be more prepared emotionally, practically and financially for looking after a young baby and look forward to the prospect. If you've split with your partner during the pregnancy or soon after the birth, you may have more difficulties. Coping with the emotional problems of separating from someone while looking after a young baby is bound to have an impact on your ability to cope. In this situation, it's more important for you to ask for and accept help.

LONE PARENTING CAN BE POSITIVE

Being a single parent is by no means all doom and gloom. You and your baby can benefit in many ways from the special relationship you'll form:
● Single parents tend to develop a much closer bond with their babies; they do not have to share their love between a partner and a child.
● Extended family – grandparents, aunts and uncles – often get more involved when there's only one parent. The baby can greatly benefit from this network of support and love.
● Looking after a baby alone is a great achievement. You'll strengthen as a person as you watch your baby develop.
● If you're single because your relationship has broken down, you have made the right decision; it's better for the baby to live with one fairly contented person than two people who are at war.

BALANCING YOUR RELATIONSHIP WITH YOUR BABY

I'm a convinced believer in showing boundless affection to babies, but as a single parent you do need to balance your relationship with your baby: some lone parents may invest all their emotions and energies into their baby and use him as an emotional crutch. Don't think that you have to be a mother and father; being a responsive parent is good enough. Your baby has no notion of lacking a second parent; he's happy enough with you, so there is no need for you to over-compensate.

ENCOURAGING INDEPENDENCE

You and your baby will have a very close and important one-to-one relationship and no-one can take that away from you, but babies need and thrive on exposure to others and should be encouraged to interact with a wide range of people. It's essential that you introduce him to other adults, and children, so he gets used to being without you now and then. This will make it much easier for you and him if you have to introduce a childminder.

CHAPTER SIX

HELPING YOUR
BABY
TO DEVELOP

Even a baby just one hour old is learning.
He's wired to recognise the human face
and can see yours quite clearly if you
hold it 8-10 inches from his.
In succeeding months he'll learn a formidable
array of skills: to hold his head up, then sit
up, crawl and stand steady by a year.
He'll acquire these skills – and many more – all
the more easily if you guide and teach him.
You are his first teacher – but not in any
formal sense. Your baby learns through play,
with games, toys and books. You're his first
playmate and his first friend.

HOW BABIES DEVELOP

Your baby will give you clear signs that a "milestone" (the acquisition of a skill) is on the brink of emerging. Be on the lookout for signs of progress. Then, and only then, match your efforts to your baby's development and give her games to help her acquire that skill – it's almost pointless to try before. With correct timing she will acquire skills at 100 per cent of her potential. If you force her too early or leave it too late, she'll acquire the skill, but not at her full capability. The main milestones are:

■ Smiling at a distance (6 weeks).

■ Discovering her hands and feet (3–4 months).

■ Blowing bubbles – this is your baby's first sign of proper speech (5 months).

■ The ability to transfer an object from one hand to the other (6 months).

■ Knowing her name (6 months).

■ Sitting unsupported (7 months).

■ "Getting" a simple joke like peep-bo (8 months).

■ Wanting to feed herself (9 months).

■ Crawling (9 months).

■ Pointing to an object with her forefinger (10 months).

■ Picking up objects with her finger and thumb (10 months).

■ Swivelling around while sitting to reach a toy (10 months).

■ Putting things into containers and taking them out again (11 months).

■ Saying her first word with meaning (11–12 months).

■ Walking unsupported (12–13 months).

ONE OF THE MOST FULFILLING aspects of parenthood is to watch and share in your baby's physical and mental development. To help your baby develop happily and to her maximum potential, you need to stimulate her to encourage her to learn new skills, while also allowing her to develop at her own pace.

NEWBORN BABIES

Your baby starts to develop from the very second she's born and she'll be longing to learn. You'll see evidence of this if you watch an infant just after birth: every baby enters the world in a state of "quiet alertness" and this state of intense focus on her surroundings can last up to an hour. She's a sponge ready to soak up information about her new environment:

● She recognizes your voice – and your partner's – immediately. She's heard these voices for seven months and switches on to them instantly.

● Your baby is born with her sight at a fixed focus of 20–25cm (8–10in); if you hold her at this distance from your face at birth, she can see you clearly and she will smile at you.

● She has an acute sense of smell and will be able to inhale and register the natural scent (pheromones) from your body.

● She'll "mouth" in response to you if she can see your face and your lips moving (at a distance of 20–25cm/8–10in); she's attempting conversation.

STIMULATING YOUR BABY

Both of you are your baby's first teachers and playmates. You must feed her with all kinds of stimulation, through play and through the way in which you interact with her, if you want to help her develop to her optimal potential. Your job is to teach her to be imaginative, adventurous, curious, helpful and generous. There is no limit to the amount of praise and encouragement you should give her as she learns new skills and begins to discover her world.

Your baby will learn by copying your actions

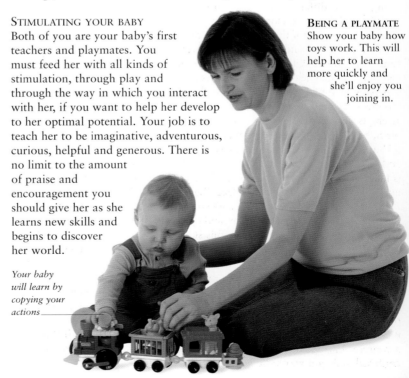

BEING A PLAYMATE
Show your baby how toys work. This will help her to learn more quickly and she'll enjoy you joining in.

HELPING YOUR BABY TO DEVELOP HAPPILY

WHAT YOU CAN DO	HOW IT HELPS YOUR BABY
SET REALISTIC GOALS	Set appropriate goals for your baby: for example, don't expect her to be able to play properly with toys designed for older babies. If you do this, it will outstrip her skills and she will become unhappy, frustrated and demoralized. Always concentrate on accomplishments, not deficiencies, and praise your baby with theatrical gestures.
BE A PLAYMATE	You are your baby's first playmate as well as her teacher. Make time to play with her whenever you can – even if it means the washing up has to wait another hour! Babies have to be shown how to do things, so get down there and join in – your baby will love it. But don't interrupt when she is engrossed in something; it's hard enough for her to concentrate and see a job through to completion, without being distracted.
ENCOURAGE SPEECH	Encourage your baby to talk – even when she's only gurgling. Keep her eyes 20–25cm (8–10in) from yours when she makes noises, especially when feeding and talking to her. That's her first experience of feeling valued and a valued baby will grow up to be a child who talks to you about everything – good and bad.
REPEAT EVERYTHING	Repeat and repeat words and actions until you're sick of it. You must tell your baby the same thing over and over again – using the same even tone of voice – and show her how to do things. It will all be worthwhile once she understands and begins to copy.

RULES OF DEVELOPMENT

Although it's wonderful to watch your baby develop, it's important not to push her beyond her limitations. She has her own timetable and it's pointless trying to set a different one. Remember the following:
● No two children develop at the same rate so don't compare your baby to other babies – even if they did walk or talk before her.
● Development is continuous, although certain skills will be acquired in a spurt while other skills slow down. For example, when a child is mastering walking, she may turn into a sloppy feeder.
● A baby won't learn to say words with meaning before she is about ten months old and won't speak until much later. She will make her own brave attempts at "talking" with babble, cries and giggles and she'll "mouth" from birth, but she'll be unable to say proper words.
● Development of the whole body is dependent on how mature the brain is and whether or not brain, nerve and muscle connections have grown. This is individual to your baby so she can't learn a skill like walking or talking until all the connections are in place. Bladder control is not possible until 18 months (see p. 157). If you have expectations of potty use any earlier, this is very likely to lead to failure and could slow down your baby's progress when she tries to acquire this skill later.
● Development proceeds from head to toe (see p. 130) so a baby can't sit until she can control her head and she can't stand until she can sit.
● Skills gradually become finer: for example, at about five months she "grasps" with her open hand; at eight months she can pick things up with her fingers and, when all the nerves and muscles have connected, she can pick up an object with her index finger and thumb.
● Be aware that over-stimulation is as bad as under-stimulation; if there is a constant barrage of noise and movement, your baby may become very confused and gain very little in terms of development.

127

POSITIVE DISCIPLINE

Teaching your baby right from wrong starts at the very beginning, but it is the way in which you teach her that will affect her physical and emotional wellbeing. You can discipline your child positively in the following ways:

■ Praising and rewarding her good behaviour and ignoring bad behaviour, especially if it occurs at meal-times.

■ Disciplining your baby through love, praise and encouragement. Never use anger and smacking – this can have a damaging effect on young children.

■ Setting useful tasks to help her understand the discipline of a daily routine – for example, encourage her to feed herself and brush her hair.

■ Holding your finger up and firmly saying "no" if your baby is likely to harm herself, others or cause damage. She'll understand this from around four months.

128

NEWBORN BABIES

From day one there are distinct differences between the behaviour and development of baby boys and girls; these differences continue as your baby grows and develops (see p. 158). When babies are newborn, the gender differences are mainly revealed by how they use their senses to perceive things and by the kind of things in which they show an interest.

HEARING
Hearing in boys is less acute than in girls, which causes them to have more difficulty in locating the source of sounds. Girls are more easily calmed down by soothing words because of their acute hearing. Whisper close to your baby boy's ear as you speak to him to stimulate his hearing and to help calm him down.

SPEECH
A baby girl uses her own voice to get her mother's attention earlier and more often than a boy. If a newborn boy hears another baby cry, he'll join in but stop crying quite quickly, whereas a girl will cry for longer.

SIGHT
A newborn girl responds enthusiastically to visual stimulation from birth. A boy quickly loses interest in a design or picture that is placed in his cot, and requires much more visual stimulation up to the age of about seven months.

SOCIAL SKILLS
Boys are as interested in things as they are in people, whereas girls show a clear preference for the human face above anything else. Later in life this female trait reveals itself as an ability to intuitively read facial expression. To encourage your son to get used to people and to help develop his social skills, hold him 20–25cm (8–10in) away from your face from when he's a newborn so that he's able to see you clearly.

BOYS AND GIRLS

THERE ARE FACTORS IN PLACE at birth that create the differences in behaviour and development between boys and girls – that's a biological fact and no amount of campaigning for political correctness will ever change it. Male and female brains work differently and we do our children a disservice if we try to force them to go against their biological grain. You can encourage your baby's individual ability if you are aware of his or her innate strengths, and by not enforcing stereotypes. Instead, help your baby to develop skills that don't come as naturally, such as language for a boy and spatial skills for a girl.

DIFFERENCES IN BRAIN DEVELOPMENT

Gender differences stem from the way the brain develops in male and female embryos. For a baby to learn and develop, certain connections have to have taken place between the right and left halves of the brain. Girls grow these connections earlier than boys (many are already in place when girls are born), which enables them to adapt faster to their new environment after birth. Connections form in a boy's brain more slowly and because of this later development, a baby boy will need slightly more help from you to reach his milestones (see p. 126).

AVOIDING STEREOTYPES

Stereotypes influence children and, worse, they tend to make people label certain qualities as inferior and superior – the latter usually being attributed to males. When children are taught to think, feel and act in line with a stereotyped model, it can stunt their personal growth. Individuality should be encouraged, regardless of gender.

DISCOURAGING STEREOTYPES IN A GIRL
● Encourage physical activities usually associated with boys, these will help your baby's muscle development.
● Make her feel important through eye contact and by using her name; this helps her to develop a sense of self.
● Don't always whisper baby talk to her.
● Don't only provide her with soft toys.
● Don't only give her dresses and pink clothes to wear.

SPATIAL SKILLS
Help your daughter to develop spatial skills by encouraging her to play with practical toys.

Encourage her to do things for herself

DISCOURAGING STEREOTYPES IN A BOY
● Stress gentleness from when he's very young.
● Let him have a doll and soft toy to cuddle.
● Don't stereotype him into the traditional male role with over-boisterous games, loud talk, loud toys and by only dressing him in blue clothes.
● Don't burden him with all that "big boys don't cry" "stiff upper lip" stuff; big boys do cry, and he's only a child!
● Little boys are naturally very loving – make him proud of that and don't sneer.
● Play down aggression by being gentle, but firm.

BEING A ROLE MODEL
You can positively influence your son by actively joining in with pastimes traditionally associated with females.

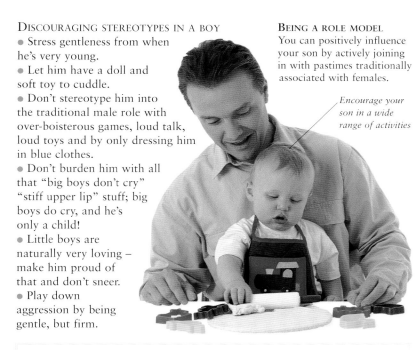

Encourage your son in a wide range of activities

FATHER

Fathers tend to be slightly guiltier than mothers of stereotyping their children. As a father you have a big influence on how your children develop and how they come to view themselves. Think about your attitude to your son or daughter and the type of activities you're encouraging.

INFLUENCING YOUR DAUGHTER
As a father, you may consciously or unconsciously reinforce your daughter's femininity. You are stereotyping her if you encourage her in activities like ballet and drama, rather than giving her a free hand or suggesting some traditionally masculine pastimes, such as football. Fathers often involve boys in "rough and tumble" games, whereas they'll be gentler with girls. Expose your daughter to all kinds of activities and let her choose. Don't fall into the trap of believing some behaviour is acceptable in boys and not in girls – you diminish your daughter if you do this. You should also be aware that your daughter is very likely to feel devalued if she sees you devaluing her mother.

INFLUENCING YOUR SON
Research has shown that your son looks to you to set his own standards of behaviour and that's a serious responsibility. You can encourage your son to develop the more attractive male qualities (such as gentleness and a sense of responsibility) rather than the less desirable ones (such as being aggressive, dominant and confrontational) simply by the way in which you behave – watching your actions will influence your son. He will imitate you in every respect and the quality of fathering that he receives from you is the most critical factor in how he views himself as a male.

129

GENDER DIFFERENCES UP TO AGE SIX

WHAT DEVELOPS	GIRLS	BOYS
NATURAL ABILITY	Girls are better at language skills like talking, reading and writing and they tend to keep this ability.	Boys are slower to develop language skills, but from a very early age they show superior spatial skills.
SOCIAL SKILLS	Girls are more sociable than boys: they are more interested in people and feelings and display this regard for others even in the first 12 months.	Boys are generally more interested in objects than people and feelings. Unlike girls, they tend to look after themselves rather than groups.
BEHAVIOUR AND PERSONALITY	Girls cope better with stress and are more conciliatory. They tend to have fewer behavioural problems than boys.	Boys tend to be more aggressive, competitive and rebellious than girls. They are more likely to develop behavioural problems.
PHYSICAL GROWTH	Girls walk earlier than boys. They grow faster and more steadily – they do not tend to have growth spurts. They gain bladder and bowel control earlier.	Boys shoot ahead physically after five years. They develop faster during growth spurts, when many skills tend to emerge over a short time.

130

CONCERNS ABOUT WEIGHT GAIN

A baby's growth is an important indicator of health and wellbeing, but don't become blinkered about weight gain – it isn't the only issue. Any real discrepancies between length and weight should be picked up at your baby's developmental checks (see p. 133), but, if you're concerned, speak to your doctor beforehand.

WHAT IF MY BABY IS NOT GAINING WEIGHT?

Some babies remain the same weight for a while and then have a growth spurt. So don't worry if your baby does not gain weight over, say, one week or appears to have lost weight. This could be due to something as simple as her being weighed at a different time of day or because she's eaten less. If your baby is ill for any period of time, she may lose weight rapidly but will regain it quickly once she's well. If she appears lively it's a good sign that she's getting enough to eat. Don't be tempted into switching to bottle feeding in the hope of improving "slow" weight gain. In fact, if you breastfeed your baby she's likely to grow faster, especially in the first few weeks.

WHAT IF MY BABY IS OVERWEIGHT?

Some babies are naturally fatter than others, which may lead to some physical development happening slightly later. If you're concerned that your baby weighs too much for her age, seek medical advice, but do not reduce her intake of food as this could affect growth and development. The aim should be to maintain her weight at the current level until her length catches up. Research does, however, show that the pattern of heart disease and obesity in adulthood can be set very early in life by being overweight from overfeeding, so never press your baby to finish off the last drops of a feed or bottle.

HOW YOUR BABY GROWS

YOUR BABY'S PHYSICAL DEVELOPMENT will be monitored closely at the developmental checks (see p. 133): growth (centile) charts, which show the rate of growth expected for your baby's weight and gestational age at birth, will be used to map her progress. In the first year she will grow faster than at any other time in her life. Physical development starts at the top, which is why her head looks large, and from the inner parts to the extremities, which is why her hands and feet look tiny. Remember, your baby's development is individual to her; don't worry if she appears to be growing faster or slower than other babies.

WEIGHT

When a baby is born, the question "How heavy was she?" comes only second in the West to "Is it a boy or a girl?". Although people will place importance on your baby's weight, it is not the only sign of growth and it is important not to use this as the only way to judge her wellbeing (see left). Your baby's weight will be monitored at the developmental checks (see p. 133); you can also have her weighed at your local baby clinic or doctor's surgery. Babies are normally weighed naked and before a feed. One feature all babies have in common is chubby arms and legs; this is due to uneven fat distribution and your baby will not lose this until she begins to use her limbs and becomes active.

THE NORMAL PATTERN OF WEIGHT GAIN

- In the first few days your baby may lose ten per cent of her birth weight.
- By the tenth day she'll have regained her birth weight.
- In the following six months she'll gain weight rapidly, at a rate of about 1kg (2lb) each month.
- In the second six months weight gain slows down and she'll put on around 500g (1lb) each month.

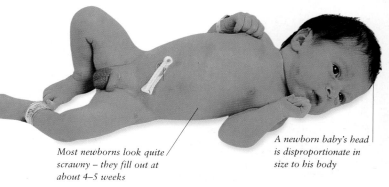

Most newborns look quite scrawny – they fill out at about 4–5 weeks

A newborn baby's head is disproportionate in size to his body

LENGTH (HEIGHT)

Your baby's size is partly due to inheritance – if you're both tall, the chances are you'll have a long baby. The biggest increase in length occurs in the first six months, after which growth slows down. If your child appears well and healthy, there's no reason for you to worry about her growth rate; any pronounced disproportion between length and weight will be investigated at the developmental checks (see p. 133).

AN APPROXIMATE GUIDE TO A BABY'S GROWTH RATE
- A newborn full-term baby is on average 50cm (20in) long.
- Her length will increase by 25–30cm (10–12in) in the first year.
- On average, boys tend to be taller than girls for the first two years.

HEAD SIZE

A newborn baby is top-heavy, with a disproportionately large head – this gradually alters over the first four years. Head circumference is monitored at the developmental checks; if the proportions do not even out, it could alert doctors to certain, rare, medical conditions.

HOW THE PROPORTIONS CHANGE
- A newborn baby's head circumference is about 35cm (14in), which is disproportionately larger than the rest of her body. By the time she is 12 months old, the size of her chest and head should have evened out.
- When a baby is born, her head makes up one quarter of the length of her body, compared to an adult's head, which makes up around one eighth.

12 MONTHS OLD

She "feels" the shape and texture of objects with her lips and tongue

A baby has to learn to sit before she can stand

SEVEN MONTHS OLD

HOW THE SENSES DEVELOP

In the first year, your baby will begin to discover her world through her senses.

VISION
Your newborn has limited, but excellent, vision; at a distance of 20–25cm (8–10in) she sees clearly, so keep your face at this distance from hers when talking or smiling and she'll respond. At six weeks her eyes focus at any distance and both eyes work together. By three months she has full perception of colours; at six months she can see more detail and by one year her vision is well developed.

HEARING
She recognizes your voice and your partner's from birth, and will turn her head when you speak, so talk to her from the very first day.

TOUCH
Babies begin by "feeling" the shape and texture of objects with their lips and tongue and then explore with their hands.

TASTE AND SMELL
Newborns have a complete set of tastebuds and can recognize their parents' smell. They only like sweet tastes and smells, which is why they love breastmilk, but they gradually accept different tastes and make their likes and dislikes known.

YOUR BABY'S FIRST YEAR
A newborn baby is floppy and has no head control. As bone and muscle develop she learns to control her head, which is the first step towards walking. Once this skill is acquired, she will learn to sit and then, by the time she is 12 months old, she should be able to stand unsupported.

Brain, nerve and muscle connections have to be in place before a baby can learn to stand

NERVE AND MUSCLE DEVELOPMENT

WHAT DEVELOPS	HOW IT DEVELOPS	WHAT IT MEANS FOR YOUR BABY
NERVE CONNECTIONS TO LIMB MUSCLES	Nerves grow slowly from the brain and spine to reach the different muscle groups in the limbs. In a newborn, connections between these nerves have not been formed so movements are uncontrolled and crude. As the nerves grow and forge connections, movements become finer and more precise.	Your baby progresses from picking something up with his fist at four months to picking up objects with his finger and thumb by ten months. As nerves grow outwards and down from the brain and spine, your baby will achieve head control and then sit, crawl and stand, before finally walking.
NERVE CONNECTIONS TO BLADDER MUSCLES	It takes at least 18 months for nerves to grow as far as the bladder. Prior to that your baby cannot have any control over how his bladder works – so don't expect it.	Once nerve connections to the bladder are in place, your baby has to "train" the bladder muscles to hold urine and then let go. This takes several months and can't be hurried.

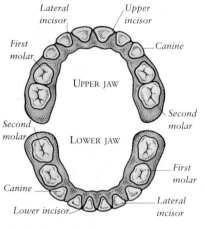

THE ORDER TEETH APPEAR
The age when teeth are cut varies, but they always come through in the same order: incisors, first molars, then canines.

132

HOW YOUR BABY'S TEETH DEVELOP

A first tooth is an exciting milestone – an indication that your baby is ready for foods other than milk, in other words, for weaning (see p. 94). Teeth usually start to come through from six months, but the age varies from baby to baby (a few babies are born with a tooth already through, while others are still toothless on their first birthday). During teething, your baby may be more irritable and more wakeful than usual (see p. 91).

HOW TEETH COME THROUGH
● The first tooth to appear is usually a lower incisor, followed straight away by its neighbour.
● Next come the upper incisors, followed first by the upper lateral incisors, then by the lower lateral incisors. There may be a delay before the first molar appears.
● After the two first molars come the canines, and finally the second molars appear.

PREVENTING PROBLEMS

You can help prevent your baby developing any teething problems:

■ Buy your baby a small, soft toothbrush and get him into the routine of brushing his teeth in the morning and at bedtime.

■ Don't give him drinks and snacks that contain added sugar. Give him plain water to drink instead of juice sometimes.

■ Never add sugar to fruit juice, and always give him undiluted juice in a beaker rather than bottle.

CLEANING HIS TEETH
Encourage your baby to clean his own teeth from an early age – he'll enjoy it!

Clean your teeth at the same time so he can copy you

DEVELOPMENTAL CHECKS

You will be asked to take your baby for a developmental check twice in the first year: at 6–8 weeks and at 8–9 months. As well as discussing any issues with you, the health worker will weigh your baby, measure his length and head circumference and then a doctor will check the baby's general health and carry out specific medical checks (see charts below).

WHAT IS THE PURPOSE OF THE CHECKS?

Many health professionals feel that "testing" babies at certain stages to see whether they are "up to the mark", is crude; now they are much more interested in the wellbeing of the whole child. When you're invited to go to a clinic, or perhaps meet a health worker at your home, you'll be asked a series of questions to establish how you're all getting on together, how you are managing and whether you've noticed any specific problems with your baby. You should think of it as an opportunity to discuss any aspects of your baby's life (not just his development) or of your life with him that seem relevant: baby checks aren't, or at least they're not supposed to be, just about ticks in boxes.

PREPARING YOURSELF BEFORE YOU GO

Make a list of questions and concerns you'd like to discuss. For example, you may have problems feeding or difficulty coping with sleepless nights. Don't be afraid to highlight problems – being a new parent is not easy for anyone and you should take the opportunity to get expert advice.

WHAT IF MY BABY HAS A PROBLEM?

It's worrying to have doubts cast over your baby's development (see p. 104). If you have any concerns or a problem is found:

■ Ask for time to sit down and talk through exactly what is wrong with your baby. Ask as many questions as necessary, especially if it is not clear what the doctor is saying. Don't be fobbed off by being told the health worker hasn't got time at the moment or that you are worrying for no reason.

■ Don't accept that you should "wait and see" – if there's any question of a problem, your baby should be referred for tests or to see a specialist straight away.

■ Get a second opinion if you are not satisfied or are still concerned.

6–8 WEEK CHECK

WHAT IS CHECKED	WHY IT IS CHECKED
HEART AND LUNGS	The breathing rate and heart rate are checked, particularly to rule out a heart murmur.
PALATE	The palate is checked at birth, and now, for completeness and to test the sucking reflex.
VISION	Your baby will be tested to see if he can follow movement and look towards light.
HEARING	A simple check will be made to see if your baby is startled by a sudden loud noise.
MOBILITY	Your baby's hips are checked for displacement and any correction needed. Head control is checked.
TESTES	If you have a baby boy, the doctor will check to ensure that his testes have descended.

8–9 MONTH CHECK

WHAT IS CHECKED	WHY IT IS CHECKED
SPEECH	Your baby should be making a range of sounds by now and his ability to do this will be noted.
VISION	Any problem should have become apparent, but the doctor may check for a squint.
HEARING	You will be asked to hold your baby, while the doctor makes noises behind to check response.
HANDLING	The doctor will give your baby a toy to hold so that he can check his handling skills.
MOBILITY	The doctor will check that your baby can sit up and is able to stand supported.
TESTES	The testes will be checked again. If they have not descended, an operation may be needed later.

BABY DEVELOPMENT
0–1 MONTH

GRASP REFLEX
Your baby will grasp anything put into her fingers and her grasp is so strong, she can take her weight.

WHAT TO LOOK OUT FOR

WHAT DEVELOPS	HOW SHE PROGRESSES	HOW YOU CAN HELP
HER MIND	• At birth, she can see clearly at a distance of 20–25cm (8–10in). • She will respond to your voice by moving her eyes and turning her head. • She will gaze at you and recognize you. • She will become quiet when you speak soothingly and distressed when you are loud.	• When talking to her, hold your face 20–25cm (8–10in) away from hers. • When you speak, let her see your mouth moving, make interesting faces and smile. Make eye contact at 20–25cm (8–10in). • Use your voice: speak in a sing-song voice, sing lullabies and laugh a lot.
HER MOBILITY	• She will turn her head: this control is the first step towards learning to walk. • By the end of the first month, the most she may be able to do is lift her head about an inch off the surface when lying on her tummy.	• Do gentle exercises to make her aware of her body (see p. 57). • Her neck and back muscles are too weak to lift her head so give her something to look at when she is lying on her back.
HER HANDLING SKILLS	• Your baby is born with "the grasp reflex", which means she will keep her fists tightly closed and grasp anything put into her fingers. • If she's startled, she'll spreads her arms, fingers and legs to protect herself.	• Your baby can't purposely hold on to anything until she loses the grasp reflex. • Gently open her fingers one at a time. • If she's grasps your fingers, she'll take her weight if you pull her up a little way.
HER SOCIAL SKILLS	• Your baby is born ready to love other people and asks for love. She longs for company and takes immediate delight in you. • She'll respond instantly to your voice and your smell. She is upset by a harsh sounding voice.	• Let her have contact with other people from when she's very young. • Be physical: make skin-to-skin contact with your baby; use your body to express love; rock, sway and dance with her.
HER SPEECH	• She "mouths" if you speak to her at a distance of 20–25cm (8–10in) because she is trying to imitate your gestures and expressions. • She's born longing to communicate and will start to make little burbling noises as a mark of pleasure and contentment.	• Talk to your baby all the time so she gets used to your voice. • Make facial expressions to match what you're saying.

STIMULATING PLAY

● Stimulate her senses with songs and by talking to her.
● Move your fingers or a brightly coloured toy through her line of vision so that her eyes and head follow your movements.
● Put a mobile over her cot.
● Do gentle knee bends and straighten her legs when you're changing her nappy; this will encourage your baby to straighten out her body.
● Place a small mirror or a clear, cartoon-style drawing of a face in her cot where she can see it when she is lying down.

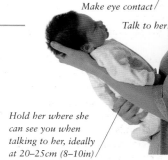

Make eye contact

Talk to her

Hold her where she can see you when talking to her, ideally at 20–25cm (8–10in)

BABY DEVELOPMENT
1–2 MONTHS

WHAT TO LOOK OUT FOR

WHAT DEVELOPS	HOW HE PROGRESSES	HOW YOU CAN HELP
HIS MIND	• Your baby begins to smile at you from a distance and bobs his head when you talk to him. • He starts to be interested in his surroundings, looking in the direction of sounds and staring at objects as though "grasping" with his eyes.	• Prop him up slightly with cushions or put him in a baby chair. Place lots of brightly coloured toys within his view. • Put a mobile over the cot – it's good if it makes a sound or has a musical box.
HIS MOBILITY	• He can raise his head to 45 degrees when he's lying on his tummy. • By the end of this month he can support the weight of his head if you hold him upright with your hands around his chest.	• Hold a coloured toy close to his head so that he has to lift his head to see it. • To teach your baby about balance, hold him upright on your knee so his legs take his own weight for a second.
HIS HANDLING SKILLS	• Your baby will no longer have a grasp reflex. • His fingers are open most of the time and he's starting to become aware of them.	• Touch, tickle and massage his hands. • Give him toys and encourage him to bend his fingers over them.
HIS SOCIAL SKILLS	• He's starting to notice people, but knows you from all others. • He smiles from a distance at six weeks and moves his whole body with excitement when he sees you.	• Make sure you give your baby frequent skin-to-skin contact and maintain eye contact when you're talking to him and, more importantly, when feeding.
HIS SPEECH	• He will begin by answering you with small throaty sounds and by the end of two months he will make grunts, cries and move his whole body in his desire to communicate with you. • He knows your voice – and your partner's – and turns his head and neck when he hears you.	• The more your baby is stimulated to talk by being talked to and encouraged to respond, the earlier he'll learn to talk and the better his quality of speech. • Talk non-stop, be theatrical with your conversations and ask questions.

135

STIMULATING PLAY

• Sing nursery rhymes and rock and sway while you hold him. Sit in a rocking chair with him or put him in a cradle.
• Show him his hands and demonstrate how to wiggle his fingers. Play "This little piggy".
• Gently rub a soft brush over his hands and fingers, especially at the tips.
• Sit him up supported at an angle of 45 degrees – this helps to increase his concentration span. Use cushions or a bouncing baby chair on the floor. Let him touch toys or objects of different textures, shapes and materials.
• Dangle, kick or bat small soft toys quite close to him, within striking distance of his hands.
• Every day have a special walk, talk and sing time with your baby. Carry him in a sling (see p. 69).

Make eye contact as you talk or sing to him

He'll wriggle with excitement when he sees you

BABY DEVELOPMENT
2–3 MONTHS

HEAD CONTROL
She can hold her head up for a short time when lying on her front.

WHAT TO LOOK OUT FOR

WHAT DEVELOPS	HOW SHE PROGRESSES	HOW YOU CAN HELP
HER MIND	• She's becoming familiar with her own body, staring at her fingers and then moving them. This is her first lesson in cause and effect. • She has a repertoire of responses to you: she smiles, mouths when you speak to her, nods, squeaks, yelps and blows raspberries.	• Show your baby her fingers so that she can study them. • Answer her with responses that are theatrical and larger than life. • Reward her attempts to relate to you with hugs, kisses and squeals of delight.
HER MOBILITY	• She can keep her head up steadily now when in a standing or sitting position or while lying on her front, but not for long. • When she is lying on her tummy, she can hold her head in line with her body.	• Encourage her to reach out for soft toys, especially when she's on her tummy. • Teach your baby about balance: hold her in a standing position with your hands around her chest, for a few seconds at a time.
HER HANDLING SKILLS	• She begins to discover her hands – she keeps them open and looks at them. • She'll hold a rattle for a few seconds if you place it in her hand.	• Encourage her to look at her fingers and to hold a rattle. • Put toys over her cot or give her a baby gym to encourage her to reach out.
HER SOCIAL SKILLS	• She turns her head to your voice and smiles because she is happy to see you. • She expresses her joy in you by waving her arms and kicking her legs.	• Keep eye contact with her when feeding – it's heaven for her to have food and your attention at the same time! • Respond positively to her overtures.
HER SPEECH	• She will begin to make simple vowel sounds, such as "oh", "ah" and "uh". • She has a repertoire of easily recognized cries to express how she is feeling: hungry, tired, lonely, bad-tempered, frustrated, angry, impatient or just wanting to be left alone.	• Imitate all the sounds she makes back to her. • When your baby cries, it is her way of communicating with you – always respond to it (see p. 88).

136

STIMULATING PLAY

● Act out nursery rhymes and play pat-a-cake.
● Play lots of simple physical games, such as gentle jerks, knee bends, arm pulls and tickling feet.
● Introduce her to small toys with different textures and say out loud to your baby how they feel.
● Lie on the floor opposite her while she lies on her tummy and looks at you – this will encourage head control.
● Enourage her to reach out for soft objects.
● Take her into the bath with you for a skin-to-skin soak and lots of water games. Encourage her to kick and splash. Make her aware of her hands by splashing them in the water, and splash your own.

Introduce her to different types of toys

Encourage her to reach out for objects

BABY DEVELOPMENT
3–4 MONTHS

FEET
In this month, your baby will discover his feet.

WHAT TO LOOK OUT FOR

WHAT DEVELOPS	HOW HE PROGRESSES	HOW YOU CAN HELP
HIS MIND	• He's curious and wants to join in. • He can recognize places and faces as familiar. • He loves the breast or his bottle and shows it. • He'll laugh by the age of four months.	• Offer a wide range of toys. • Explain everything you see and do. • Pin photographs of yourselves in his cot with a safety pin.
HIS MOBILITY	• He loves sitting up now with a little support from you or cushions. • If you gently pull him into a sitting position, he will bring his head up in line with his body. • If he is lying on his tummy, he can look straight at you now.	• Sit him up with cushions for support. • Pull him gently up into a sitting position to strengthen his back and neck muscles. • Play games that make your baby swivel from the waist and offer toys that he is able to reach easily.
HIS HANDLING SKILLS	• He's starting to control his hands and feet and will start reaching for his toes. • He moves his hands and feet together. • He crosses his feet and puts a foot on the opposite leg.	• Put toys in his hands when he reaches for them or he will overshoot. Make him reach for things in every position. • Give him rattles so that he can make noises with his hands.
HIS SOCIAL SKILLS	• He looks at and smiles at people who talk to him – he hasn't learned shyness yet. • He knows you and your partner and people he sees regularly, such as grandparents. • He loves company and cries when left alone for long. He knows warmth, love and the opposite.	• Encourage his sense of humour. Laugh with him, share the joke and imitate everything he does. Don't be afraid to over-act all your responses. • Encourage emotional development: laugh when he laughs and cry when he cries.
HIS SPEECH	• He'll squeal with pleasure. • He's learning all the basic tones of voices. • He says "m", "p" and "b" when unhappy and "j" and "k" when happy.	• Repeat sounds back at him – "M, m, m you're not happy are you". Speak in a tone of voice that is appropriate.

137

STIMULATING PLAY

● Play "peep-bo" and hiding your face games. When playing "peep-bo" stay slightly to one side so that your baby has to swing his trunk to find you.
● Put objects on a string over his cot and pram so that he can examine them – one day he'll reach out and knock one.
● Amplify his experiences by talking to him about what you see and do. Add as much detail about each object and activity that you can.
● Place a rattle in your baby's hand and shake it a few times. He will be intrigued by its texture and by the sound that it makes.
● Play tickling games to encourage his laughter.

Gently pull him up when he is lying on his back

BABY DEVELOPMENT
4–5 MONTHS

EXPLORING WITH HER MOUTH
Your baby will put everything into her mouth, especially her hands. She is exploring with her lips and tongue.

WHAT TO LOOK OUT FOR

WHAT DEVELOPS	HOW SHE PROGRESSES	HOW YOU CAN HELP
HER MIND	• Your baby loves games – she learns skills from them by copying what you do. • Her concentration is expanding. She spends a long time examining things. • She smiles at herself in the mirror. • She moves her arms and legs to attract you. • She pats her bottle when feeding.	• When she attracts your attention respond to it; this will encourage good behaviour. • Turn your body theatrically towards her. Let her know you're attending to her by focusing on her: move towards her, bend down and make eye contact. • Call her by her name all the time.
HER MOBILITY	• She has now mastered full control of her head. Although it's quite steady, it may wobble if she moves suddenly.	• Give her plenty of rocking motion. This will promote head stability and aid her when she begins walking.
HER HANDLING SKILLS	• She puts things into her mouth, such as toys, her fist, her feet, as it's the most sensitive area. • She grasps large toys with both hands and begins to use the little finger side of her hand to grip things. She sometimes can't let go.	• Don't try to stop her putting her hand in her mouth – it's natural. • Play with her toes and guide them to her mouth. • Play give and take games with toys.
HER SOCIAL SKILLS	• Your baby is beginning to be shy with strangers (this is the first sign of her emerging "self"), but she still smiles at people she knows.	• Introduce her to all visitors so that she gets used to strangers and the concept of friends.
HER SPEECH	• Her language is very colourful: she tries to "talk" by blowing, babbling, squealing, laughing, and she says "ka" in an attempt to sound like you. • She uses facial expressions to communicate.	• Imitate all her sounds with changes of pitch and volume. If she listens, stimulate her with new sounds and name them.

STIMULATING PLAY

• Play lots of games with her, especially those that involve clapping.
• She loves crumpling paper – give her sheets of old lining paper or lots of tissue paper that crackles.
• Hide her face under a towel for a second then whisk it away and say "peep-bo" – she'll squeal with delight.
• Look out for your baby holding her hands up and her arms wide – this means that she wants to play.
• Let her look at herself in a mirror while you hold her – talk to her and help her to recognize herself and you.
• Play rocking games while she is sitting on your lap, dance with her and gently swing her.
• Encourage her to open her fingers by playing giving and taking away games. Always give her the object when she reaches out.
• She will reach for her bottle to feed herself. Let her hold it and then try to get her to give it back to you.

Gently rock her on your lap to help develop balance and mobility

She now has head control

BABY DEVELOPMENT
5–6 MONTHS

SITTING SUPPORTED
Encourage him to sit by propping him up with cushions.

WHAT TO LOOK OUT FOR

WHAT DEVELOPS	HOW HE PROGRESSES	HOW YOU CAN HELP
HIS MIND	• He gets excited if he hears someone coming. • He expresses his discomfort or insecurity. • He makes lots of attention-seeking sounds and raises his arms to be picked up. • He loves meal-times, showing preferences for different foods and making his particular likes and dislikes very clear.	• Respond to his call as soon as you hear it. Shout out that you're coming, then go towards him and say his name. Hold out your arms as you approach him. • Keep using his name every time you speak to him. • Encourage him to try different foods.
HIS MOBILITY	• He's now strong enough to take the weight of his upper half on his arms. • He can sit for a few minutes supported on the floor with lots of cushions.	• Play bouncing games with your baby. Get a baby bouncer if he likes it. • Lie next to him on the floor and crawl around. It will encourage him to copy.
HIS HANDLING SKILLS	• He now has the ability to transfer objects from one hand to another. • Holding one toy in his hand, he'll drop it to take hold of another. • He'll hold his bottle.	• Show him how to let go and drop things and how to pass a toy from hand to hand. • Play give and take games – this will also encourage him to share. • Give him finger foods, such as rusks.
HIS SOCIAL SKILLS	• He starts to make assertive advances: pats your cheek, scratches and slaps. • He explores your face with his hands – it means "hello", so say "hello" back and smile. • He's possessive of you and may be very wary of people he doesn't know.	• Show your baby new gestures, stretch out your arms to him and he'll lift his too. • Make expansive gestures and pitch your voice to match. He will copy you. • Avoid leaving him in a room with strangers.
HIS SPEECH	• He blows bubbles (this is his first real speech). • He now says "ka", "da" and "ma" all the time and a new sound emerges: "ergh". • He seems to understand a bit of what you say.	• If he appears to understand you, ask if he does, repeat what you said and praise him.

139

STIMULATING PLAY

• Demonstrate cause and effect. Push a ball to him while he's sitting up and say "the ball is rolling".
• Play weight-bearing games: these encourage him to take more and more weight on his legs, which helps to strengthen them. Hold him on your lap or on the floor, gently bounce him up and down and you'll feel him push off.
• Blow "raspberries" on his tummy when you're changing his nappy or getting him dressed after a bath – encourage him to copy the different noises you make.
• Reward him for holding out his arms by playing lifting games – squeal with delight as you lift him and swing him around.

Weight-bearing games will strengthen her legs

BABY DEVELOPMENT
6–7 MONTHS

MOBILITY
Your baby can now bear her weight on one hand when she's lying down on her tummy.

WHAT TO LOOK OUT FOR

WHAT DEVELOPS	HOW SHE PROGRESSES	HOW YOU CAN HELP
HER MIND	• She starts off conversations and you'll understand many of her own sounds. • She knows her name and who she is. • She may want to feed herself. • She anticipates repetition and imitates you.	• Encourage her sense of self by showing your baby her reflection in the mirror and repeating her name over and over "That's Oona, that's you". • Have conversations with her.
HER MOBILITY	• She can now bear weight on one hand when she is lying on her tummy. • She can lift her head when lying on her back. • When you hold her up she can take all her own weight on straight legs and hips.	• To encourage her to take her weight, play lots of standing games. • Place a toy above her while she's on her back and encourage her to lift her head to reach out for it.
HER HANDLING SKILLS	• She reaches out for objects using only her fingers now. • She holds on to a toy if she reaches for another. • She bangs the table. • She's becoming much more accurate when she feeds herself with finger foods.	• Let her try to feed herself from a dish with her own baby spoon. Continue with finger foods (make cheese cubes smaller and smaller) to encourage fine finger movements. • Give her plenty of toys that are easy for her to hold.
HER SOCIAL SKILLS	• Your baby loves other babies and stretches out to them in friendship. • She may cry if she's left with anyone other than you or your partner, especially if it's someone who she doesn't know.	• Give her physical affection; she can't be loving to anyone (including herself) if she doesn't have a bank of love to draw on. • Keep introducing her to strangers and give her time to adjust.
HER SPEECH	• She now has very clear syllables with actions, "ba", "da" and "ka". • Cries have high and low pitches and a nasal sound has appeared.	• Make every sound back to her to make her feel important.

STIMULATING PLAY

● Encourage her sense of self by playing games with her things and using her name: for example, say "That's Oona's dress" and "Whose teddy is this? It's Oona's".

● If she's wary of strangers now, introduce them gradually.

● Develop her sense of humour with simple jokes like tickling; play "Round and round the garden, like a teddy bear".

● To encourage her to pull her tummy off the floor, play at aeroplanes. Lay side by side on your front and lift your arms and body – and your baby's – off the floor.

● Play touching games: use every opportunity to touch your baby and let her touch you; for example, she'll love it if you let her explore your face.

Hold a mirror up so that she can see herself, and say her name

BABY DEVELOPMENT
7–8 MONTHS

FINGER-THUMB GRASP
Your baby will try to pick up objects using his thumb and fingers in a "pincer" movement.

WHAT TO LOOK OUT FOR		
WHAT DEVELOPS	**HOW HE PROGRESSES**	**HOW YOU CAN HELP**
HIS MIND	• He's showing signs of determination; he'll keep going after toys he can't quite reach. • He concentrates hard on discovering what he can do with his toys – he's learning all the time about the properties of various objects.	• Encourage him to retrieve a toy for which he has to stretch. • Play water games in the bath. • Give him plastic containers to pour, empty and fill over and over.
HIS MOBILITY	• He'll sit rocking his body backwards and forwards to try to reach a toy. • He loves standing when supported. If you stand him on your lap, he'll jig about. • Lying on his front, he'll try to wriggle forwards.	• While he's sitting, sit a little way from him and hold your arms out. He'll try to shuffle along on his bottom to reach you. • Hold him upright as much as possible. • Get him to reach a toy while on his front.
HIS HANDLING SKILLS	• He loves making any noise by banging. • He'll try to copy you if you clap. • He can hold any toy firmly in his fingers, and will shake a rattle. • He will point to objects – this is the first stage of him learning the finger-thumb grasp.	• Give him spoons, pan lids, or a toy drum so that he can use his hands to bang and make a noise. • When he's sitting on the floor or in his cot, make sure that he has lots of toys to reach for, pick up and explore.
HIS SOCIAL SKILLS	• He will respond fully to sociable games such as "Pat-a-cake" or "This little piggy". • He doesn't like it when you're angry and will respond accordingly. • He's clear what "no" means and responds to it.	• Make him feel valued by using his name in every situation. This will help him to develop a sense of himself. • When you need to say "no", say it firmly and use a different tone of voice.
HIS SPEECH	• He plays games with his mouth and tongue, blowing "raspberries" and smacking his lips. • He may combine two syllables such as "ba-ba" and "da-da", though not with meaning.	• Play sound games to convey meaning – "quiet" (whisper) or "loud" (shout).

141

STIMULATING PLAY

• Play and sing word games to encourage him to vocalize. Say rhymes over and over again always with the same emphasis and move your body; he'll start to copy you and use his.
• Use all kinds of safe household items as toys, for example, plastic or wooden spoons, pans and brushes. Show your baby how to use each one. Banging games will be huge fun.
• Always answer his needs and cries; this breeds self-confidence and self-esteem.
• Sit with your baby on the floor and encircle your legs around him. Fill the circle with his favourite toys.
• Lie on the floor and encourage him to climb over you.
• Play clapping games – encourage him to copy you.

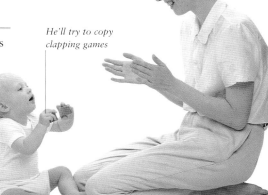

He'll try to copy clapping games

BABY DEVELOPMENT
8–9 MONTHS

LEANING FORWARDS
Your baby will have mastered the skill of leaning forwards to reach objects.

WHAT TO LOOK OUT FOR

WHAT DEVELOPS	HOW SHE PROGRESSES	HOW YOU CAN HELP
HER MIND	• Your baby loves familiar games and rhymes and laughs at the right times. • She can anticipate movements. • She will turn her head to her name and hold out her hands to be reached.	• Help her to understand life on a day-to-day basis by explaining all routines. Use meals and bathtimes as cues for special activities – "Now it's time for lunch", "Now it's time to have your bath".
HER MOBILITY	• She can take her weight on her legs, if supported. • She can sit for 10 minutes, lean forwards and sideways and stay balanced. • She can roll from side to side, but can't get up from a sitting position to stand.	• Help her to stand from a sitting position, bend her hips and knees for her. • Help her to cruise round the furniture by having pieces close together. Encourage her to hold on to a low piece of furniture.
HER HANDLING SKILLS	• Her movements are becoming more refined. • Her fingers are used for exploring – she puts things in her mouth much less. • She has the ability to lean forwards and pick up small things easily.	• Show her how to stack bricks on top of one another or side by side – she's learning about volume as well as fine movements. • Give her a soft cooked pea to pick up between her finger and thumb.
HER SOCIAL SKILLS	• She's shy with new faces and may be reluctant to be picked up by people she doesn't know. • She remembers people she has got to know well, even if she hasn't seen them for a few days	• Talk to her on the telephone if you have to be away from home at all. • Get her a toy telephone to play with. • Help her get to know the baby-sitter.
HER SPEECH	• She's understanding more and more of what you say so repeat "Yes, that's what daddy means: it's cold outside, brrrr". • She'll start to add "t", "d" and "w" sounds. • She might make one animal sound if you do.	• Repeat words that start with t, d and w. • Repeat all her sounds back to her. Name everything. • Read animal stories and make the noises.

STIMULATING PLAY

● Read a book or magazine – babies especially love colour supplements with commentary from you.
● Get lots of noisy toys (wooden spoons, metal pots and pans or a toy drum). It helps her to understand how to exert some control over things and herself and develops her understanding of cause and effect.
● Name parts of your body and ask her to copy.
● Crawl beside your baby and imitate her movements to encourage her to do the same.
● Show her how you can put one brick on top of another. It takes great skill and she won't achieve it by herself for at least another month or so, but she'll enjoy knocking the bricks over and scattering them about the floor!

Playing with bricks will help her to develop her hand control

She can pick up small objects easily

142

BABY DEVELOPMENT
9–10 MONTHS

CRAWLING
He will begin by leaning forwards on to his hands and knees.

WHAT TO LOOK OUT FOR

WHAT DEVELOPS	HOW HE PROGRESSES	HOW YOU CAN HELP
HIS MIND	• Your baby is getting used to rituals; they order his life and make him feel secure. • He'll wave bye bye. • He'll put his foot out for a sock – he's longing to be helpful! • He knows teddy and dolly. • He'll look around corners for a toy.	• Try to keep to some sort of routine so that your baby can get used to it. • Show him how to dress and undress, so that he begins to understand the concept of a daily routine. • He should have toys such as teddies or dolls that are "like baby".
HIS MOBILITY	• He's discovered mobility. • He moves forward on his hands and knees and loves changing positions. • He can twist his trunk around quite confidently.	• Hold out your arms, call his name and encourage him to crawl to you. • Offer your fingers for him to pull himself up on, then lift his foot on and off the floor.
HIS HANDLING SKILLS	• He reaches for objects with his index finger and will master picking up something small, such as a raisin, with his thumb and index finger. • He'll let go of objects deliberately. • He can build a tower of two bricks.	• Point to objects for him. • Put toys on the tray of his high chair and encourage him to throw them over; you can tie them on. • Ask him to roll a ball to you.
HIS SOCIAL SKILLS	• He shows affection by pressing his face and head against yours and hangs on to you tightly. • He'll give you a toy if you ask him for it, but become angry if you take it away.	• Teach about hugs – let's both have a hug together – he's learning reciprocity. • Teach sharing: ask him for a bit of food and show him how nice he is for sharing it.
HIS SPEECH	• Your baby begins to make lots of consonant sounds. • He chatters away in the rhythm of speech, without meaning.	• Name absolutely everything. • Face your baby when you speak to him so that he is able to read your lip movements.

143

STIMULATING PLAY

• Rock him on your knee and pretend to drop him – he'll enjoy "falling" as long as he's safe.
• Set aside a time each day for reading: read real story books and point out pictures. He'll learn to look at pictures the right way up and begin to recognize pictures of objects.
• Play hide and seek by hiding yourself or a toy.
• Give him lots of bath toys – plastic jugs, beakers and sieves as well as floating toys like boats and ducks.
• Give him his own doll and teddy and show him how to dress and undress it.
• Give him squeaky toys, horns and bells.
• Stack blocks or cubes of the same size on top on one another and side by side for him to see.

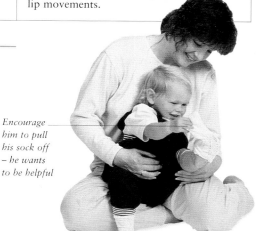

Encourage him to pull his sock off – he wants to be helpful

BABY DEVELOPMENT
10–11 MONTHS

CONTAINERS
She'll love to put items into containers and take them out again.

WHAT TO LOOK OUT FOR		
WHAT DEVELOPS	**HOW SHE PROGRESSES**	**HOW YOU CAN HELP**
HER MIND	• Your baby will point things out to you. • She loves dropping toys off her high chair, then looking for them. • She asks to be picked up. • She learns through opposites: keep showing her examples, such as in and out, here and there and over and under.	• Read different kinds of books and magazines to her. • Encourage her concentration span by telling her a simple storyline. • Pick her up if she reaches out to you. • Keep demonstrating cause and effect, by pushing over bricks or splashing water.
HER MOBILITY	• She's crawling or shuffling at great speed. • If you support her standing, she'll lift one leg. • She's completely balanced while sitting.	• Place a toy right behind her to make her twist around – it's okay, she's got the skill. • Position her so that she can crawl or shuffle.
HER HANDLING SKILLS	• Your baby loves taking things out of containers and putting them back. • She will hold something out to you if you ask for it.	• Play giving things to each other and then taking them away, but don't *force* her to relinquish something. • Take her hand and point to objects.
HER SOCIAL SKILLS	• She knows her name and knows who Mummy and Daddy are when you use the words. • She's got a wonderful sense of humour: play little jokes all the time and laugh at her attempts to make you laugh.	• Use laughter to show your approval and silence to mean the opposite: this is gentle baby discipline and she'll soon catch on. • Demonstrate social rituals, such as kissing and waving goodbye.
HER SPEECH	• Your baby is now beginning to imitate real speech sounds. • She may start to attempt one word with meaning – "Dada" when Daddy appears is often the first.	• Keep saying "Mama". • Repeat "Dada". Use association, for example: "Dada has gone to work".

STIMULATING PLAY

• Play games using the hands, such as "Incy-wincy spider" and "Jack and Jill" – buy a book that shows you the movements.
• When reading, name several items on each page and go over them in the same order each time you read. Let her turn the pages.
• Babies love babies, so introduce the concept of parenthood through pictures of other babies, puppies and kittens.
• Encourage her to practise putting in and taking out by giving her a wooden spoon and bowl or bricks and a basket.
• Play games with bricks: she will attempt to make a tower of bricks and you can demonstrate cause and effect by knocking them down and saying "all fall down".
• Encourage her to pull herself up to standing by holding a favourite toy just out of reach.

Help her to learn by showing her how toys work

BABY DEVELOPMENT
11–12 MONTHS

FEEDING
By this age your baby will be much more adept at feeding himself.

WHAT TO LOOK OUT FOR

WHAT DEVELOPS	HOW HE PROGRESSES	HOW YOU CAN HELP
HIS MIND	• He loves jokes and will do anything for a positive response like a laugh – this will make him feel good about himself. • He knows about kissing and wants to kiss you.	• Laugh when he finds something funny. • Let him kiss you, but don't ask him to kiss strangers. • Talk enthusiastically about your activities.
HIS MOBILITY	• He can walk if you hold one hand. • He'll walk if he pushes a sturdy trolley, or he'll hold on to furniture to steady himself.	• While he's cruising, encourage him to launch off by calling him. • Make sure the furniture is steady.
HIS HANDLING SKILLS	• He is getting better at feeding himself. • He can rotate his hand to turn toys over. • He loves throwing things away. • He makes lines with a crayon. • He holds on to two things in one hand.	• Keep putting two blocks into his hand. • Encourage self-feeding of soft but non-runny food with a spoon. Give him his own special dish and spoon. • Give him crayons and paper.
HIS SOCIAL SKILLS	• He knows who he is. • He becomes quite possessive of his toys and resents them being removed. • He loves social gatherings as long as you or someone he is familiar with carries him. • He'll give you things if you ask for them.	• Introduce him to lots of babies. • Encourage him to share. • Encourage affection by cuddling his doll. • Leave him with a baby-sitter occasionally. • Sit him in his high chair at the table or playpen in the room in which you're sitting.
HIS SPEECH	• He follows conversation and makes sounds in the gaps. • He may say one word, such as "dog", with meaning, pointing when he sees a dog. • He can make you understand he wants something and what it is.	• Teach him "thank you"; he may be able to say "ta". • Congratulate him when you understand what he's saying.

145

STIMULATING PLAY

• Read simple stories about animals and their young to encourage his interest in other "babies". All babies love this and you can use this opportunity to make references to you and your baby and how much you love him and will protect him.

• Give him non-toxic coloured crayons and large sheets of plain paper on the floor, to encourage him to draw.

• Encourage him to stand unaided by holding him steady, then letting go for a second or two.

• Concentrate on the names of objects and name parts of the body. Point to parts of your body and he'll copy.

• If he uses the furniture as support to get around the room, place it slightly further apart to encourage him to bridge the gap. Be ready to help in case he loses his balance.

As you are reading, point to objects and name them

CHAPTER SEVEN

BALANCING
FAMILY
AND WORK

You may have always planned on returning to work after your maternity leave, even so it takes some organisation on your part and cooperation on the part of your partner. It also depends on whether your employer (and his) can accommodate flexible working, job sharing, tele-working and part-time working but all, by law, have to try. One condition of being a working mother is that you feel pulled in many directions at once and that you're not fulfilling any of your roles as well as you'd like. Making concessions can be difficult and sometimes frustrating, but as long as your baby has your undivided attention when you're with her, rest assured she won't suffer from having a working mum.

WORK AND PARENTING

WHEN IS THE RIGHT TIME?

Aside from legal requirements (see p. 160), your baby's needs and your feelings will, to an extent, dictate when you're able to return to work:

■ If you want to continue breastfeeding, practise expressing enough milk for your baby's needs (see p. 72). If you intend to stop breastfeeding, you need to introduce the bottle in good time.

■ Think carefully about whether you feel ready – physically and emotionally – to return to work.

WORK OPTIONS

Look at all your options to work out which would suit you best.

PART-TIME/JOB-SHARING
Part-time can be the best of both worlds, as you have time with your baby and the stimulation of work, but you also have the pressure of both. If you can be part of a job-share, you may be better able to continue to build your career.

WORKING FROM HOME
You have to be self-disciplined and that means arranging some child care (see p. 150). If the baby is in the house, you're more likely to be easily distracted.

CAREER BREAK
You may decide to have a career break for a couple of years. Make sure putting your career on hold is what you really want and that you've thought clearly about all the implications.

FATHER AT HOME
If you want to return full-time, it may be an option for your partner to be the main carer (see p. 154).

IF YOU PREPARE for returning to work well in advance, the transition period should be easier for all of you. As a couple, you need to ensure that you've made adequate child care provisions, decide how you'll adjust your routine and accept that the change in lifestyle may be unsettling at first, especially for the baby.

MAKING THE DECISION

You may decide while you're pregnant that you want to return to work at the end of your maternity leave (see p. 160). Once the baby is born, however, it's normal to feel unsure about leaving him, especially as this is likely to coincide with the time that you're just settling into being a mother. On the opposite end of the scale, you may be surprised to find that you actually miss work and are ready, after a few months, to take a break from the domestic routine and return to an adult environment. Of course, there may simply be no decision for you to make – financially, you may have to work.

WHAT TO CONSIDER
Whatever you decided while pregnant, it's important to look at your financial and domestic situation once the baby is born and for you and your partner to weigh up the advantages and disadvantages of your return to work:
● What type of child care can you afford? Have you checked what is available in your area?
● After covering the cost of child care, does your salary leave enough extra to make it worthwhile? (Don't forget to take travel costs into account.)
● Is it feasible to return to your old job as it was and also devote enough time to your baby? For example, does your job involve lots of overtime or travel away from home?

CONCERNS
For the past few months you'll have been focused on preparing for the birth and then looking after your new baby. Once you have to think about returning to work, you're likely to have concerns and mixed feelings.

Feeling guilty You may feel guilty (especially if you can't wait to get back to work), but don't. Just because you're a working mother doesn't mean you're a bad mother. There is no point in staying at home with your baby if it doesn't fulfil you – it will be more beneficial to him if you're happy and contented when he does see you. Also, don't forget how your baby will benefit from the additional income.

Losing your confidence If the last few months of your life have mainly consisted of nappy changing and entertaining a baby, you may doubt your ability to readjust to a working environment. You may worry that you have lost your touch and that everyone got on fine without you. A couple of months after the birth, try to ease yourself back into work mode by catching up on what has been going on in your industry and by talking to colleagues. Nearer the time, go into the office (without the baby, if possible) even if it's just to meet someone for lunch, so that it isn't such a shock when you return. You'll soon realize that not much has changed in the time you've been away.

WHEN YOU'RE BACK AT WORK

It may take a few weeks to settle back into work. You'll just about have worked out a routine with your baby at home and then suddenly have to adapt to a different timetable and concentrate your mind on a different set of priorities. You'll also, for the first time, be doing your job while having to handle added pressures and responsibilities at home.

MAKING THE TRANSITION

AREA OF CHANGE	HOW TO MAKE IT EASIER
PREPARING YOUR BABY	Introduce your baby to the childminder, starting with a couple of mornings each week and gradually building it up, or take him to the nursery for a trial run. You should also start to adapt his feeding routine in good time.
ADAPTING TO A CHANGE OF ROUTINE	Trying to juggle work and looking after your baby can be difficult. Establish a routine in the mornings and evenings so that you are sharing the baby care and chores equally. You'll soon find a routine that works.
COPING WITH TIREDNESS	No-one who is consistently deprived of sleep can be expected to cope adequately with a job, so you must take it in turns to care for your baby during the night. If one of you is in part-time work, still organize a pro-rata arrangement.
FOCUSING ON WORK	It's an acquired skill not to think about your baby while you're at work. If you've made the best arrangements you can for his welfare, any energy you now dispense on worrying is wasted and sells you and your employer short.
SETTLING YOUR BABY	The fact is your baby will *have* to settle and he will. What you can do is prepare yourselves for his reaction and, during the time he's with you, be reassuring and comforting to him. Make sure he has whatever comfort object he loves.

CAREER CONSIDERATIONS

People often assume that a woman's first priority will be her child and, in some situations, they're right: when push comes to shove, it's quite often the mother's employment that takes the strain and not the father's. If your partnership is different, you're probably going to have to demonstrate this several times before it's recognized. How your career is affected may also depend on your employer's attitude: set the ground rules early on by talking to your manager and telling him or her that you're committed to your job, but that your responsibilities at home mean you'll need a certain amount of flexibility. Explain that you need to leave on time (although, ideally, collecting your baby should be equally divided with your partner), but that with sufficient notice you're prepared to work extra hours, if necessary.

FATHER

If you've agreed as a couple that your partner should go back to work, then you must be accommodating. The routine at home will change if you're both working full-time and you must prepare yourself for this.

HOW YOU CAN HELP

■ Be supportive to your partner. She's very likely to find the transition to going back to work a strain and she may be distressed by having to leave the baby. Try to plan in advance as much as possible and give her time to adjust.

■ Share the responsibility. Don't just assume that your partner will sort out child care problems. The carer or nursery should have telephone numbers for both of you (including mobiles), so that you can easily share the responsibility if a problem arises.

■ Share the chores. Your partner may have been doing most of the care while she was at home full-time, but now she's back at work this should become more equal. Alternate doing the domestic chores, getting up during the night and collecting your baby from the childminder.

149

EMERGENCIES

You both have to agree on a strategy for emergencies, such as your baby or the childminder being ill. In the absence of a replacement carer, such as a grandparent, there's no alternative to one of you taking time off work. If either of you feels that your job merits priority, then this is something that must be stated and agreed in advance of the problem arising.

CHILD CARE

HIDDEN COSTS

When you're weighing up the cost of child care, don't just look at the daily or hourly rate. It's worth considering the following:

■ Are there transport costs?
■ Are your baby's meals provided?
■ What are the additional costs associated with a live-in carer?
■ Would it be cheaper to employ a nanny if you have twins?
■ Are there hidden emotional costs, such as feeling indebted, if you're using a friend or relative?

W HEN CHOOSING CHILD CARE, most parents are restricted by what they can afford. Ideally, as part of your decision to have a baby, you will have discussed your options or, if not, have some idea of what would suit you once the baby is born. Finding and choosing a carer is mainly dictated by practical and financial considerations, but there are also emotional issues involved: leaving your baby for several hours each day with someone new is difficult so, for your own peace of mind, it's essential that you're as happy and confident as possible about the type of care and carer you've chosen.

150

CHILD CARE OPTIONS

TYPE OF CARE	DESCRIPTION	ADVANTAGES	DISADVANTAGES
RELATIVE	You may decide to leave your baby with a member of your family, such as a grandparent. Encourage him or her to involve your baby in outside activities, such as a playgroup.	• Usually a cheaper option. • Your baby is with someone who loves her. • You are less likely to have strict time restraints, but don't abuse this.	• It can be difficult if there are disagreements. • You may worry more about your baby forming a close relationship with that person.
CHILDMINDER	A childminder looks after several children at one time in her own home. She is likely to be very experienced, especially if she has her own children.	• You can often pay by the hour to suit your budget. • Your baby will mix with lots of children, which will help to develop social skills.	• No training is required. • She may have limited resources. • You can't take your baby if she's ill.
NANNY	A nanny cares for your baby at home and may live with you. Interview a prospective nanny together – you both have to get on with her and observe her with your baby.	• A nanny is professionally trained and qualified. • Care takes place at home, which will help your baby to settle and is more convenient for you.	• A nanny is expensive (you're responsible for her tax and insurance), but consider a nanny share. • Beware of domestic tensions if the nanny lives in.
DAY NURSERY OR CRECHE	There are very few local authority nurseries, so you'll probably have to pay for private care. If you're lucky, an all-day creche may be available at your workplace.	• Your baby is with other babies and care is based around developing skills. • Nurseries and creches must be registered and often employ qualified carers.	• Can be expensive and there will be limited places. • You'll have to collect your baby at an agreed time. • You can't take your baby if she's ill.
AU PAIR OR MOTHER'S HELP	This is a student from another country who lives with you as part of the family. She will probably want to attend language classes and is only suitable if you work part-time or from home.	• Care is provided in the home, which is convenient. • Cheaper than a nanny. • When your baby is older, the au pair may be able to teach her a second language.	• Not professionally qualified, and not suitable for the full-time care of a baby. • Works limited hours. • There will be additional live-in costs.

WHAT TO LOOK FOR IN A CARER

Once you've decided on the type of child care you'd prefer, you need to look around for the best carer. If you plan your child care well in advance, you'll have more choice. If you leave it too late before you finish maternity leave, you may be restricted by what is available. Ask the person or institution that you're considering lots of questions to find out the type of care that will be provided, and thoroughly check the facilities. If you're unhappy or unsure, follow your instincts and look elsewhere.

Qualifications and references A nanny or nursery nurse should have accredited training with a proper qualification (NNEB in the UK). If you're using a childminder or a nursery, check that the person or institution is registered with a local authority. Remember, au pairs are not professionally trained. Ask a potential au pair for the name of another employer you could speak to and at least two written references. Always try to talk to the referees on the telephone to gauge more of an idea of the person's suitability.

Level of care Check how many babies are looked after at one time and the carer to child ratio. Even if your baby will not be receiving individual care (with a nursery, creche or childminder), she should still be given enough care to be stimulated and to encourage her development. Check the space and resources available, such as the kitchen and sterilizing equipment, the play area and the types of toys offered. With all types of care, ask what kind of activities your baby will be involved in on a day-to-day basis.

Interaction with your baby Always invite a potential carer to spend time with your baby so you can see how they interact. Watch to see what she says while holding your baby and how your baby reacts. Ask her questions, such as her thoughts on discipline to check that they match your own.

Commitment It can be confusing and distressing for a baby to have a change of carer. Check that the person or institution will be able to provide relatively long-term care. An au pair may only be available for a short time and is likely to have other commitments while she is staying with you.

YOUR RELATIONSHIP WITH YOUR CARER

However sure you are about employing your carer, it's advisable to discuss and agree on all aspects of caring for your baby from the outset:
- A trial period before you agree to a full contract is a good idea.
- Write down your requirements so that you can agree on some ground rules; especially with regard to telephone use and visitors for live-in carers.
- Find out the carer's thoughts or the institution's policy on discipline.

THE CARER'S RELATIONSHIP WITH YOUR BABY
Leaving your baby with a carer is likely to come at a time when you've just settled into being a parent and feel particularly close to your son or daughter. Your carer will also form a close relationship with your baby, but this doesn't mean you're any less important and you're by no means replaced. Your baby is capable of being close to – and accepting the attention of – more than one person: in fact it's beneficial if this happens because the more love, attention and stimulation she receives the better she'll develop. Babies often go through periods of time when they favour certain people (see p. 111); if your baby seems closer to her carer it's probably only a phase. Your baby may also seem unsettled now and then, but don't read too much into this. However, if it continues for more than a week or two, spend time with the carer and your baby together to try to pinpoint any problems.

TRIAL PERIOD

Investing money in nursery fees or your childminder's wages before you return to work, so that you can settle in your baby gradually, will pay huge dividends:

■ Your baby will have time to become familiar with her new surroundings and her new carer.

■ You'll be able to gauge the impact of the new regime on your baby and find ways of soothing her if she becomes unsettled.

■ You'll be able to sort out logistic hitches without the pressure of neither of you being available.

■ If you introduce your baby to her new carer gradually, the emotional impact of handing her over should be less once you actually return to work.

151

IF THINGS GO WRONG

If the child care situation doesn't work out, it can be disappointing and problematic, especially if your carer lives with you. You should, however, try to treat the problem professionally as you would with any working relationship:

■ It's best if issues are dealt with quickly; ignoring problems will only make matters worse and lead to resentments building up.

■ Talk to the carer and try to reach a compromise. Agree to see how things go and, depending on the problem, set a time limit. If, after this period, you have not resolved the matter, it may be in everyone's interest to terminate the employment.

■ Decide on a set notice period at the beginning; this is also advantageous to you because, if your carer is the one who decides to leave, you won't suddenly be left in the lurch.

MOTHER

Remember, play does not have to involve sitting down and playing with toys; often just being with you is fun for your baby.

WHAT YOU CAN DO

■ When you get home from work, make a habit of picking up your baby straight away and keep him on your hip as you walk around the house doing things.

■ Exaggerate your pleasure at seeing him, talk to him the whole time, make eye contact, laugh a lot, play little jokes and enjoy each other.

■ Try to spend ten to fifteen uninterrupted minutes playing with your baby each evening.

■ Later in the evening, read the paper or a book together so that you both relax. Read out items and show your baby pictures to involve him.

■ If you're really tired have a bath together. A skin-to-skin soak is good for both of you.

AN HOUR EACH DAY

An hour of time spent playing with your baby each day becomes rewarding and fulfilling for all of you. What's more, a baby who gets the undivided attention of his parents for an hour a day acquires self-esteem and self-confidence and becomes a generous, loving and well-adjusted child. This does not have to be a solid hour – in fact, your baby will not concentrate for this period of time; it could be two half-hour periods or four quarter-hour periods as long as he has your undivided attention at these times. Your baby loves routine and will get excited about his playtimes as they approach.

SPECIAL TIME WITH YOUR BABY

IF YOU'RE WORKING PARENTS, the time spent at home as a family becomes not just important, but precious – and that applies as much to fathers as mothers. Play is essential to your baby's mental and physical development, and nothing will make him happier than to play and have the attention of his parents at the same time.

THE IMPORTANCE OF PLAY

As well as being a parent, you are your baby's playmate; this is especially true in his first year when he may not have had much opportunity to interact with other children. Every game you play with him is magical and every lesson becomes worth learning, so time spent in games, no matter how simple, ensures that your baby is avidly learning and acquiring skills. Do not underestimate how important play is to your baby: it's his full-time job; a job that requires great concentration and expenditure of energy. It's harder than most adult work because everything is new and fresh lessons are learned all the time. These lessons, however, are made easier and are more fun if he can enjoy them with his favourite playmates – his parents.

WHY PLAY IS ESSENTIAL

● Your baby investigates his world through play.
● It stimulates and excites him and is the best use of his time.
● For the first few years of his life it is the only way he learns.
● It is an integral part of his physical and mental development.

GETTING THE MOST OUT OF PLAY

To maximize the rewards that play can bring, it's important to make the time to join in activities with your baby and encourage him in play that will stimulate his development.

Investing time Formal play isn't necessary, but some planning does reap dividends so try to make play a part of your morning, evening and weekend routine so that your baby is getting at least an hour of playtime in total from both of you each day (see left). A baby has a very short attention span so don't expect him to sit playing happily while you cook the dinner. Fifteen minutes invested in playing with your baby before you begin a task will pay off; if you only give him five minutes of your time he's more likely to become attention seeking when you're busy doing something else.

Stimulating development Babies start acquiring skills from the very moment of birth. These mental and physical milestones (see p. 126) emerge at particular stages as your baby's brain and body develops. It follows that these are optimum moments for you to introduce games that encourage particular skills to flourish, so make sure you vary the activities that you play with your baby: for example, physical games encourage mobility; singing helps to develop speech; playing with toys such as building blocks helps your baby to become more dextrous.

MAXIMIZING YOUR TIME

If you work full-time, try to take advantage of any spare moments you have to spend time with your baby. It helps if you're organized and can prioritize: if you're both in high-pressured jobs it's easy to let work take over and work an extra hour at the beginning or end of the day, but this hour is invaluable time you could be spending with your baby.

WEEKENDS

If you're at work all week, your weekends will be very precious. Don't bring work home with you; if it's not there you can't do it, which means you can spend time with your baby without feeling guilty. Try to get out as a family at least one of the days at the weekend; if you're in the house, you're more likely to get distracted with other things. Keep to your baby's weekly routine as much as possible – at around nine months he'll begin to understand that certain things happen at certain times.

MORNINGS

It can be one mad rush in the mornings if you're trying to get yourselves and your baby ready, but most babies do wake up early so use this opportunity to spend time together. If you don't have time for proper play, sing and talk to your baby as you change and dress him. Try to sit down to breakfast with him – he'll enjoy you being sociable.

EVENINGS

Working full-time will make you tired in the evenings. Try to establish some sort of routine for when you get home because as well as having time with your baby, it's important that you both have time to yourselves and time together as a couple (see p. 114).

Leave work on time Try to get into the habit of leaving work on time. It's unfair on your partner and the baby if either one of you is always home late, leaving one parent to do everything. Don't take advantage of the childminder – an extra hour in the evening is a lot when she's been looking after the baby all day.

Divide the chores One of you should cook and the other wash up so that you both have time to spend with the baby.

Choose relaxing activities It will be difficult to get your baby to bed if he's very excited. Read or sing to him to calm him down before you put him to bed. Remember, he's had a busy day playing and he's probably tired too!

RELAXING TOGETHER

Play doesn't always have to be energetic. Settle into a comfortable chair in the evening and read a story to your baby. This is a relaxing and enjoyable activity for both of you.

see p. 81

FATHER

Your baby will look forward to you coming home in the evenings. Reward him by showering him with attention and showing him how special he is to you.

WHAT YOU CAN DO

■ Develop a special routine that becomes a welcome ritual for when you get home from work. It could just be holding out your arms for your baby to walk or crawl to you, or picking him up immediately, walking around with him and telling him about your day.

■ Try to find time each evening to spend ten or fifteen minutes playing a game.

■ If you like to read the paper in the evening, let your baby sit with you, read to him and let him have his own bit of paper to crumple.

■ Have a bath with your baby (see p. 81) before getting him ready for bed; this can be relaxing for both of you.

■ If you don't have much time with your baby on weekday mornings, try to make a special effort to dress him and give him breakfast at the weekend.

153

TIME-SAVING TIPS

To maximize time with your baby in the evenings:

■ Try to prepare some weekday meals at the weekend.

■ Record any early evening programmes and watch them once your baby has gone to bed.

■ Save any long telephone calls until after your baby's bedtime.

■ Eat mid-afternoon sometimes so that it's possible for you to wait later for your evening meal.

FATHERS AT HOME

MOTHER

Being the breadwinner while your partner stays at home can lead to conflicting emotions, even when it's a decision you're sure about.

HOW TO HELP YOURSELF
Society as a whole still pressures women to be the main carer and it's difficult not to be affected by this. You may feel guilty, and envy other women who have more time to spend with their babies. Try to be confident in your decision or accepting of your predicament, and spend as much as possible of your spare time with your baby. It can be stressful if your family relies on you for its income; find ways to relax and try not to let this pressure turn into resentment.

HOW TO HELP YOUR PARTNER
Make sure your partner has time out to relax, see his friends and spend time with you (see p. 114). Don't leave all the chores to him just because he's the main carer.

HOW FRIENDS REACT

Most of the flak that fathers at home have to dodge comes in the form of ridicule from male friends. Many traditionally minded men find it threatening that the "house husband" is independent and strong enough to flout the social conventions that are sacrosanct to his more macho brothers. They like to hang on to these conventions because it gives them security. But if you're a man who is strong enough to have made the decision to be a full-time parent, you'll no doubt be strong enough to take the flak!

SOME COUPLES ARE SUFFICIENTLY LIBERATED – and brave enough – to overturn the traditional pattern of family life. They're opting for a reversal of roles in which the mother becomes the breadwinner, while the father acts as a "house husband", caring for the baby and running the home. Just as women only needed the opportunity to demonstrate their competence in the workplace, men who become the main family carer are finding that they only needed to be given the chance to demonstrate that they are just as capable as women of loving and bringing up their children at home.

MAKING THE DECISION

For many couples, the decision to reverse roles is made because they feel that their baby will benefit from having a full-time parent at home and, because the mother is earning more, it makes sense for the father to be that person – especially if his work is something he can do from home. When a parent stays at home full-time, a couple will be financially worse off than if both work, but this is often compensated for by an improvement in their quality of life and is seen as a worthwhile investment in their child. A man may be forced to stay at home due to a job loss; even if this is only short-term, it can often be an invaluable opportunity for him to spend time with his child and take on the role of primary carer.

A LEARNING PROCESS

Those people who make a stand on the traditional roles of father and mother as being "natural" are missing the point completely and to divide parental labour along the lines of gender is completely redundant. Looking after a baby is a learning process for all new parents, whether they're male or female, so don't let anyone tell you otherwise. Remember the following:
● Women are not born with an innate ability to change nappies and dress babies: they possibly appear more confident at it because they're made to feel that they should know what to do.
● Looking after and nurturing a baby is a learned skill and to begin with it's as difficult for a mother as it is for a father.
● Men are not at a disadvantage when it comes to caring for a baby: if you're a father who has decided to stay at home to be the main carer, you have as much chance at being good at it and raising a happy, confident and intelligent child as your partner.

PARENTING
If you're a couple who have chosen the father at home option, you are hopefully committed to parenting in general rather than fathering or mothering (see p. 11). It's only sensible to base your family set-up on your mutual strengths rather than be captive to stereotypes that may well conflict with your personalities.

THE ADVANTAGES

As a father who chooses to stay at home, you'll form a close bond with your baby and have a chance to watch and enjoy her development at an age that most men miss out on. This role will enable you to express your affection and feelings in ways that are difficult when you're in the more traditional male role. Giving up a full-time job to be a carer will enable you to change your priorities and release you from the pressures of being the main provider for your family. This leaves you with more of yourself to offer your baby and partner, which can be hugely beneficial to the family as a whole.

HOW YOUR CHILD IS AFFECTED

To a baby her mother and father are interchangeable. The baby only knows parental love and care – it doesn't matter who is doing the giving. The advantage of a man being the main carer is that he can offer a positive role model to his children free from the commonest kind of stereotyping. A son will grow up feeling comfortable with the emotional side of his personality and he'll follow his father's lead in having an independent spirit unpressured by prevailing social mores. A daughter, of course, will seek out the same well-balanced kind of men as her father – and that's no bad thing.

BEING THE LONE MAN

The main problem for most full-time parents is isolation and since a large proportion of people are working during the day, adult company can be found largely with others looking after children. As these are usually women, this can cause a problem for the full-time father. It's pointless to pretend that people interact with the opposite sex in the same way as with their own, but it's likely that a man with enough flexibility and confidence to become the main carer in the first place will move fairly easily into this predominantly female world. While some mothers may be surprised to find their ranks as full-time child carers joined by a man, few will be hostile. The "house-husband" is usually a bit of a nine-day wonder whose presence is very shortly taken for granted. Most men are welcomed, although some are the victims of maternalism of the "let-me-help-you-love variety", which can be as irritating as the "leave-that-to-me-darling" paternalism practised by some men.

AN EQUAL SHARE

Some couples decide that they'll both work part-time or one or two days at home, so that they both have a mix of parenting and work. This is possible if the job can be done at home or part-time, but with the technological revolution it is becoming an option for more and more people. The downside is that it may mean both of you putting your careers on hold, but many couples feel that it's the right choice; at least it prevents either person having to give up a career altogether. The advantages include:

■ Both of you have real quality time with your baby a couple of days each week, which will mean you'll form an equally close bond with her.

■ You'll both have a strong appreciation of the frustrations involved in being in sole charge of your baby and the problems of juggling work and home.

■ The baby benefits from building a close relationship with both of her parents.

■ You become a real team by dividing things equally; this prevents the resentments that often build up in the classic mum-at-home set-up.

BEING ACCEPTED
Over time, a full-time father will stop being the token male and become just another parent, who shares the same pleasures and problems of parenthood as his female friends.

LOOKING TO THE FUTURE

156

YOUR CONSTANT ROLE

Your role as nurturer means respecting your child, and offering support without foregoing your own principles. It takes many forms.

COMFORTER
You can only help your child to cope with emotional or physical pain by acknowledging it, and offering comfort when it's needed.

PLAYMATE
Play is a serious business for your child, and the best play is inter-active. No amount of passive amusement in front of a television set can compensate for active play with other people, the most important of whom are his parents.

LIMIT-SETTER
The first limits you set for your baby will be to prevent him hurting himself; later, these limits will prevent him from hurting others as well. Never be apologetic about consistently setting reasonable limits, but try not to do so in a punitive or accusatory manner. Rather than saying "no" all the time, help him to understand your reasons for restraint.

TEACHER OR ROLE MODEL?
The role of teacher is crucial for any parent; but it isn't formal teaching: you do it by example. Your child will learn behaviour from you, so you can't shrug off responsibility for an errant school child or truculent teenager – he learnt about life from you.

AUTHORITY FIGURE
Don't confuse authority and power: power results from the use or threat of force; authority comes from a person who has influence over, and receives consent from, others without force. Your child will accept your authority if he also sees that you are fair, competent, loving and reasonable.

YOUR BABY HAS NOW COMPLETED his first year of life; he's beginning to communicate with language, he's mobile (perhaps even taking his first steps), he's feeding himself and asserting his personality as a full member of the family. He's growing up, so your role as parents will be changing too, and it'll continue to change as he progresses on to school and ultimately to adolescence and adulthood. As the months and years pass, under your care he'll become more and more independent, but he'll always need you both as his permanent bedrock of security, sympathy, friendship and love.

YOUR BABY GROWS UP

The main change you will see, and must be prepared to accept, is that your baby is becoming a person in his own right, with personality, preferences and a will of his own. He will gradually acquire a sense of place in the family, a sense of independence and, most importantly, a sense of self-worth. Not all these changes are straightforward for you. On the one hand, they are all signs of growing maturity and so should be welcomed. On the other hand, some aspects of his growing up may lead to clashes with you and could result in a battle of wills that needs careful handling. Then again, his frustration at wanting to out-perform his ability may express itself as tantrums that leave you bewildered, perplexed and sometimes helpless (see p. 158). Tantrums, nonetheless, are a crucial milestone; he cannot become a reasonable, self-controlled child without experiencing them.

A HIERARCHY OF NEEDS

Keep in mind the basic needs that will help your child to grow and develop normally. Health, of course, is a pre-requisite, but you also have to try to provide the right sort of environment for him to reach his full potential – physically, emotionally, socially and intellectually. All children have a hierarchy of needs, starting from the very basic need for survival. You could think of your child's needs in terms of a pyramid: the solid base is provision of the food, drink and shelter needed for *survival*; then comes *safety*: protection from harm; a sense of *belonging*: your child feels wanted and secure, leading to *self-esteem*: no-one can feel good about himself if he feels unloved. Near the top of the pyramid comes *actualization*: understanding his place in the world – with a fully-developed sense of *self* as the pinnacle that can't be achieved without the rest in place.

BUILDING CONFIDENCE These fundamental building blocks help your child reach his full potential.

SELF
ACTUALIZATION
SELF-ESTEEM
BELONGING
SAFETY
SURVIVAL

BECOMING INDEPENDENT

Your child's burgeoning spirit of self-reliance is more important than you may think because so many good things can flow from it. Without a secure feeling of independence, a child can't relate to others, share, be reasonable, outgoing and friendly, have a sense of responsibility and eventually respect others and their privacy. Many other qualities stem from his belief in himself – curiosity, adventurousness, being helpful, thoughtful and generous. With such qualities people will relate well to him and he'll automatically get more out of life. What you pour in as love, expresses itself as self-worth and belief in himself. Love, of course, is not the only spur; you can encourage him practically as well.

Helpfulness Ask him to fetch things for you, such as the shopping bag or the dustpan, so that he feels useful.

Decision-making Give him small decisions to make, like which toy to play with or which cup to use, so he can use his judgment and rely on it.

Sense of identity Ask questions about his preferences, solicit his opinion to give him a sense of identity and importance.

Physical independence Give him slightly more and more difficult tasks – like jumping up and down, throwing or kicking a ball, so he can feel pleased with the strength and co-ordination of his body.

Emotional independence Show him that he can trust you: you always come back after leaving him, you always comfort him when he's hurt, you always help him when he's in difficulties.

Co-operation "We can do it together" is a motto that you should keep repeating – it breeds faith in your baby's own efforts. When he overcomes an obstacle or succeeds in a task on his own, he'll experience the thrill of achievement – especially if you heap praise on him.

ACHIEVING CONTROL OF HIS BODY

Many parents believe that they can set a clock for their baby to achieve bowel and bladder control. Those parents are doomed to frustration. Your baby's timetable has nothing to do with your expectations – only with his speed of development. Bowel and bladder control are undoubtedly important milestones between dependent baby and independent child, but they can't be reached until other areas of development have been achieved. This is why I dislike the label "potty training"; no child can do something until he's ready for it and, once ready, no child needs training.

WHEN HE'LL BE DRY

At around 18 months and no earlier, your child might start to tell you that he can feel himself passing urine. He can't hold it, he can't wait, he has no control over it. He'll give you a sign; he'll point to the nappy and vocalize to draw your attention to it. Then, and only then, do you start a gentle programme of encouragement. Your daughter will probably have achieved bladder and bowel control by the age of two, and be dry at night by three; it may take your son longer. Being dry all night can take some children a long time – it's quite normal for a boy not to achieve full control until he is four or five. Never scold your child for wetting the bed, or having an accident during the day, especially if he's been "dry" for a while. It could be a sign of illness or emotional distress, so think about the underlying causes. Being angry with your child for something over which he hasn't much control will just upset him and make the problem worse.

BEING REASONABLE

This heading disguises a few personal comments on discipline in young children. I have to disguise it because what I believe to be good discipline has little to do with the usual punitive interpretation of the word.

RE-DEFINING DISCIPLINE
Good discipline has nothing to do with a parent forcing a mode of behaviour *on* a child; it's about encouraging reasonable behaviour *from* a child. Your aim should be to create a desire to behave well most of the time, rather than to conform to an arbitrary adult code out of fear, weakness or resignation.

ENCOURAGING GOOD RESULTS
Hitting a child to make him obedient is no more efficient than belabouring a worker on the production line for being too slow. The basic tool of good personnel management is praise for good results, not penalizing poor results, and so it should be for children.

START FROM THE BEGINNING
It's easier if you start how you mean to finish; discipline doesn't just happen at, say, three years old. It's been building from birth and is based on reasonable behaviour expressed by you.

PARENTAL RESPONSIBILITY
Children are born with an over-whelming desire to please; if they lose that desire, my view is that we parents must take responsibility. If you think you're doing everything right, but still have a difficult child, you may be being too easy on yourself. Look at what you think of as "right", and ask yourself if it is right for your child.

BEING CONSISTENT
Work out your joint attitude to discipline, and be consistent in your response. A child who gets different reactions from each parent will be confused about what his limits really are, and his behaviour will reflect this.

TEMPER TANTRUMS

By the time she's about two, your child's will is well developed, but her ambitions far outreach her capabilities. The resulting combination of stubbornness and frustration can be explosive, resulting in the classic temper tantrum. There are ways to cope:

■ Accept temper tantrums as normal. Better still, see them as a cry for help. Having your child throw a fit of screaming, kicking and crying is upsetting at the best of times, and sometimes publicly humiliating. If you're firm, gentle and have a steady nerve, you'll nurse her out of them; to do that you have to realize that she's not being wilfully naughty – she simply can't control herself.

■ Don't shout, smack or get angry. She needs you to help her regain control. A temper tantrum means she's saying, "Help me. Protect me from myself." Your very quietness should calm her down.

■ A really upset child can frighten herself by the sheer strength of her uncontrolled emotions, so cuddle her close; be firm – she will struggle.

■ Be businesslike; she's trying to elicit a dramatic response but she'll calm down if you're cool.

■ If this doesn't work, say you're going to leave the room or walk where she can't see you, but you can see her. Do as you promised and the screaming will stop; it usually does without an audience. (If members of the public form a scandalized audience you may have to carry her outside.)

■ Try to stay where you can see her as much as possible, and be ready to prevent her from hurting herself or others.

CAUTION
Some children develop breath holding attacks that may be frightening, but most are brought to an abrupt end by a firm tap between the shoulder blades.

GENDER DIFFERENCES IN DEVELOPMENT

It's clear from the previous page that bladder and bowel control is one obvious area of development where there may be a marked difference between boys and girls (although there will always be exceptions to the rule). However, many gender differences are imposed on boys and girls by adults' own prejudices about what boys or girls are expected to be like (see p. 128), and so it's not always clear whether the recognized differences are solely due to nature or nurture. However, differences in the rate of development of certain skills between boys and girls throughout childhood and into adolescence have been measured by researchers (see chart below). Being aware of these differences may help you to understand your children better, which can then enable them to move forward at an appropriate rate and also help overcome any difficulties before they become problems. It can also help to avoid the sort of gender stereotyping that doesn't allow girls to be adventurous or boys to show affection.

SOME DEVELOPMENTAL DIFFERENCES

GIRLS	BOYS
As toddlers, girls are better at hopping, rhythmic movement and balance.	At school age, boys are usually better than girls at running, jumping and throwing.
Girls are slightly faster than boys at some aspects of early language ability. They learn to read and write, and grasp grammar and spelling, earlier than boys.	Most boys talk later than girls, and take longer to make complicated sentences. They have more reading problems by adolescence, and are less adept at verbal reasoning.
Girls are more emotionally independent than boys and are also more sociable and form close friendships from an earlier age.	Boys are more emotionally dependent than girls, and tend to have more behavioural problems before and during adolescence.
There's little difference in strength and speed between girls and boys until puberty, but from that time fat to muscle ratio is greater in girls.	At adolescence, boys become stronger and faster than girls and have more muscle and bone, less fat and larger hearts and lungs.
Physical growth is faster and more regular; girls mature at adolescence earlier than boys.	Physical growth tends to go in uneven spurts; boys reach puberty later than girls.
Girls may be slightly better at arithmetic than boys before they reach adolescence, after which the trend reverses.	At every age boys are better at spatial visualization and, from adolescence, tend to be better than girls at mathematical reasoning.
In early childhood, girls generally appear to be more willing to obey adults' requests.	From toddlerhood, boys are more aggressive socially, and more competitive than girls.

WIDENING HORIZONS

As your child grows and develops, she'll become increasingly sociable and need contact with other people in order to develop natural curiosity and intellectual growth. She'll get these from the everyday interaction she has with you, your friends and their children, with grandparents and other relatives. But it's also a good idea to let her meet other children of her own age with you at a creche or parent and toddler group, and later to think about playschool or nursery as a way of preparing her for formal schooling in the future. Although your child may not start to form strong attachments – real friendships – until she's approaching three years old, she'll enjoy playing alongside other children. This will enable her to start finding out about giving and sharing, and to begin exploring the enormous potential for creativity in joint imaginative play.

EXTENDING YOUR FAMILY

Once you're settled as a family with one child, it's natural to think about whether or not you're going to extend your family and, if so, how long to wait. As with all family matters, there's no hard and fast rule about this. It suits some couples to wait until their first child is old enough to attend a nursery, or even until she's at full-time school. For others, a smaller gap seems better, but bear in mind that children have been found to benefit from a minimum gap of two and a half years. You also need to take into account work commitments and financial considerations, as well as your own health; a mother who had a strenuous labour and birth, or perhaps a Caesarean section, would probably want to feel that her body is completely back to normal and has had time to become "hers" again, before embarking on another pregnancy. Age also has significance, although nowadays this doesn't have much bearing on the ability to bear and look after children. However, biology is against you: the older you are, the longer it's going to take you on average to conceive again (see p. 18), so you may not want to wait too long before trying for another baby.

THE IMPACT ON YOUR CHILD
Whatever the length of time between the two (or subsequent) births, it's important that you think carefully about the impact on the older child, and that you introduce the idea to her sensitively and in good time. Even a teenager can feel displaced by the arrival of a new baby, something that may well happen if you've entered a new relationship and one of you already has children (see p. 123). Your decision to extend your family must always be inclusive: your first child is a fully paid-up member of your family unit and deserves to be treated as such, whatever her age.

A FINAL WORD

Long after your child can cook herself a meal, iron her own clothes and has set off along the golden road to Samarkhand, she'll still need both her parents to nurture her. True nurture caters not only for her material wants but also offers continuing and unconditional love, and it's a lifelong commitment. If this unconditional love is combined with reasonable limits and guidelines, you'll both help her to mature into an individual who is sensitive to the needs of others, but remains independent of mind, confident and open to all the possibilities that life can offer.

SIBLING RIVALRY

Jealousy is a normal emotion for a small child to feel if her security appears threatened by the arrival of a new baby. Although you can't guarantee to avoid some jealousy, the best way to help her cope is to prepare her for the new arrival and to keep on showing her that her place in your affections is quite safe.

BEFORE THE BIRTH
Talk to her about the new baby as soon as your tummy looks really swollen. Let her touch your tummy whenever she wants to, but especially to feel the baby kick. Refer to the baby as *her* baby, and ask if she'd like a brother or a sister to get her involved. If you know the sex in advance, tell her so she can start to identify with the new baby. Get her to show love and affection openly by reading parent and baby animal books together, by encouraging her to be gentle with other babies, and by exchanging lots of cuddles.

AFTER THE BIRTH
When she visits you in hospital for the first time, make sure you aren't holding the baby – have your arms free for her and wait for her to ask to see the baby. Give her a present from the baby. Share bath and feeding times so that she can show you how helpful she is and be praised and rewarded by you. Put aside at least half an hour a day when you give her your full attention one to one, without the baby. Keep telling her how much you love and treasure her.

THE FATHER'S ROLE
Some feelings of displacement are inevitable, but a father really comes into his own when the new baby arrives. You'll be able to reassure your elder child that you still love her. You're ideally placed to arrange special treats and activities. With your attention and love, you'll enable your first-born to negotiate the choppy waters of sibling rivalry and you'll have cemented a life-long friendship.

USEFUL INFORMATION

T HE FOLLOWING SECTION provides information to enable you to maximize the resources and benefits available to you during your pregnancy and after the birth. It also includes a summary of the health care procedures and recommended immunization schedule for your baby, and details of specialist organizations that offer help and support.

MINIMUM RIGHTS

Regardless of how many hours you work or how long you've been employed, you're entitled to:

■ Working conditions that are safe for your unborn child: any risk must be removed, or you must be removed from it, if necessary by moving you to a suitable alternative job or suspending you on full pay.

■ Time off work without loss of pay to attend antenatal appointments and classes.

■ The right to keep your job; you cannot be dismissed as a result of your pregnancy.

■ Minimum maternity leave and pay (see right and opposite).

ADDITIONAL BENEFITS

You may be eligible for other benefits to help you support yourself and your baby:

■ If you're a single parent, you may be entitled to one-parent benefit, but not if you co-habit.

■ If your income is low, enquire about the possibility of Income Support, Family Credit, Maternity Payments, Housing and Council Tax Benefits and Health Benefits.

■ If you or your partner are on Income Support, unemployed or disabled you may be entitled to a Maternity Payment. This is a single payment for you to buy necessities for your baby.

■ Once your baby's birth is registered and you've got a birth certificate, you can make your claim for weekly child benefit.

FINDING OUT YOUR MATERNITY RIGHTS

Becoming a parent means changing your status from a legal and economic point of view, as well as a personal one. Sometimes the changes contingent on becoming a parent can affect your working and economic life in a very complicated way, but help is at hand. The important thing is to start making enquiries and getting help from the appropriate bodies early on in your pregnancy – don't leave it until you're 35 weeks pregnant, or you may find yourself losing out. Many women have additional maternity rights provided by their individual employer. It's a good idea to read your contract and staff handbook, especially if you work in a large company, so that you can check your entitlements. If you are confused about anything, make an appointment with your personnel officer and talk it through to find out exactly what is offered by your company. To qualify for maternity leave and pay you need to obtain the appropriate forms from your midwife, GP or local Social Security office and apply by the deadlines (see chart, opposite).

MATERNITY LEAVE

You have the right to 14 weeks minimum maternity leave, and extended maternity leave if you've worked for your company for a certain period. When you return to work you're entitled to return to the same job.

WHAT YOU NEED TO DO
You need to write to your employer at least 21 days before you start your maternity leave, stating you are pregnant and giving your estimated delivery date. If you are going on extended maternity leave (see below), you must also state in writing that you intend to return to work after the birth. If your employer requests it, you must provide a copy of your maternity certificate (form MAT B1; in Northern Ireland, form MB1) which you can get from your midwife. Your employer may also write to you at any point from 11 weeks into your leave asking you to confirm your intention to return to work: to keep your right open, you must reply in writing within 14 days and state very clearly that you wish to return. At least 21 days before you return, you must notify your employer in writing of your proposed return date.

EXTENDED MATERNITY LEAVE
If you've worked for your current employer for two years continuously at the 11th week before your baby is due, you're entitled to extended maternity leave of 40 weeks in total. There's no statutory requirement for your employment to continue during this extended period, although there has to be good reasons and proper procedures for it to be terminated.

MATERNITY PAY

If you have worked for the same employer for at least 26 weeks by the end of the 15th week before your baby is due, you are entitled to Statutory Maternity Pay (SMP). This is a weekly payment paid for a maximum of 18 weeks starting when you leave work. You can get it even if you don't intend to return to work after the birth. You can decide how soon you want to stop work, and hence how early you start your maternity pay – week 11 before your estimated date of delivery is the earliest you can start getting SMP, and you can, if you wish, work right up to the week of your baby's delivery. SMP is 90 per cent of your average pay for the first six weeks; after that it's paid at a basic rate for up to 12 weeks. However, many companies – especially larger ones – offer better deals for women taking maternity leave.

IF YOU DO NOT QUALIFY

If you aren't entitled to SMP, but have paid National Insurance contributions for at least 26 of the 66 weeks before your baby's estimated due date, you can get Maternity Allowance. This is paid for up to 18 weeks starting any time from 11 weeks before your baby is due, and is paid at two rates – the lower for self-employed or unemployed women, and the higher rate for women who are in employment. If you don't qualify for SMP or Maternity Allowance, but have paid some National Insurance contributions over the previous three years, you may be entitled to Incapacity Benefit, a weekly benefit paid from six weeks before the birth until two weeks after.

REGISTERING THE BIRTH

You are legally required to register the birth within 42 days (three weeks in Scotland). A registrar may be available in the hospital; otherwise you will have to go to a Registery Office. If you were married at the time of the birth, either parent may register. An unmarried mother must attend, and if the father wants his details entered he must accompany her. You need to give delivery details; the baby's names; parents' names, addresses, occupations and dates of birth; the number of previous children; and marriage date. You'll be given a copy of the entry (you may buy further copies), and a medical card so that you can register your baby with a doctor.

161

RIGHTS AND BENEFITS SUMMARY

WHEN	WHAT YOU NEED TO DO	WHY YOU NEED TO DO IT
WHEN PREGNANCY IS CONFIRMED	If you're working, inform your employer. If you're not entitled to SMP, find out about Maternity Allowance (MA).	To establish eligibility for SMP and so that you can organize paid time off for antenatal visits.
3 WEEKS BEFORE FINISHING WORK	Confirm to your employer, in writing, when you intend to stop work and also give him your return date.	By confirming your intentions to your employer, you protect your right to return to work and to get SMP.
14 WEEKS BEFORE YOUR BABY IS DUE	Ask your doctor or your midwife for a maternity certificate (form MAT B1; in Northern Ireland, form MB1).	The maternity certificate must be given to your employer to confirm your right to maternity leave and pay.
11 WEEKS BEFORE YOUR BABY IS DUE	This is the earliest date that you are allowed to finish work, start your maternity leave and receive SMP.	You are entitled to claim your SMP and Maternity Allowance once you have stopped work.
AFTER THE BIRTH TO SIX WEEKS	You have to register the birth by the time your baby is aged six weeks (three weeks, in Scotland). You can claim child benefit.	Register to get a birth certificate, and NHS and child benefit forms. After six months, child benefit won't be backdated.
7 WEEKS AFTER YOUR BABY WAS DUE	You should write to your employer at this time to confirm that you are intending to return to work.	The letter of confirmation that you intend to return to work protects your right to do so.
3 WEEKS BEFORE RETURNING TO WORK	You should write to your employer at this time to inform him of the actual date that you intend to return to work.	Again, writing to your employer with your return date protects your right to return to work.
29 WEEKS AFTER BIRTH	Your leave is officially over by this date, which means that you must return to work.	If you don't go back by this date, you may lose your right to return at all.

162

HEALTHCARE PROFESSIONALS

You'll be looked after by a series of professionals throughout your pregnancy and after the birth.

GENERAL PRACTITIONER (GP)
If you're not registered, sign up with your GP as soon as you find out you're pregnant. She'll confirm your pregnancy, if needed, and refer you to the hospital.

MIDWIFE
The midwife is responsible for your antenatal care and will run antental classes. A midwife will be with you during labour and deliver the baby, and she will monitor you and the baby for about two weeks after the birth.

HEALTH VISITOR
A health visitor is a qualified nurse with specific training in child care. She advises on your baby's health and development and arranges any further help. She visits you at home from about ten days after the birth to answer any questions you have and examine the baby. She is also available on the telephone or at the clinic if you need additional help.

HEALTH BENEFITS

During pregnancy and for the first year you will be eligible for health benefits, qualifying for more if you are on a low income:

■ You are entitled to free NHS dental care and free prescriptions while you are pregnant and for a year after your baby is born, regardless of your income.

■ If you are on a low income, your entitlements may also include free eye tests, vouchers towards spectacles, assistance with travel to your hospital, as well as milk tokens and vitamins. Contact your Social Security office for details.

HEALTH INFORMATION

Your baby's health will be closely monitored so that any problems can be picked up as early as possible. To protect your baby from certain illnesses, you will be advised to have him immunized from when he is two months old.

HEALTHCARE RECORDS
A record of your pregnancy, labour and delivery is kept as well as anything from your medical history – or your family's – that could affect your child. Once the baby is born and the birth is registered, you will be given a NHS form to fill in so that you can register your baby with your doctor (see left). Details of your baby's growth and development are recorded and updated at the regular checks (see p. 133); charts are used to record his weight, height and head circumference to check that he is, on average, developing at the correct rate. You will be given a copy of your child's health records and they will be passed to his school to monitor his health throughout his childhood.

IMMUNIZATIONS
Some parents are anxious about the possible side effects that may occur as a result of a vaccination. If you have concerns, it's important to talk these through with your GP and health visitor. The risk of complications in all cases is extremely small; the risk of harmful effects from the diseases themselves is much more serious. Your baby will not be immunized if he was premature or has a fever. If he has had side effects from a previous vaccination, the GP may delay or stop further immunizations, depending on the severity of the reaction.

IMMUNIZATIONS IN THE FIRST YEAR

AGE DUE	VACCINATION	HOW GIVEN	SIDE EFFECTS
TWO MONTHS	• Polio	• By mouth	• None
	• Hib (haemophilus influenzae type b) • DTP (diptheria, tetanus and whooping cough)	• Injection • Combined injection	• Possible lump at injection site; fever; slight risk of high fever and convulsions.
THREE MONTHS	• Polio	• By mouth	• None
	• Hib • DTP	• Injection • Combined injection	• As above.
FOUR MONTHS	• Polio	• By mouth	• None
	• Hib • DTP	• Injection • Combined injection	• As above.
12–15 MONTHS	• MMR (measles, mumps, rubella)	• Combined injection	• Fever; rash; slight risk of high fever and convulsions.

USEFUL ADDRESSES

LABOUR AND BIRTH SUPPORT

The Active Birth Centre
Bickerton House
25 Bickerton Road
London N19 5JT
0207 482 5554
http://www.activebirthcentre.com/
Runs classes and workshops to prepare you for pregnancy, birth and parenthood.

Independent Midwives Association
1 Great Quarry
Guildford
Surrey GU1 3XN
01483 821 104
http://www.pobox.com/~ima.uk/

SUPPORT FOR YOU AS PARENTS

Association of Breastfeeding Mothers
PO Box 207
Bridgwater TA6 7YT
020 7813 1481
http://home.clara.net/abm/

Association for Postnatal Illness
25 Jerdan Place
London SW6 1BE
020 7386 0868
http://www.apni.org/

BLISS
89 Albert Embankment
London SE1 7TP
020 7820 9471
http://www.bliss.org.uk/
Help for parents with special care babies.

British Agency for Adoption and Fostering
200 Union Street
London SE1 OLX
020 7593 2000
http://www.baaf.org.uk/

Contact a Family
170 Tottenham Court Road
London W1T 7HA
020 7383 3555
http://www.cafamily.org.uk/
Advice and support for parents whose children have special needs.

Cry-Sis
BM Cry-Sis
London WC1N 3XX
020 7404 5011
Help and information for parents with a baby who has sleep problems.

Gingerbread National Office
16–17 Clerkenwell Close
London EC1R 0AA
020 7336 8183
http://www.gingerbread.org.uk/
Help and advice for one-parent families.

La Leche League (Great Britain)
PO Box BM 3424
London WC1N 3XX
020 7242 1278
Advice for women who are breastfeeding.

National Childbirth Trust (NCT)
Alexandra House, Oldham Terrace
London W3 6NH
020 8992 8637
http://www.nct-online.org/

National Childminding Association
8 Masons Hill
Bromley BR2 9EY
020 8464 6164
http://www.ncma.org.uk/

Meet-a-Mum Association (MAMA)
Waterside Centre, 26 Avenue Road
London SE25 4DX
020 8771 5595 (7–10 pm Mon–Fri)
Support for new mothers.

National Stepfamily Association
Chapel House, 18 Hatton Place
London EC1N 8RU
0990 168388 (helpline)

Twins and Multiple Birth Association (TAMBA)
Harnott House, 309 Chester Road
Little Sutton
Ellesmere Port CH66 1QQ
01732 868000
http://www.tamba.org.uk/

MATERNITY RIGHTS

Association for Improvements in the Maternity Services (AIMS)
5 Portholl Road
Brighton, BN1 5PD
01753 652 781
http://www.aims.org.uk/

Maternity Alliance
45 Beech Street
London EC2P 2LX
020 7588 8582 (Mon–Thurs 9–2.00)
Information and advice about welfare and employment rights, and benefits.

SPECIAL NEEDS

Association for Spina Bifida and Hydrocephalus
Asbah House, 42 Park Road
Peterborough PE1 2UQ
01733 555988
http://www.asbah.demon.co.uk/

Council for Disabled Children
8 Wakley Street
London EC1V 7QE
020 7843 6000
http://www.ncb.org.uk/

Cystic Fibrosis Trust
11 London Road
Bromley, BR1 1BY
020 8464 7211
http://www.cftrust.org uk/

Down's Syndrome Association
155 Mitcham Road
London SW17 9PG
020 8682 4001
http://www.dsa-uk.com/

The National Eczema Society
163 Evershot Street
London NW1 1BH
020 7388 4097
http://www.eczema.org/

MENCAP
123 Golden Lane
London EC1Y 0RT
020 7454 0454
http://www.mencap.org.uk/

National Deaf Children's Society
15 Dufferin Street
London EC1Y 8UR
020 7250 0123
http://www.ndcs.org.uk/

Royal National Institute for the Blind
224 Great Portland Street
London W1N 6AA
020 7388 1266
http://www.scope.org.uk/

Scope (formerly the Spastics Society)
12 Park Crescent
London W1N 4EQ
0800 800 3333 (helpline)
http://www.scope.org.uk/

163

INDEX

ACKNOWLEDGMENTS

THE PUBLISHER WOULD LIKE TO THANK:

For their kind permission to reproduce photographs:
(c=centre; t=top; b=bottom; l=left; r=right)
AKG: 10crb; Collections: Anthea Sieveking 46bl, 59b; Sally & Richard Greenhill: 42b, 45b; Science Photo Library: Ron Sutherland 50b.

For help in producing the book:
Sue Callister, Keith Davis, Glenda Fisher, Mae Hau, Ian Merrill, Robert Newman and Tanya Tween for design assistance; Adam Moore and Rajen Shah for DTP work; Andy Crawford and Steve Gorton for additional photography; Elizabeth Burrage and Liz Jones for make-up; Joanna Moorhead for research; Claire Cross, Clair Savage and Anna Scobie for editorial assistance; Caroline Green for proofreading; Hilary Bird for the index.

For help and information:
Habitat, Early Learning Centre and Mamas and Papas for loaning props; the National Stepfamily Association and the British Association for Adoption and Fostering for advice.

For modelling:
Jacqui and Rosalyn Burton; Luke and Ziz Chater; Karl and Thomas Clowes; Rosie and Sarah Crouch; Lisa and Richard Czapnik; Angie and Chloe Elstone; Meredith and Tim Ericson; Ann and Kealey France; Imogen, Phoebe, Rohan and Sophie Harris; Oulimata Jagne; Joanna, Morgan, Niall, Rosie and Sarah Johnson; Kerry, Georgina and Sam Joseph; Nazrin, Neda and Nassar Khalili; Guenevere, Micheal and Suzanne Kiely; Adele King; Amber and Amelia Lecoyte; Maggie and Rebecca Mant; Jo Marceau; Cathy and Felix Miles; Claire and Thomas Moore; Alfie and Juliette Norsworthy; Darcie, Eva, Marea, Zak and Pat Oyrzynska; Katie Paine; Alastair, Linda and Matthew Partner; Ragen and Tina Patel; Vicky Phillips; Tim Pilcher and Megan Pilcher-King; Caroline and Marco Pinit; Ian and Kathy Redington; Jo and Shekinah Reuben; Nathan and Marvin Sackey; Ann and Joshua Simpson; Annabel Storr; Amanda and Zachary Stuart; Lawrence and Harry Taylor; David and Zachary Ward; Max and Sonia Whillock; Martin Wilson; Emilie Woodman.